Kuwabara Payne McKenna Blumberg Architects

KUWABARA PAYNE MCKENNA BLUMBERG ARCHITECTS

with contributions by
George Baird
Thomas Fisher
Mark Kingwell
Mirko Zardini

Dedicated to Detlef Mertins (1954-2011)
who helped frame our practice and our
architecture in ways that illuminated and
inspired what we are doing and the material
reality of the ground we have staked out.

CULTURE & MEMORY

CAMPUS & COMMUNITY

VERTICAL NEIGHBOURHOODS

INTEGRATED DESIGN

MIRKO ZARDINI
Foreword

1 Architecture, particularly between the 1960s and 1980s, played a significant role in shaping Canada's cultural identity and social values. During this period, buildings and landscapes were seen as indispensable tools capable of, and partly responsible for, defining the character of pioneering public programs and private ventures conducted by the Centennial celebration in 1967 when the country commemorated the 100th anniversary of the Canadian Confederation. The energy of architecture throughout this stage resided mainly in a long-held 'sense of engagement in a social contract, a contract between architect and client, with the obligation to create an environment that enhances life and allows the inhabitants to develop to their highest potential.'[1]

2 The commitment to this social agreement produced a series of large-scale projects which, regardless of their use or location — the city fabric or the open landscape — possessed clear public and urban qualities. The significance of these contributions — from the Simon Fraser University campus in British Columbia (Arthur Erickson, since 1963) or Scarborough College in Toronto (John Andrews, 1963-1969) to Place Bonaventure in Montreal (Affleck, Desbarats, Dimakopoulos, Lebensold, Sise, 1964-1967) or Robson Square in downtown Vancouver (Arthur Erickson, Cornelia Oberlander, 1973-1983) — has not been fully acknowledged and figures like Arthur Erickson or Cornelia Oberlander have not received the international recognition they deserve in the history of post-war architecture.

3 The richness and intensity of this period went well beyond idealism and testified to the power of architecture when embodying a program based on a large welfare state responsible for providing universal social services. But this national venture no longer holds and, at present, Canada seems to be going through a very different historical phase. Similarly, architecture, no longer driven by synchronized state and private policies, is going through a so-called moment of transition and searching for major agendas.

4 In the middle of this generalized intellectual drifting, the landscape — 'soft, neutral, and continuous — unanimously understood as good, reliable, and therefore not open to critique'[2] — is becoming the only safe theme on which to act. And Canada is no exception. Here, too, a sentimental, often intensified, version of the landscape is becoming the recurrent theme in architecture. Projects that celebrate this vision often describe fluid environments devoid of conflict, places where not only architecture is brought closer to the landscape — highlighting features like climate, geography, topography and ecological soundness — but where landscapes becomes more architectural. These works often account for new ideas about sustainability and ecology that have transformed the very definition of the natural environment, including the landscape, and turned them once again into a myth; the effortless integration of architecture, nature and users. This 'organic view' usually disregards the positive values that arise from the basics of the contemporary city: conflict, excessive variety, irregularity, intricacy and extraordinariness. In fact, upon closer inspection, some of these operations are subordinated to ongoing broader agendas — with local and global ambitions — attempting to anesthetize profound, intricate social and environmental conflicts.

In addition to the passivity of transformative industries and the real concerns posed by conservation and the enrichment of Canada's natural resources and landscapes — including political issues like energy production, pollution, land and water protection and management, material extraction, agriculture, forestry or fishing — it seems that the country's main challenges lie within urban environments, particularly with what the government defines as medium and large urban population centres. It is in these centres where 20 million people, 67 percent of the population, concentrate, where conflicts, basic needs and collective ambitions need to be negotiated for the better, where 50 percent of the aboriginal population resides,[3] and to where more and more immigrants are attracted.[4]

Detail of commissioned series of photo murals by Pascal Grandmaison for customized Skyfold partitions in Torys LLP Offices, Toronto

5 This is the environment and the circumstances in which KPMB's architecture is positioned and, more importantly, the conditions KPMB's projects engage with. The firm, founded by Bruce Kuwabara, Thomas Payne, Marianne McKenna and Shirley Blumberg, in 1987, is a practice concerned with redefining the intricacies of the contemporary cities and metropolises. Fascinated with the public realm and the possibility of producing an enduring civic legacy, KPMB operates mainly through projects still rooted in the endangered tradition of architecture in Canada to honour an implicit social contract.

KPMB's work is well-known for its particular way of responding to heterogeneous users and urban contexts, manipulating diverse programmatic requirements, and engaging historical buildings. The flexible use of a late-modern language, including a 'mixture of extensions, critique and correctives'[5] is not only a formal choice but the instrument used to articulate these very diverse conditions. In fact, through this conventional language, KPMB is able to present a subversive and defiant attitude. For instance, they often refuse to define the city block in the traditional way. Instead, they integrate and improve the character of the city streets and public spaces by freely assembling activities, circulation, uses and volumes. Likewise, KPMB organizes skillful and unusual combinations of programs, in a single site, vertically and horizontally. As well, they embrace a mix of cultural institutions and private developments, commercial and residential uses, and private and public spaces, in an honest effort to stimulate and support urban diversity. Both strategies are evident in their recent academic and cultural buildings in Toronto and Montreal downtowns. In contrast, projects by KPMB engaging with existing buildings are often organized through a series of graceful operations, producing new cohesive elements that connect the new and old with the city fabric.

6 To be sure, the contemporary metropolis is the 'landscape' architects are being called upon to shape today. Residential projects, public and private institutions, education and research facilities, work and leisure spaces, all constitute the urban environment and will continue to do so despite the regression of the state's involvement. The contemporary city is the stage where conflicts are mediated in different ways and potential resolutions tested. It is the stage where new social contracts and public consultation help decide the quality of the built and natural environments. It is the stage where designers can articulate the voice of multiple communities into unexpected thoughts and projects that will help to define the future of daily life in Canada — and elsewhere.

References

1. Excerpt from *Canada: Urban Architecture and the Social Contract*, notes by Phyllis Lambert for a lecture at Princeton University, February 28, 2002.

2. Mirko Zardini, 'Seemingly Seamless,' in *Landform Building*, ed. Stan Allen and Marc McQuade. Baden: Lars Müller Publishers, 2011 p. 61.

3. John Ralston Saul, *A Fair Country: Telling Truths about Canada*. Toronto: Viking, 2008, p.282.

4. Data source: Statistics Canada, Census of Population, 1851 to 2006, http://www.statcan.gc.ca/subjects-sujets/standard-norme/sgc-cgt/urban-urbain-eng.htm (accessed July 14, 2012).

5. Detlef Mertins, 'Toronto Style,' in Phyllis Lambert, Detlef Mertins, Bruce Mau and Rodolphe el-Koury, *The Architecture of Kuwabara Payne McKenna Blumberg*. Basel, Berlin, Boston: Birkhäuser — Publishers for Architecture, 2004, p. 17.

Gardiner Museum, detail at main entrance looking towards neoclassical façade of adjacent Lillian Massey Building (1908-1912)

MARK KINGWELL

Building Cities, Making Friends:
A Meditation in Five General Propositions

> Like a bad concert hall, affective space contains dead spots where the sound fails
> to circulate. — The perfect interlocutor, the friend, is he not the one who constructs
> around you the greatest possible resonance? Cannot friendship be defined as a
> space with total sonority?

> — Roland Barthes, *A Lover's Discourse: Fragments*[1]

I am much taken with this image from Barthes's poignant, fragmentary, nuanced engagement with the plight of the lover, stranded at the limits of language. All love is a kind of wish, and here we see the core of all human longing, the desire for someone who will listen. There is no better figure of friendship than the implied construction of the good concert hall, the one where there are no dead spots, where I am always heard because you, the friend, have created a space so sonorous and resonant that my merest whisper is heard in the rear balcony.

Friendship, especially of the intimate sort that Barthes has in mind for the lover, may seem an odd keynote for a discussion of urbanism and architecture. But I want to suggest that the prospect of such intimacy, the space of total sonority, is the regulative ideal of all great cities, the goal, perhaps finally unreachable, towards which all effort is aimed. The construction of a resonance that allows each one of us to know that we are heard, that we have a friend in the existence of the city itself.

The image is resonant in another, more obvious way in the current context, of course, because the impressively varied practice of KPMB now includes one of the best, most resonant concert halls to be found in the city where I live, Koerner Hall, part of the Royal Conservatory of Music renovation of 2009. I was able to visit the site of this construction before it was completed, and climbed the scaffolded height to stand inside what would eventually become the elaborate wave-wood ceiling of this exemplary space. That is, I was able to stand inside one of the design elements that make for sonority, that enable resonance, in the finished hall. That moment of suspension within a not-yet-finished architectural project remains, for me, a crystallized memory of what it means to build a city, to create the material conditions of shared dwelling. And now, when I step into the hall's lobby, which floats over Philosopher's Walk and embraces downtown Toronto as if we were in a living room — or a shared playground — I see again the genius of this design.

The meditative origins, the warm materials palette, the creation of a community space and not just a building: these traits are characteristic of the KPMB practice. More than any other firm, KPMB has sounded the keynote of urban renewal in Toronto, their home base. But projects in other cities and towns are equally significant makers of sonority. If we believe Aristotle, that a just city must be, in some sense, a city of friends, the architectural interventions of KPMB are more than commissions or projects; they are exercises in civic humanism. Buildings become, in effect, miniature cities, gathering their surrounding spaces, large and small, unto themselves. From the modified college cloister of the CIGI Campus in Waterloo, Ontario (2011), with its stunning cantilevered entrance and warm interior spaces for conversation and instruction (which converts the loose edge of a small town into a vibrant urban site), to the capacious Vaughan City Hall (2011), Canada's National Ballet School (2005), the renovated Gardiner Museum (2006) and the TIFF Bell Lightbox (2011), we observe again and again the material conditions of community.

By that phrase I mean at least the following five necessary features of city building: (1) a strong connection to existing urban geography — even if, as in the Vaughan project, for example, the surrounding area is anti-aesthetic or bare; (2) the artful reinterpretation of traditional elements and forms (the courtyard, the quad, the bell tower, the café); (3) the creation of public space within buildings as well as between them, forming interior crucibles of shared citizenship; (4) program design that makes

Koerner Hall, Royal Conservatory of Music

Model of New Babylon (1959–1974), metal, plexiglas and wood, the anti-capitalist 'city of play' designed by Situationist architect Constant Nieuwenhuys

for frequent mixing and social interplay; and, perhaps above all, (5) a sense of play, the ability to create spontaneous situations and encounters among people, to achieve even in workmanlike spaces a creative, non-utilitarian dérive — a drift.[2]

Since these five features may seem obvious, even as their realization is in fact far from common, allow me to expand on them with a series of expansive theses which I believe the city-building practice of KPMB brings to our attention. Thus a meditation, philosophical and architectural, in the form of five general propositions …

General Proposition No. 1: The city is a philosophical extension of the human person.

This proposition is valid along at least two distinct vectors. First, the city is an extension of human action in the same way that Marshall McLuhan meant when he said that communications media are 'extensions of man.' Media enables a routine transcendence of the limitations which inhere in the human sensorium. Unaided, I can see only what is revealed to my eyes, hear only what lies within range of my ears, and so on. But with the aid of a telephone, or a television, or a telegraph — with, to be sure, a computer or tablet but also, for that matter, with smoke signals or a walking stick — I can experience a vastly expanded range of possible stimuli beyond my meagre bodily range: events, stories, intimacies. Media offers us an extended body, a body stretched and attenuated across large distances in space and time.

The built environment of the city is, by the same logic, a massive and complex extension of the human body. It allows me precisely to pursue all the bodily tasks of human life that make for the complex achievement of personhood: to shelter and work, to move and interact, to eat and drink, to remember and forget, to live, love and die. Not all of its extensions are strictly sensory, as in communications media as such; instead, the city is what we might call the ur-medium or super-extension of man. The city offers ways of getting somewhere, places to get, places that are neither here nor there. The person, in the form of his or her body, perforce negotiates these spaces on a daily basis — and so comes into contact with other persons, other bodies, doing the same. The city is thus the physical manifestation of our desires and purposes, both responsive to what we think we want and constraining, shaping, of what we come to want.

It has been a commonplace at least since Aristotle (him again!) that first we create cities, and then they create us. Winston Churchill's much-quoted line to the same effect, where the term 'buildings' appears in the place of 'cities,' is both less general and offered without proper provenance. He is not wrong, but the deeper point — the point that lurks in Aristotle's sense of the city as an expression of organic norms encoded in the natural and social world (really there is no bright division between them) — is that buildings affect other buildings as well as affecting people. Cities are composed of complexes of desire, not all of which are entirely conscious at the level of the individual user or even creator of buildings.[3]

The general proposition is valid in another, perhaps less obvious sense, however. It is related to the first but requires a little more philosophical flexibility to accept. It is this: the city is, like the human person, subject to a version of the mind-body problem. That problem, with us since Descartes, concerns that apparently mysterious causal linkage between one substance, the mind, which is wholly immaterial, with another, the body, which is wholly non-mental. (The Homer Simpson version goes like this: 'Mind? No matter. Matter? Never mind.') How is it possible that the human person, apparently

TIFF Bell Lightbox, Toronto International Film Festival Group

possessed, somehow, of both a distinct mind and an ambulatory body, is able to function? On the premise of two distinct substances, this should not be possible; and yet, the evidence is overwhelmingly in favour of its being not only possible, but trivial. People do things each and every day, blithely unaware that there is any problem at all concerning the interaction of the mental and the material.

We need not tarry here with Descartes's proposed solution to the problem (a neatly evasive reference to a mysterious substance-interface performed in the pineal gland), nor with the many decades, indeed centuries, of debate that this problem has spawned. What we can do, instead, is note that there is a rather obvious solution to the mind-body problem, which is in fact dissolution: the premise of two wholly distinct substances is flawed from the start. Human consciousness is not, despite philosophers' long-standing penchant for abstraction and out-of-body thought experiments, ever divorced from its embodiment; by the same token, the human body is not best conceived as some inanimate machine which receives a jolt of life from the ghostly inhabitation of mental activity. This point can be made as a matter of logic, as Gilbert Ryle did: his dismissive phrase 'the ghost in the machine' for the Cartesian orthodoxy is deployed in my previous sentence.[4] It can also be made positively, via the introduction of an alternative view.

There are several such alternatives, but the most persuasive is some version of what has come to be called phenomenology. On this view, it is impossible to conceive of human consciousness without an awareness of the facts of embodiment. Consciousness just is a sense of being somewhere, in place, that complex immersion of self within a horizon of spatial and temporal awareness. To be myself (to be anyone at all) is to presuppose, as a condition of life's possibility, a sense of in front and behind, here and there, then and now. That premise — and not some division of substances manufactured in the laboratory of runaway meditation — is the philosophically significant fact about human persons. And it is realized in a host of daily actions and experiences, from the skillful but mostly implicit negotiation of myself through a doorway — together with the loss of memory that such a threshold-crossing may entail! — to the complex bobbing and weaving required to traverse a busy sidewalk or railway-station concourse.[5]

We may seem to have wandered some distance from cities, and architecture, and architects. But not really. For a city entertains and then solves — or rather, dissolves — its own version of the mind-body problem in just the same way. A city is not reducible just to its built forms: on the analogy, its matter or 'body.' But neither is the city merely the sum total of its citizens and their desires: again, per analogy, its consciousness or 'mind.' And just as neither of these reductions can be validly enacted, since each limits the reality of the city as a living thing, an achievement, it is likewise the case that the city is not best conceived as some troubled interaction between the two aspects. Indeed, the sense of division between built forms and citizen-desires is precisely the premise that requires dismissal. Phenomenology sees the human person as embodied consciousness; good urban theory views the city the same way.[6]

From the left: Empire State Building in New York, Eiffel Tower in Paris, and the John P. Robarts Research Library at the University of Toronto

General Proposition No. 2: The architect is an instinctive phenomenologist of the city.

Architecture concerns the unfinished text of the city: the city is never over, always begun anew, ever layered. Architecture creates public space even when its projects are nominally private — an office building rather than a park or institution — because the architect's intervention is made within the shared fabric of the city. That noun 'fabric,' so often used without full awareness, creates a trace of meaning worth following, a thread to tease out: a fabric is not just textile but, instead, any made thing, that which is fabricated. The shared urban fabric is the making, the project, which engages and concerns us all. The city, the made thing which we inhabit, is our collective project. But the architect has a special status within this shared fabrication.

That master of the paradoxical thought, Pascal, said this about our status as thinking reeds — 'the most feeble thing in nature,' but blessed with the significant, indeed transcendent ability to consider ourselves: 'It is not from space that I must seek my dignity, but from the government of my thought. I shall have no more if I possess worlds. By space, the universe envelops me and swallows me up like a point; by thought, I envelop the world.'[7] Here consciousness flies out and back in an instant, and the occupation of space is revealed for what it is: a speculation by consciousness about consciousness, a thought about the very fact of thinking. This moment of reflection — which is the moment in which consciousness experiences itself as self — is architecture's business and highest achievement.

But (one might object) surely architecture is about solving technical issues in the deployment of space, heating and cooling, and program, the negotiation of site and client desire? Of course it is. But to what purpose? If architecture is not a form of speculation about life, the occasion for thought, it has failed its ultimate mission. That is why, contrary to the usual narratives of ego and mannerism, the real objections to signature style or grand formalist gestures in an architect are not about humility but, instead, concern rigour of thought. The architect who indulges style over conversation — with the adjacent buildings and streets, with the citizens, with the city — has failed to engage the philosophical responsibilities of the architect. He or she may have failed other responsibilities as well: aesthetic, political, ethical; but these are predicated on the more basic failure to think.

One therefore looks at this urban thought in action — in Concordia University's integrated complex combining faculties for engineering, computer sciences, visual arts and business (2005 and 2010), for example, with its deft vertical integration of an otherwise inchoate campus stranded in a downtown neighbourhood that has heretofore lacked a coherent identity — and feels a power of thoughtful consideration, the way design is executed at the service of community and use. Other campus projects — for Centennial and George Brown colleges (2004 and 2012), future works at M.I.T., Princeton and Northwestern universities — demonstrate the same sensitivity to gathering and listening. Indeed, we might say that here campus and city become specular partners: the urban college or university folded into the city surround, but also the isolated campus made into a miniature city.

Campus in Latin means field, and the first university campuses were not the quads and towers but the fields on which they sat; now, a campus is a field of thought, a field of possibility, at once delineated and opened by the built forms in which we work, speculate and converse. Discourse, realized in matter, enabling discourse.

General Proposition No. 3: Not all great architecture is great urban architecture.

The reason for this distinction should be obvious. There are great architects and (it follows) great buildings which do not concern themselves with city building. Such buildings may inhabit cities, or stand in their precincts, but they do not engage and converse with the city. Hence these are buildings that do not build the city — they are not part of its shared fabric. It is possible for such buildings to be monuments, in Aldo Rossi's sense, but only in the somewhat violent sense that they take up and redistribute the existing surround without regard for its history of effects. We might, indeed, distinguish here between violent monuments and benign ones, the latter embodying more of Rossi's sense that a city could be memorialized and extended by the monumental in architecture.[8]

Thus one might include in the former, violent category such examples as the Eiffel Tower in Paris and the Daniel Libeskind Lee-Chin Crystal renovation of the Royal Ontario Museum in Toronto, and in the latter category the Empire State Building in Manhattan and, in Toronto, the John P. Robarts Research Library at the University of Toronto. Note that the distinction is not a function of modest elevation or of accommodating style: the Empire State soars but nevertheless manages to engage and (we might say) shelter its island home; the concrete brutalist mass of Robarts is surprisingly warm, even welcoming. The affectionate nickname it has earned from students at the University of Toronto — Fort Book — communicates benign monumentality better than any amount of theoretical discourse.[9]

The conclusion I mean to derive from these rather tendentious examples (for what examples are not tendentious when we speak of architecture and theory?) is that sometimes, maybe often, the 'bold' or 'original' architectural statement is precisely the one that does not succeed in building the city. There is surely a place for signature buildings and insistent gestural design in all great cities — one might even argue that no city can be truly great without the spirited conversation, or controversy, that inevitably erupts around such buildings. But they do not, themselves, make the city; in fact, they are parasitic upon another kind of architectural genius, namely the sort that intervenes in and subtly extends existing conversations, not splashing but rippling the waters of urban life.

Pedestrians may not stop on the street to take photographs of such buildings, but one must concede at a certain point that this is the point. A photographed building may be a mere oddity, a sport, a folly. More nuanced regard may be present in the form of quiet approval, pleasant engagement, calm beauty. This is the stillness of perfect form, which yet works a sly magic on the viewer and user, stretching the boundaries of consciousness in ways more powerful for being less jarring.

General Proposition No. 4: Urban architecture is, above all, the creation of place.

There is a line from David Young's play *Inexpressible Island*, about the bare survival of a Royal Navy expedition to Antarctica, which has stayed with me since I saw the original production in 1997. In the drama, based on historical events, six men are lost in the extreme landscape near the South Pole at the same time that Robert Scott's ill-fated *Terra Nova* expedition is perishing of cold and starvation. The six figures in the play will all survive, barely, the brutal eight months of winter, only to find their story overshadowed by the harrowing tale of Scott's failure. The play is about many things, including class and spirituality, but mostly it shows the weirdly inspired madness that can descend on human beings undergoing desperate conditions of life. Towards the end of the winter, the small unit's medical office, headed by Dr. Levick, descends into a kind of philosophical delirium.

'Nature, in the form of man, begins to recognize itself,' Levick says, ostensibly to his command officer, Lieutenant Campbell, but really to himself. 'That's what we're doing here in the South, Lieutenant. We are all artists, of a kind. We are giving nature back to herself.' And, later: 'As much as anything that's

Scene from David Young's play *Inexpressible Island* (1997), based on the experiences of the marooned scientists who were part of Captain Scott's Antarctic expedition in 1912

Members of Scott's party at the South Pole, January 18, 1912. From left to right: Wilson, Scott, Oates (standing); Bowers, Edgar Evans (seated)

what has carried us here on this pilgrimage. The South Pole is an idea. A place that is no place. The final nothing.'[10]

There is much to consider in these lines, as in the whole play. The South Pole is an abstraction, a notional point created only by the world-defining Cartesian geometry of the Mercator Projection. It is both real and not real: a place that is not a place, something that does not exist for humans yet can be fixed, and visited for the first time (as we know, it would be Scott's tragedy to find that Norwegian rival Roald Amundsen had beaten him to the spot). Thus this is a pilgrimage of the mind, carried out by the body. A modern spiritual journey, a hejira defined entirely by lines, angles and national identity. But it is also a work of art: the creation of that place where the mind and the body meet — perhaps to perish — where the universe becomes aware of itself in the form of human consciousness. Nature, in the form of man, begins to recognize itself.

All creation of place exhibits this eerie mixture of abstract and concrete, of material and mental. And so we return again to the basic phenomenological awareness of embodied consciousness, but now tied even more closely to the idea of place, of being in place by deploying the conditions of possibility for place-making. Anywhere — and, it follows, nowhere — can be a place. As long as we are there, to think and talk, to listen and respond. The world, once conscious of itself in the form of human making, is a vast concert hall. What sounds there is not the divine music of celestial spheres, as the ancient Greek mathematicians believed, but the sound of one human after another issuing the daily plea: to be heard, to be understood, to be accommodated.

And, invoking another play about survival, extremity and madness, we know that the opposite condition, the poor, bare, forked condition of human alienation, is precisely the lack of place: the heath, where Lear must go mad because he is not, finally, heard. Reason not the need!

General Proposition No. 5: The creation of place is the gift of play.

A gift is given without expectation of return. In the true gift economy, wealth is measured not by how much one has accumulated but by how much one has given away. Truly to give, to give beyond all exchange or reciprocity, is to be irresponsible, creative, ironic, spontaneous, available. It is to play, in the sense that great art and great philosophy are forms of play.

Place-making is play-making. In one sense, to make a place is to create the material conditions of experience, to create the phenomenological clearing; but a place is not a place without my being there, my finding myself there, being in place. Further, place-making does not end with the subjective experience of either the one-in-place or the maker-of-place. For it is the nature of places to keep on giving, to create and renew, again and again, the conditions of their own possibility. Places are, in a sense, living things, maintained in time by experience and enjoyment. That is what it is for a place to be a place. This is what it means to clear a space for us to play in.

City halls, educational buildings, cinematic complexes — functionality varies according to task. Place-making, and hence city building, transcends all specific functionality. It speaks to engagement, not program, freedom rather than function.

It is in such places that we may find — or (as we sometimes say) make — friends. There may be in actuality no perfect interlocutor as described by Barthes, but the well-built city gives us the chance, over and over, to try and find that comprehensively resonant friend. The one with whom we can play. The one who will listen while we drift together, continuously.

References
1. Roland Barthes, *A Lover's Discourse: Fragments.* Paris: Éditions du Seuil, 1977; New York: Hill & Wang, Richard Howard, trans., 1978, 2010, p. 167, from the fragment 'No Answer: mutisme/silence.'
2. Though I borrow here the term favoured by the Situationists, there is no need to align the sort of city building I am discussing, with its feet firmly rooted in reality, alongside the utopian New Babylon 'city of play' advocated by Ivan Chtcheglov and Constant Nieuwenhuys. Still, there is something compelling about the vision of a city designed entirely for homo ludens, a city where, as Chtcheglov puts it in his 'Formulary for a New Urbanism,' 'the main activity of the inhabitants will be CONTINUOUS DRIFTING.' Chtcheglov promises an 'aesthetic of behaviours' but also a 'complete phenomenology of couples, encounters, and duration.' Along the way, he reserves some choice words for Le Corbusier: 'Some sort of psychological repression dominates this individual — whose face is as ugly as his conception of the world — such that he wants to squash people under ignoble masses of reinforced concrete, a noble material that should rather be used to enable an aerial articulation of space that could surpass the flamboyant Gothic style. His cretinizing influence is immense. A Le Corbusier model is the only image that arouses in me the idea of immediate suicide. He is destroying the last remnants of joy. And of love, passion, freedom.' (See http://www.bopsecrets.org/SI/Chtcheglov.htm.) Chtcheglov first drafted the 'Formulary' in 1953, when he was 19, under the name Gilles Ivain; it was published in the first issue of *Internationale Situationniste.* He spent five years in a psychiatric ward after being committed by his wife, and died in 1998.
3. A somewhat hostile review of my book *Nearest Thing to Heaven: The Empire State Building and American Dreams.* New Haven: Yale University Press, 2006, suggested that the claim there — namely, that the Empire State had in a sense 'caused' the people of New York to construct it, given the logic of the 'race for the sky,' contemporary technological advances, and so on — was evidence of my having been 'bamboozled' by fashionable French theory. No, just taking Aristotle seriously.
4. See Gilbert Ryle, *The Concept of Mind.* New York: Hutchinson & Co., 1949.
5. The congruence between phenomenological theory and clinical psychological findings is a growth industry in academia. Just one example: a 2011 University of Notre Dame study found that doors and other spatial thresholds created 'event boundaries' in episodes of experience or activity, prompting changes of consciousness that might, for example, present as changes of mood or, notoriously, temporary loss of memory. Hence the common experience, even absent dementia, of arriving in a room and not knowing what brought you there, or what you came to fetch. One of the study's authors offered this advice: 'Doorways are bad. Avoid them at all costs.' (Misty Harris, 'Study shows doors can be linked to memory loss,' *The National Post* [November 9, 2011]).
6. This is an extremely brief rehearsal of arguments that I make at length in *Concrete Reveries: Consciousness and the City.* New York: Viking Press, 2008.
7. Pascal, *Pensées*, #348.
8. Aldo Rossi, *Architecture of the City.* Cambridge, MA: MIT Press, 1982. It is worth noting that Rossi considers himself, after a fashion, a structuralist devotee of Barthes.
9. But for more theoretical discussion, see Mark Kingwell, 'Monumental-Conceptual Architecture,' *Harvard Design Magazine* 19 (Fall 2003/Winter 2004) and also *Nearest Thing to Heaven*, ed. cit., passim.
10. David Young, *Inexpressible Island.* Winnipeg: Scirocco Drama, 1998, pp. 116 and 120.

GEORGE BAIRD

Maturity: a Commentary

Design practices in architecture evolve over time. Some firms — perhaps even a majority of them — reach a plateau of design ambition, and then remain there — or perhaps even lose some part of the intensity of ambition that typified them in earlier years. Some other firms continue to seek new design challenges, and to recast the images that they have already attained in the public eye. Among the admirable firms to be found in the second category is surely Kuwabara Payne McKenna Blumberg.

Certainly one bellwether project in the evolution of the firm has been the new headquarters complex for the National Ballet School on Jarvis Street in downtown Toronto. Here, the firm was presented with an extraordinarily complex set of site circumstances. First of all, the overall site was split in two by the developer, Context Developments, with the west half accommodating a high-density residential project (designed by the Toronto firm Architects Alliance), and the east half accommodating the Ballet School. And this was only the beginning of the complication of the commission. The east half of the site already included some existing facilities of the Ballet School, as well as two important heritage structures, one from the mid, and the other from the late 19th century. Together with their joint venture partner, Goldsmith Borgal & Company Ltd. Architects, KPMB has accomplished an astonishing feat of design integration. The new buildings for the Ballet School brilliantly complement the two preserved and reused heritage buildings, as well as both the low-rise and high-rise residential structures to which they abut. And while all of this is true, the principal massing element of the Ballet School projects striking images of the rehearsing young dancers in their practice space, out into the void of Jarvis Street itself.

In the corpus of current work of the firm, the Ballet School has recently been joined by four other remarkable and — to my eye — tonally similar projects. These are the renovated and expanded Gardiner Museum of Ceramics, the new municipal complex for the City of Vaughan north of Toronto, the new administrative headquarters building for Manitoba Hydro in Winnipeg, and the extension to the Rotman School of Management at the University of Toronto.

There are a number of features of the design for the addition and alterations to the Gardiner Museum that prompted me to read it as another bellwether of subtle new design tendencies at KPMB. First was the insistent vocabulary of rectilinear cubic volumes, which, as I saw it, bespoke a newly evident minimalist approach to the deployment of architectural massing. Then there was the treatment of the skin of the building, combining surfaces of carefully cut stone with others of fritted glazing. Together, these produced a dramatic new pictorial effect, in which the surfaces of the elemental, minimal forms of the building seemed to create an almost shimmering visual oscillation.

This vocabulary of elemental, minimalist volumes, as I see it, is developed even further in the new City Hall for Vaughan, a complex — partly three storeys and partly four storeys high — comprising three administrative pods of floor area, wrapped around a fourth volume which accommodates the council chamber. In this case, the opaque surfaces of the tectonic volumes in question are clad in a terracotta-coloured ceramic panel. For their part, the surfaces of adjacent volumes that are glazed are fabricated of glazing sections that are a deep matte-black colour. Then too, the glazed surfaces of those of these building volumes that face either south or west are overlaid, in their entirety, with horizontal ceramic louvres that match exactly the colour of the ceramic panels on the opaque façades. For me, these louvres generate a shimmering, oscillating pictorial effect that is even more dramatic than the one at the Gardiner Museum. The net result of this is that the City Hall complex hovers on the landscape of suburban Vaughan with a very powerful symbolic presence.

Detail of façade at Canada's National Ballet School (opposite); detail of west elevation at Vaughan City Hall (bottom)

Manitoba Hydro Place, south elevation

But of course, the dramatic skin of the Vaughan City Hall does not only produce a powerful pictorial effect; it also signals KPMB's expanding interests in environmental sustainability. The louvres in question, for example, play an important role in controlling sun penetration to the building's interior, whilst still permitting extensive views outwards.

Then too, the building's interior is organized around three vertical atria surmounted by clerestories. These atria function as powerful foci of the building's system of public space at the same time that they serve as stacks for a passive system of natural ventilation throughout the building's various workspaces on all three floors. In short, at Vaughan, the formal and pictorial qualities that are so compelling at the Gardiner Museum are joined by an environmental agenda, not to mention by a vigorous continuation of the firm's long-standing interest in the social orchestration of interior public space within its designs for large buildings.

This last comment leads me in turn to consideration of what is one of the firm's most important commissions to date: the new administrative headquarters building for Manitoba Hydro on Portage Avenue in downtown Winnipeg. A unique project in a wide range of respects, Manitoba Hydro is first and foremost a result of a client's resolute commitment to produce a building of the highest achievable environmental sustainability. At Manitoba Hydro, KPMB had their first experience of working on a project in an integrated design process with a wide roster of fellow consultants, including, most notably, Thomas Auer, partner in the distinguished international consultancy Transsolar KlimaEngineering. The result of Manitoba Hydro's deep commitment to environmental achievement, combined with the intensely integrated design process, is a building of quite astonishing urban presence and environmental performance.

Like the Vaughan City Hall, Manitoba Hydro manifests KPMB's characteristic double commitment to both the compelling social orchestration of interior public space, as well as to the achievement of an extraordinary level of environmental performance. To begin with the orchestration of interior public space, one can note how a generously proportioned, naturally-lit galleria passes through the entire plan of the building from Portage Avenue, Winnipeg's major downtown shopping street, to Graham Avenue behind it, where a hub of public transit routes for the city is located. Mezzanines overlooking this galleria provide access to a whole series of publically accessible meeting rooms and recreational terraces, as well as to a pedestrian bridge to an adjacent shopping mall complex. As a result, Manitoba Hydro makes a major contribution to downtown revitalization in Winnipeg, whilst maximizing the use of public transit to get its 2,000 employees to work.

As for environmental performance, the collaboration between the KPMB design team and Auer has led to one complementary innovation after another. Geothermal heating and cooling, storage of solar power available in Winnipeg's very cold but very sunny winters, and a sophisticated passive system of natural ventilation stretching over all 18 floors of the building all combine in a provocatively compelling way.

Then too, the exterior skin of Manitoba Hydro represents a further development from what the firm was able to accomplish at Vaughan City Hall. Here the almost animate, shimmering oscillation of the skin is accomplished not by louvres, but by a precocious set of glazing systems. One of them — the one that clads the outer surfaces of the two office slabs that rise into the Winnipeg sky — is fitted with a regular pattern of opening vents in both its outer and its inner skin. The ends of these same slabs are clad with a fritted triple-glazed system behind which are located three stacked atria to serve as buffer zones within the building's passive ventilation system. Then too, the two 18-storey splayed office slabs are surmounted on the building's Portage Avenue façade by a solar chimney that rises above the roof to exhaust surplus heat and at the same time serves as the marker of the building on the city's downtown skyline. Water features throughout the public and collective spaces of the complex contribute to humidity control of the interiors at the same time that they animate the interiors and provide a pictorial filigree to them.

Unlike that of the building for Vaughan, Manitoba Hydro's skin does not produce its iconic pictorial presence through unexpected material selection and chroma. Instead, it has an almost *sachlich* quality that is, as far as I can tell, quite new to the oeuvre of KPMB. In this sense, it is the newest aspect of the firm's fascinating current shift of its established professional image. One looks forward to seeing to what extent this newly *sachlich* tenor will be manifest in upcoming projects of the firm. Indeed, it has occurred to me that a striking precedent for the synthesis of voluptuous filigree and *sachlich* elements can be found in Chareau and Bijvoet's superlative Maison de Verre from 1930 in Paris.

Joseph L. Rotman School of Management Expansion, west elevation

Now under construction on the campus of the University of Toronto is the last of the three buildings I propose to discuss: the extension to the Rotman School of Management. Here, in many respects, the design ambitions for the project are opposite to those of the previous two I have discussed. Where Vaughan was intended to generate a powerful urban symbol for a diffuse suburban municipality badly in need of one, the Rotman Expansion seeks to insert a substantial quantity of floor space in an unavoidably vertical format, whilst not overwhelming the tight and highly charged setting of the established University of Toronto campus that surrounds it. Where Manitoba Hydro sought to serve as an icon for its client in downtown Winnipeg, Rotman seeks instead to insert itself as discreetly as possible amidst a group of already existing buildings, some of them quite historic, and others major architectural masterpieces. Thus the massing of Rotman is quite deferential, and the iconic presence the building exudes is achieved — rather like Vaughan — through material selection and chroma. Again, like Vaughan, the massing of Rotman is quite minimalist in configuration, and the darkness of the material palette of its minimalist volumes makes for a rather haunting exterior aspect.

Then, inside, one encounters a remarkably bold staircase configuration, which is intended to play multiple social roles for the complex. First, it establishes a strong interior visual link to the atrium of the existing, adjacent Rotman building; second, it provides a strong vertical spatial centre for all the classroom and office space the new building provides to Rotman's faculty and students; and lastly, it provides easy vertical movement between the three floors at the base of the complex that house the majority of the building's most public facilities.

Taken as a set of four, these projects do, indeed, for me, show a mature architectural practice in architecture. By now, the varied influences of Kahn and Myers, of Stirling and Scarpa are quite distilled. It is heartening to see the firm pressing hard to expand its horizons further still, and to raise the bar for its own design performance. It prompts one to anticipate future projects of KPMB that will continue to break new ground, for themselves, for their clients and for their fellow architects.

THOMAS FISHER

Opposable Minds

In his book *The Opposable Mind*, Roger L. Martin, Dean of the Rotman School of Management at the University of Toronto from 1998 to 2013, refers to F. Scott Fitzgerald's definition of 'a first-rate intelligence' as someone who has 'the ability to hold two opposing ideas in mind at the same time and still retain the ability to function.' Martin sees that ability, 'to hold two conflicting ideas in constructive tension … to think our way through to a new and superior idea,' as not just a characteristic of a first-rate intelligence, but also of a creative mind.[1]

In many ways, every architect has this creative ability to some extent. It defines design thinking: the capacity to envision a possible future different from the present, to conceive of and then create something that doesn't yet exist. Some architects, obviously, do this better than others; we have only to look at the designed environment around us to see that. But few architects deploy their 'opposable minds' as clearly and exemplify that first-rate intelligence as thoroughly in their work as KPMB.

Opposable Architecture

This seems entirely appropriate, since KPMB have, among many other projects, designed an addition to the Rotman School of Management, giving physical form to the ideas that have made that school an international leader in integrating design thinking into business decision making. So let's start there in tracing the opposable minds of KPMB. Like much of the firm's work, the Rotman project comprises an addition to the school's existing building, which invariably means that KPMB's architecture must address the 'constructive tension' between the existing and the new.

At Rotman, the addition consists of a sleek, glass-wrapped office block that appears to hover above the adjacent business building and two historic brick buildings, while holding its own against the towering university library across the street. By pushing the office block back from the street and pulling the new, two-storey, glass-walled event space forward, KPMB maintains the intimate scale of the streetscape. The firm's design solution also pulls the life of the street and the school into the new building with a continuous stair — painted a hot pink — that moves people up through the addition's atrium. Using the new to enhance the old, increasing the density of a building while reducing its scale, opening up to the outside in order to draw people in — such opposable ideas show how great design accommodates differences and resolves conflicts in ways that are superior, making new 'wholes' out of disparate parts.

A short walk from the Rotman School, you see how KPMB applies that thinking in a variety of settings. Woodsworth College, an early KPMB project (1992), comprises a U-shaped addition that runs behind existing historical structures, with a generous, glass-door-lined corridor opening out to a new courtyard in the buildings' former backyards. The addition also wraps around a voluminous utilitarian building that now serves as a gathering space. You hardly see this project from the street and yet KPMB's background building unifies the foreground ones, and like a giant clamp, holds them all together.

Around the corner, you come upon KPMB's renovation of a historical stone building into the Munk School of Global Affairs (2012). Apart from a discreet rear entry lobby and stair-and-elevator addition, the firm's work here occurs mainly in the building's interior. And yet, the same opposable thinking prevails. Spaces once separated by a centre hall now open onto each other, allowing the school to accommodate larger groups or host big events, while also closing off parts into discrete rooms. Large digital screens and comfortable furniture allow students and faculty to have their own gathering places and yet remain linked. And, as you climb to the top of the building, rather than find a dark attic, you come upon a sky-lit space that draws people up to it. Knowing what people assume about the world, opposable minds like those of KPMB can play off those expectations to create something new and compelling. Where you might expect discrete rooms, you find flowing space; where you might expect darkness, you discover light.

Joseph L. Rotman School of Management, detail (opposite); exterior (top); staircase (centre); Woodsworth College cloister (bottom)

Further down the street, across from the firm's elegant residential tower One Bedford (2009), stands KPMB's extraordinary, extensively awarded Royal Conservatory TELUS Centre for Performance and Learning (2009). Once again, the firm has used an inherently opposable situation to great effect. Having renovated the historic brick-and-stone McMaster Hall, including its former memorial hall, into a small performance space, KPMB then added a gorgeous concert hall behind the original building, separated by a street-like, day-lit atrium. They also pushed a rehearsal hall and ticket booth forward to front Bloor Street, announcing the new addition and defining a forecourt for the entire ensemble.

The new and old parts of this project contrast and complement each other at the same time. The flowing wood interior of the concert hall recalls the sinuous handrail of McMaster Hall's wooden main stair while the addition's smooth stone cladding refers to that of the original building. And yet the addition clearly announces its difference. Unlike the massive walls of McMaster Hall, the multi-storey glass-walled lobby of the concert hall opens out to the adjacent Philosopher's Walk, turning a once under-appreciated passage on the University of Toronto campus into an active and much-used open space. Likewise, the conservatory theatre, often used for rehearsals, has large windows overlooking the street, bringing back-of-the-house activities to the fore and opening up the once fortress-like facility to passers-by.

Further down the street and around the corner, you come to another widely awarded KPMB project, the Gardiner Museum, also an addition to an existing historic building. The opposable mindset proves most valuable when confronted with the most difficult problems, and that proved to be the case here. KPMB faced the challenge of renovating the parking garage into additional museum space, adding a new entrance far back from the street and enticing visitors to want to climb up to the public event spaces on the top floor. And the firm had to do all of that on a budget that was very modest for a museum.

They did so by designing an inviting entry plaza that draws in people from the street to a series of stone-wrapped, glass-walled, box-like spaces. One of these box-like rooms projects over the entrance as if reaching out to museum-goers to welcome them in, while the others step back as if echoing the climb visitors will take through the vertically stacked galleries up to the top floor dining and event space. And once inside, you find your view directed back outside to the neighbouring brick and terracotta buildings, which act as a life-size display for this museum devoted to ceramic art. The museum serves the city and the city serves the museum in a nicely opposable way.

Opposable Urbanism

Few blocks anywhere in North America contain so many different kinds of buildings by one architectural firm, all varied in their expression and yet all extraordinary in their sensitivity to the opportunities and challenges of making additions or alterations to existing structures. Taken together, these buildings, like almost all that KPMB have designed, envision a new kind of city, one that Bruce Kuwabara has labeled 'Ourtopia.' As he defines the term, 'Ourtopia is situated between an unattainable utopia and a dystopian future … attainable through the transformation of the ideal into the real with a plurality of thought and action.' [2] You could also define Ourtopia as taking the idea of opposability, so evident in KPMB's buildings, to the scale of the city.

The very word Ourtopia makes it clear what city Kuwabara has in mind: KPMB's home turf of Toronto. The geographer and Rotman School faculty member, Richard Florida, describes Toronto as a global innovation centre, at the core of the 12th largest mega-region in the world, with what he calls 'messy urbanism — high-rise condos next to ramshackle Victorians, luxury

Royal Conservatory atrium and entrance off Philosopher's Walk; Gardiner Museum (top to bottom)

boutiques next to mom-and-pop shops.'[3] That 'messy' urbanism also means innovative urbanism, the kind of urban environment that attracts creative people and inspires creative ideas.

Kuwabara sees the necessary ingredients of a creative city like Toronto including an openness to 'complexity and heterogeneity ... (as) a fundamental condition of civil society ... (an) open-ended urban grid ... (that) promotes interconnectivity — of individuals, communities, institutions, economies, and events ... public debate ... (that) stimulates ... a vocal public, passionate clients, visionary architecture, and engaged patrons, critics and citizens ... an appreciation for heritage fabric ... and an annual cycle of cultural festivals.'[4]

KPMB has realized this urban vision in several of their projects. With Canada's National Ballet School, for example, they have created not only an extraordinary dance facility, but an entire piece of urban fabric, a microcosm of Ourtopia. Occupying a site in a part of Toronto that had seen better days, this project consists of a school located in an existing historical structure connected by a bridge to a new multi-level dance rehearsal and performance building. To help pay for the facility — one of the best of its kind in North America — developers have constructed high-rise residential buildings at the back of the site, with an internal street and drop-off area mid-block.

That mix of uses not only made the project financially feasible, but it also reflects the complexity, heterogeneity and interconnectivity that help spur innovation in a city as well as the appreciation of history and of the arts that encourage creativity in a culture. The National Ballet School has a buzz that draws in not just pupils, but the public as well, with rehearsal spaces visible from the lobby and with access through the building from the street to the residential structures behind it. Everyone — students and spectators alike — seem to engage in a kind of dance there in a wonderful example of messy urbanism in action.

You see the same sensibility in KPMB's commercial and corporate work as well. For them, the city comes first and the buildings follow suit in enhancing the energy of their urban settings. At the firm's design for Manitoba Hydro's headquarters in Winnipeg, KPMB and their associated architects and consultants have oriented the building not only to maximize its solar exposure in order to achieve their ambitious sustainability goals, but also to create a pedestrian passage through the block, connecting the city's main commercial street to the new public plaza on the south side of the site. That pedestrian space, with its indoor waterfalls conveying the source of Manitoba Hydro's power as a public utility, not only serves as the building's lobby, but also has enough height and width to double as a gathering place for private ceremonies and public events.

That desire on the part of the company to give back to the public also drove the building's remarkable energy-saving strategies. Stacked, six-storey-high atria on the south side of the tower let in fresh air, which the sun warms and a drip water wall humidifies before it gets drawn through the building's raised floors and up and out through the solar chimney on the north side of the structure. To further temper the indoor space, radiant floors and ceilings draw heated or cooled water from the building's extensive geothermal array, while operable windows in a double-glass wall allow employees to adjust the temperature of their work space. Such strategies make this tower not only one of the most sustainable high-rise office buildings in North America, but also an excellent example of leadership on the part of a public utility that utilizes one of the cleanest sources of energy available: water power.

The opposable city, in which public and private parties cooperate to create something more than either can by themselves, also exists in KPMB's commercial development work. In the firm's design for the TIFF Bell Lightbox and Festival Tower, they accommodate a public venue for the Toronto International Film Festival, including three cinemas and two screening spaces, as well as a private development: a 38-storey residential condominium tower. While the private development helps pay for the public benefit of the theatres and adjoining atrium, KPMB reverse the emphasis, setting the condominium tower back and pulling the five-storey cinema complex forward to the

Manitoba Hydro Place, south-east corner view

main street. This not only relates the complex better to the lower-rise buildings around it, but also foregrounds the structure that will draw in the greatest number of people.

Inside, KPMB have treated the 'Lightbox' like an extension of the city. The three-storey atrium features a red-painted box with a large window into the theatres' control booth, along with black zinc-clad cinemas and street-like circulation spaces between them. A café and restaurant, also designed by KPMB, add energy to the space and provide places for people to go before and after screenings.

These are the kind of facilities that will characterize the 'messy urbanism' — the opposable city — of the future. They don't fit neatly into any one building type or financing source, and yet, because of their hybrid nature, they bring to urban life exactly the kind of unexpected juxtaposition of activities that propel a population to think and act in creative new ways and that prompt innovators to see opportunities that others have missed. Any city can become Ourtopia, but cities like Toronto have a definite head start in part because of the vision of a firm like KPMB.

Opposable Place-making

Nor does this only have to happen in cities. KPMB have shown how suburban locations or sites far from the mixed-use density of downtown Toronto can have an equally creative mix of program and activities. Roger L. Martin's notion of the opposable mind is just that — a mindset that can occur wherever one chooses to apply it. And KPMB have demonstrated how creative opposable thinking can bring enormous value even to some seemingly unlikely locations.

You see this in some of the city halls that KPMB have designed. The Kitchener City Hall, a project in 1993 that brought KPMB to the attention of an international audience, offers an economically struggling city not just a new civic centre, but also an energetic and optimistic work of architecture that embodies the hopes of its leadership. Located on the main commercial street in Kitchener, the U-shaped building embraces a public plaza and skating rink that provide a sense of openness and play. You can't help walk down that main street without stopping to watch what is happening on that plaza.

The asymmetrical form of the building itself, with its glass-clad administrative tower, its stone-clad lower wings, and its central, day-lit rotunda providing public access to city services, convey the vitality of a city administration willing to support a work of this quality. 'Every building implies a city,' says Bruce Kuwabara, who led the design team on this project, and you can clearly see it here.[5] Composed of a diversity of parts, open at a variety of points, accommodating a range of activities in a building that, itself, looks like a loose assembly of dynamic elements — the Kitchener City Hall not only implies a city; it expresses what this city wants to be.

An even more unlikely location for a creative city hall occurs in Vaughan, one of the fastest growing suburbs in the greater Toronto area. As in Kitchener, KPMB won a design competition to design the Vaughan Civic Centre, in part because of their vision of how it would anchor a new municipal campus for this growing city, with a large open space, a new public library and a new chamber of commerce building. Driving through Vaughan, you don't expect to see the city hall's campanile tower, which terminates the main commercial street and stands in stately contrast to the visually chaotic quality of that suburban environment. The grand steps and plaza that lead up to the building from the parking area only reinforce that sense of municipal monumentality.

Inside, Kuwabara's notion of the building evoking a city comes through clearly. KPMB have organized the U-shaped facility around a series of street-like atria, with a main hall providing

TIFF Bell Lightbox north-east view from street and interior view from second level at atrium; Kitchener City Hall (top to bottom)

access to the most frequented public services and the city council chamber, with its sculptural seating area enabling the public to remain in close contact with council members. In the other two wings, narrower atria bring daylight deep into the building and allow those occupying the offices around them to open their windows as they would on a city street. These street-like spaces in the building do not just imply a city; they have the feel of a city, with people able to see each other and run into each other in myriad ways.

City halls have diverse programs almost by definition, given the range of activities they encompass, but you see KPMB's skill at mixing programmatic elements in private and non-profit facilities as well. Their design of the Centre for International Governance Innovation (CIGI) Campus places the Balsillie School of International Affairs around a central courtyard, and links it to a pavilion structure containing an auditorium, a café and public spaces. The pavilion is located next to the former Seagram Museum, a restored 19th century barrel warehouse that was readapted for the offices of CIGI. Although surrounded by three Governor General Award-winning buildings, the CIGI site seems very suburban, with extensive open space, a lot of cars and few pedestrians surrounding it — all the more reason why the building needed to have an urban quality.

That urbanism in a suburb is just one of a number of opposable qualities in this complex. Others include the massing and materials of the new building echoing those of the old warehouse next door, the openness of the entrance contrasting with the cloistered quality of the courtyard, and the diversity of internal spaces compared to the repetitive pattern of windows on the exterior. All of that and more lead to a completely surprising and delightful experience of the building, which continually counters your expectations and initial impressions. The building's combining of two different fields — public affairs and law — also has the promise of hybrid activities that can give birth to new ideas and new disciplines.

That opposability of disciplines, able to keep different ones in tension in order to generate new ones, pervades KPMB's academic work. Their Mike & Ophelia Lazaridis Quantum-Nano Centre at the University of Waterloo (2012), for instance, combines two related but different fields — quantum computing and nanotechnology — into one building. Each discipline has its own section, with the quantum computing building having alternating vertical bands of vision glass and mirrored glass, slightly angled to create their own visual 'quantum leaps' as you move around it. The nanotechnology section, in contrast, has a mirrored glass skin with an exterior hexagonal structure that carries some of the load of the building and echoes the molecular structure of carbon used so extensively in this form of engineering.

A brick-clad base, echoing the form and material of the neighbouring buildings on campus, holds these two glass buildings together visually, and more importantly, provides a meeting place for faculty and students working in these fields. A linear atrium in this base allows people to move from the ring road to the centre of campus, while also offering spaces for scientists to interact with each other and with the public. Universities once housed different disciplines in their own separate buildings, but projects like this show how much the academic community has become as full of opposable minds — able to keep apparently contradictory fields in mind at the same time — as creative firms like KPMB.

21st Century Creativity

Many in the architectural community look at the work of KPMB and see what appears to be a very clean, simple and straightforward modernism. A few even interpret their work as nostalgic, harkening back to the optimistic form-making that characterized modern architecture in North America after World War II, when the U.S. and Canada emerged as dominant global economies and modernism came to represent the rational and technological prowess that brought both countries to such prominence.

Vaughan City Hall; CIGI Campus; Mike & Ophelia Lazaridis Quantum-Nano Centre at University of Waterloo (top to bottom)

A deeper look at KPMB's architecture, however, reveals the superficiality of that reading of their work. While their buildings have many of the hallmarks of modern architecture — the simple forms, minimal details and asymmetrical compositions — the underlying ideas in this work show how much it differs from mid–20th century modern architecture. The latter almost always insisted on purity, separating functions, forms, spaces and materials in ways that ensured that one thing did not contaminate another. KPMB's work does just the opposite. It hybridizes functions, juxtaposes forms, combines spaces and mixes materials in ways that encourage interactions, knowing that out of such mash-ups come the kind of creativity and innovation that we need to thrive in a global economy.

Roger Martin, in *The Opposable Mind*, contrasts 'conventional thinking' with the 'integrative thinking' that creates new products and services. Integrative thinkers, he writes, 'take a broader view of what is salient,' they 'welcome complexity because they know the best answers arise from complexity,' they 'keep the entire problem firmly in mind while working on its individual parts,' and they 'search for creative resolution of tensions, rather than accept unpleasant tradeoffs.'[6] KPMB has some of the best integrative thinkers in architecture today and for evidence: look at the work!

References

1. Roger L. Martin, *The Opposable Mind, How Successful Leaders Win Through Integrative Thinking*. Boston: Harvard Business School Publishing, 2007.

2. Bruce Kuwabara, 'Ourtopia: Ideal Cities and the Role of Design in Remaking Urban Space,' in: Paola Poletto, Philip Beesley and Catherine Molnar (eds.), *Ourtopias: Cities and the Role of Design*. Toronto: Canadian Design Research Network, Design Exchange, Riverside Architectural Press, 2008, pp. 7–20.

3. Richard Florida, *Who's Your City? How the Creative Economy is Making Where to Live the Most Important Decision of Your Life*. New York: Basic Books, 2008.

4. Kuwabara, *Ourtopia*.

5. Ibid.

6. Martin, *The Opposable Mind*.

Engineering and Computer Science and Visual Arts Integrated Complex, Concordia University, detail of stair and LED wall leading from metro into the building (opposite)

CULTURE & MEMORY

The purpose of art is not the release of a momentary ejection of adrenaline but rather the gradual, lifelong construction of a state of wonder and serenity.

Glenn Gould

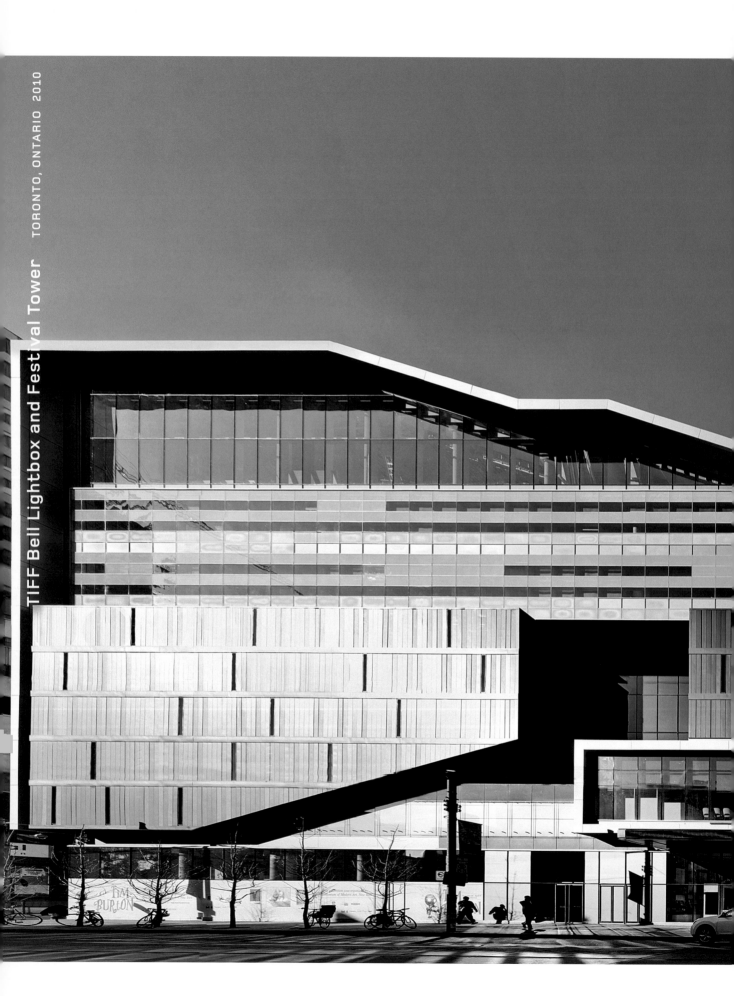

Founded in 1976, the Toronto International Film Festival (TIFF) is recognized as the most important film festival after Cannes and the most successful public film festival in the world. For almost 30 years it operated its programs from a circuit of 200 venues throughout the city. In 2003, TIFF embarked on a capital campaign to create a year-round public destination for individuals engaged with and passionate about film. The Reitman family — acclaimed filmmaker Ivan Reitman and his siblings Agi Mandel and Susan Michaels — donated a prime undeveloped site in the heart of downtown Toronto. The King and John Festival Corporation was formed to develop a mixed-use project combining the TIFF cultural institution with a residential point tower. The design was selected through an invited competition.

The Bell Lightbox and Festival Tower also function as urban infill, transforming an empty lot into a cultural and social landmark. The winning design competition scheme included a 46-storey tower, but city planners required the tower to defer to the post-modernist 27-storey-high Metro Hall located diagonally across from the Bell Lightbox. However, the client and architects argued that a taller tower would create an urban landmark for TIFF and provide an appropriate statement of the value of TIFF to the economic vitality of the city. They also demonstrated the benefits of the tall height for optimizing horizontal real estate. The City deferred with a slight reduction in height to 42 storeys.

Site The project occupies a full urban block at the northwest corner of King and John Streets in the heart of Toronto's media and entertainment district.

Program The Bell Lightbox comprises 17,570 square metres of multi-use, flexible space over five storeys to accommodate the ebb and flow of up to 2,000 volunteers throughout the year. It includes five cinemas for a total of 1,300 seats, an exhibition gallery, café, restaurant, retail shop, education studios and cinemas, administrative and production spaces and a film reference library and archives. The residential tower is 32 storeys high above the podium for a total of 42 storeys and 37,550 square metres.

Kuwabara Payne McKenna Blumberg Architects, Design Architect / Kirkor Architects & Planners, Architect of Record

Concept

The design concept creates a hybrid architectural expression that negotiates the cultural image of the street-related Bell Lightbox against a commercial residential image for the Festival Tower. It also responds to the competition terms which required an epic scale to create a city of film that would elevate the cosmopolitan profile of Toronto's media and entertainment precinct as well as reflect the heterogeneity of the city's multicultural population. The transition between the cultural institution and the residential development occurs at the point where the roof of the Bell Lightbox meets the base of the tower. The roof is stepped to provide an outdoor amphitheatre and terrace for screenings and events and formally references the roof of the Villa Malaparte, a classic icon of film and architecture.

The Bell Lightbox is a horizontal podium building with an open plan structure typical of the 19th century industrial lofts that characterize the historic fabric of downtown Toronto. Its footprint is set to the corner of the intersection of King and John Streets and extends the width of the entire block. The base is transparent while the upper portions are expressed as a composition of projecting volumes and textured surfaces contained within a massive, continuous frame that traces the geometry of the stepped roof. A café on the ground floor and a bar/restaurant with an outdoor balcony terrace on the second level vertically animate the north-east corner of King and John Streets. To foreground the institutional presence of TIFF, the residential tower is set back from King Street with its entrance flush with John Street.

The interior is treated as an urban set organized around a three-storey atrium with a suspended master control booth. Individual cinema volumes are treated as buildings within the building, and the spaces between them as urban laneways. The public circulation route is choreographed to culminate at a ramp leading to the cinemas on level three. On the fourth and fifth levels administrative and production spaces, library and archives are organized around a second, light-filled atrium.

Materials

The exterior combines clear, fritted and translucent glass panels that express the interior program of theatres and public gathering spaces to the street. The suspended master control booth is framed in red and the volumes of the five cinemas are clad in black zinc. The cinema interiors are dark and unadorned to focus audiences on the art of film.

Outcome

The Bell Lightbox contributes a strong urban attractor for tourists and visitors, fulfills City of Toronto Green Standards for high urban density and enriches the cultural vitality of downtown Toronto. The 42-storey condominium tower contributes a clean, contemporary figure to the evolving silhouette of Toronto's urban skyline to the west. The trafficable roof with the grand terraced stair provides the city with a new outdoor event space. More significantly, the Bell Lightbox brings together TIFF's programs under one roof for the first time in its history to ensure the long-term sustainability of this important institution.

View of TIFF Bell Lightbox and Festival Tower looking east to the historic downtown district of Toronto's Financial Core (top); competition model with detail of rooftop terrace with monumental stair (bottom)

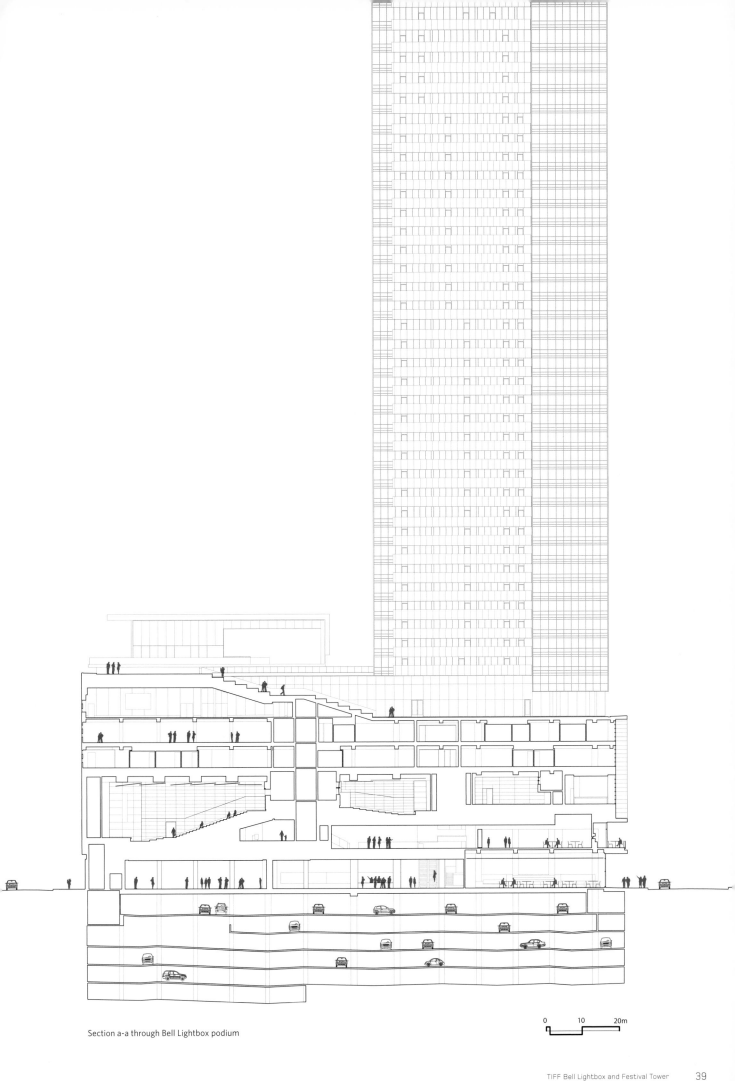

Section a-a through Bell Lightbox podium

0 10 20m

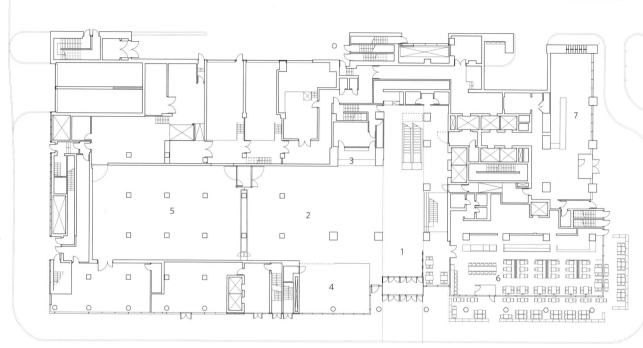

Ground floor

1 main entrance
2 atrium/lobby
3 box office
4 gift shop
5 gallery
6 Canteen Restaurant
7 condominium tower lobby
8 bridge/ramp
9 concession

10 balcony
11 theatre — 361 seats
12 theatre — 550 seats
13 theatre — 227 seats
14 bar/lounge
15 LUMA Restaurant
16 Green Room

Central atrium (bottom) and Canteen Restaurant
at street level (opposite)

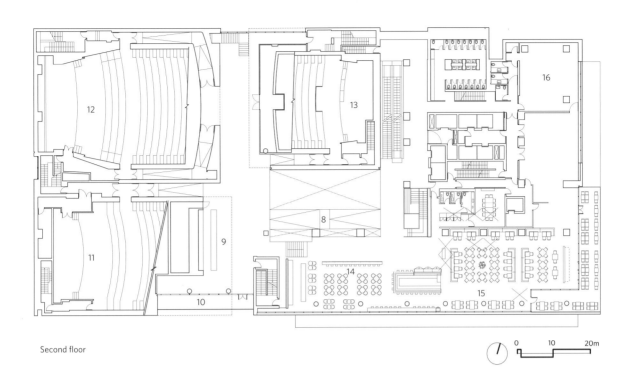

Second floor

The impact of the overall mass on the street was resolved by setting the tower back from King Street and integrating it into the base of the five-storey Bell Lighbox (top); view from top of Metro Hall looking north-west during grand opening (opposite)

The Royal Conservatory of Music (RCM) is one of the largest, respected music education institutions in the world. In 1991, the architects developed a master plan to support the RCM's stated mandate 'to develop human potential through leadership in music and arts education.' The master plan recommendations were phased over time to focus on the restoration of the exterior heritage fabric while funding for a larger expansion was secured. Over time the master plan was revised to reinvent the RCM as a hybrid educational institution and cultural destination.

Site Since 1962, the RCM has occupied a family of Victorian era buildings on Bloor Street West in an emerging cultural precinct in mid-town Toronto. The site is adjacent to the Royal Ontario Museum on Bloor Street, and surrounded on three sides by University of Toronto properties including Philosopher's Walk, a green landscaped north-south pedestrian path that links Bloor Street to the university campus. It is also around the corner from the Gardiner Museum.

Program The total program includes 17,280 square metres of new construction and restoration and adaptive reuse of the heritage Ihnatowycz Hall (1881). The new addition includes 60 teaching and practice studios, the Conservatory Theatre rehearsal hall and the 1,135-seat Koerner Hall performance venue.

Concept Conceived as 'a series of great rooms' for music, the design emphasizes the primacy of acoustics and reinforces the RCM's vision to foster creativity through innovative academic programs. The siting, massing and elevation of the new addition, a light transparent volume set above a low masonry wall, defers to the 19th century heritage buildings on Bloor Street. Its footprint is shifted away from the historical buildings to minimize impact to the heritage fabric. Three storeys of glass lobbies overlooking Philosopher's Walk and teaching and rehearsal studios wrap Koerner Hall. The space between new and old is adapted as an atrium/pedestrian route connecting the Bloor Street and Philosopher's Walk entrances.

A smaller-scaled addition at the west edge contains the main entrance from Bloor Street, with the Conservatory Theatre on the upper level.

The heart of the expansion is the Michael and Sonja Koerner Concert Hall. Developed in collaboration with Sound Space Design and Anne Minors Performance Consultants of London, England, Koerner Hall is designed as an ideal venue for a diverse range of music, as well as lectures and screenings. Its shape is inspired by the classic 'shoe-box' with two balcony tiers above the main orchestra level, and a third technical balcony.

Curved wood balcony fronts and walls form a sculpted 'liner' within the rectangular volume. A wooden veil of curved oak strings forms the backdrop for the chorus at the first balcony level and is lifted over the stage below the fixed acoustic canopy, extending into and over the full length of the hall at the technical balcony level. The wood strings undulate and are acoustically transparent to distribute sound and light over the stage and audience.

Materials Contemporary building systems emphasize transparency and lightness to create a dynamic counterpoint to the polychromatic masonry walls of the heritage building. Within Koerner Hall, every material was selected for acoustic considerations. The balcony fronts are shaped solid oak ribbons curving in three dimensions for acoustic sound dispersion. Custom bronze-cast glass light fixtures highlight their surface. The black ribbon wall tiles are shaped fibre-reinforced plaster tiles cast in a silicone mold with the texture derived from an original casting of plaster in rough fabric.

Outcome The new centre has generated synergies with a range of arts organizations in Toronto and is a highly frequented destination for students and parents, as well as the general public. Koerner Hall continues to be lauded by world class performers such as Yo-Yo Ma for the seamless fusion of architecture, engineering, acoustics and beauty.

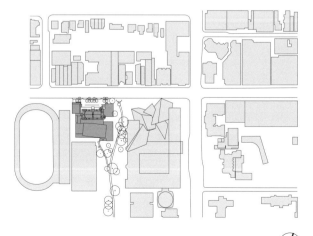

East entrance from Philosopher's Walk (opposite)

Located beside the Royal Ontario Museum, the RCM offers an essay in opposites to the explosive geometry of Daniel Libeskind's 'Crystal' expansion next door. While the RCM addition is substantial in scale and size, it deliberately is conceived as a backdrop to the historic buildings on Bloor Street.

The space between the historic and new building is enclosed to create a sky-lit pedestrian court. Glass and steel interventions act as a counterpoint to the polychromatic façades of the heritage building. The new envelope is clear glass set into minimal saw-cut joints in the existing walls.

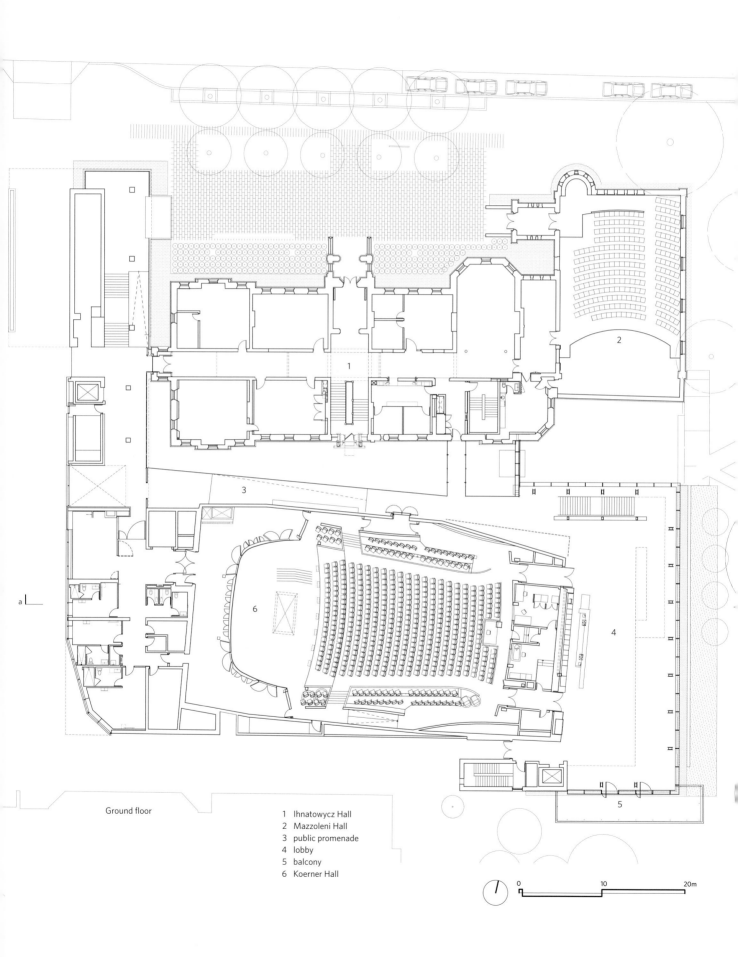

Ground floor

1 Ihnatowycz Hall
2 Mazzoleni Hall
3 public promenade
4 lobby
5 balcony
6 Koerner Hall

0   10   20m

The curved wood strings of the concert hall
are fabricated of solid oak strips in a jig from a
3D CAD model and twisted to distribute sound
over the stage while remaining acoustically
transparent over the audience in order to permit
the sound to fill the full volume of the space.

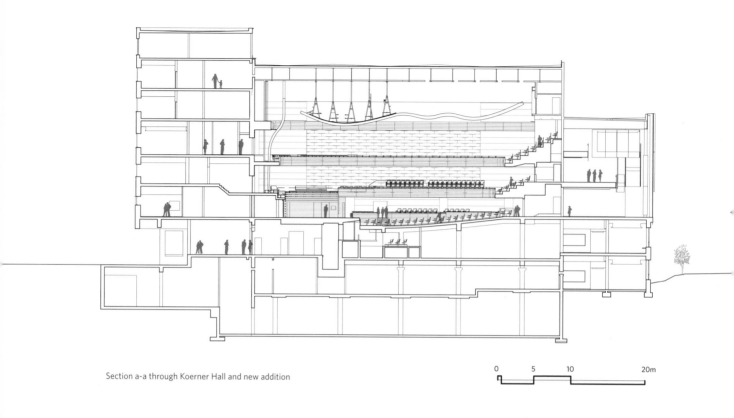

Section a-a through Koerner Hall and new addition

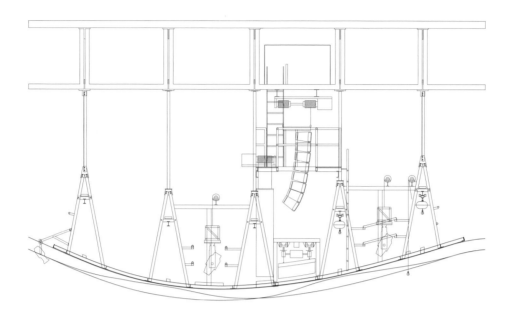

Detail section through acoustic reflector

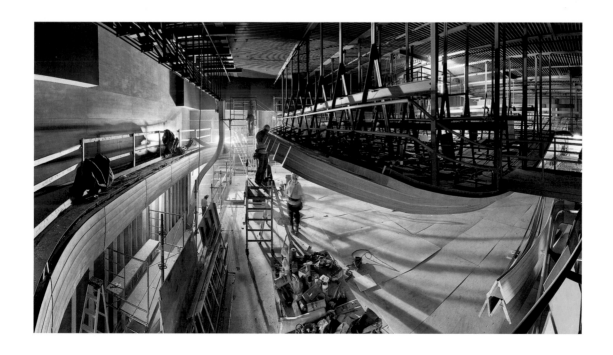

The 1,135-seat Michael and Sonja Koerner Concert Hall features an undulating wood 'veil' integrated with acoustical and technical devices. Natural oak, dark plaster planks and bronze details provide texture and warmth. The stage is proportioned to accommodate a range of performance groups and includes a generous stage extension for large orchestras.

Gardiner M

The expansion and reimagination of this small museum dedicated to ceramic arts was catalyzed by the need to address functional deficiencies that were impairing its cultural profile in the city. The transformation occurred within a limited budget and a very tight urban site. The challenge was to negotiate these requirements while preserving the intimate scale of the original building designed by architect Keith Wagland in 1983.

Site Located across University Avenue from the Royal Ontario Museum, immediately north of the University of Toronto's downtown campus, and around the corner from the Royal Conservatory of Music, the Gardiner is a significant presence in one of Toronto's evolving cultural precincts. The building is set within a niche formed by the limestone wall of the neoclassical Lillian Massey Building (1908–1912) to the north and the red brick façade of the Queen Anne-style Annesley Hall student residence (1901–1903) to the south.

Program The program involved 4,300 square metres of strategic additions and renovations. Within the existing building, this includes a new entrance vestibule, an expanded museum shop and a contemporary ceramics gallery. The third floor addition accommodates a flexible exhibition space, a café/restaurant and multi-purpose event space. The former underground parking garage was converted into ceramic studios and curatorial space.

Concept The design sets the museum in conversation with its surrounding urban context. The original two-storey museum was designed to zig-zag back from the street to protect views of the adjacent neoclassical limestone façade. To create a bolder urban presence for the Gardiner, the second floor is expanded and projected 2 metres and includes an outdoor terrace on its roof. The west exterior was re-landscaped with terraced platforms that step down to University Avenue.

Materials The original pink granite exterior was replaced with black granite and limestone cladding and louvres on the upper floors of the west and south façades. A new light grey limestone skin seamlessly wraps existing and expanded spaces together and transitions into a screen of limestone solar louvres over the glazed spaces of the upper floors. Steel and concrete block were used for the third floor addition, which is expressed as a light-filled pavilion. The interiors were refinished in limestone, oak and white drywall to foreground the diverse collection that ranges from pre-Columbian artifacts from the Americas to Renaissance majolica and modernist-era ceramic objects such as a Picasso vase.

Outcome The transformation has allowed the museum to originate and host international exhibits of contemporary works and attract significant collections, including the Macdonald collection of Japanese-influenced European porcelain deemed among the best collections of its type in the world.

The intimate scale of the museum is preserved and the reconfiguration of the plan and circulation draws visitors to previously unimagined views of the façades and pediments of the adjacent heritage architecture, and the city beyond.

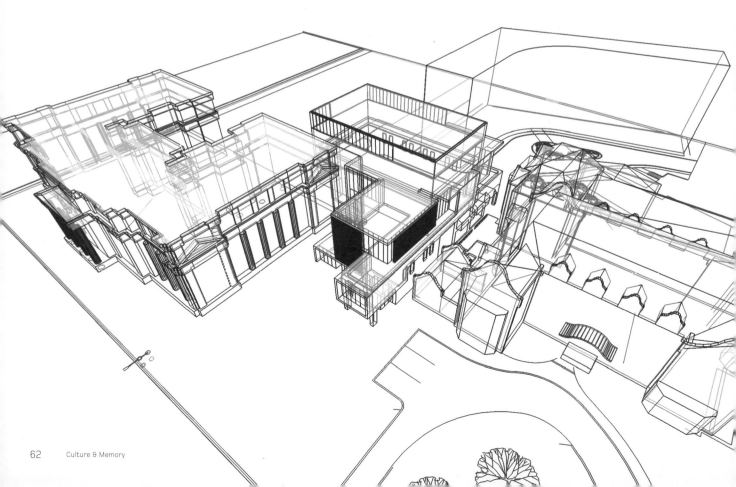

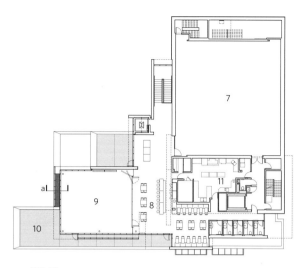

Third floor

1 entrance
2 reception
3 lobby
4 retail space
5 contemporary ceramic gallery
6 permanent collections gallery
7 temporary exhibition space
8 restaurant/bar
9 multi-purpose room
10 outdoor terrace
11 kitchen

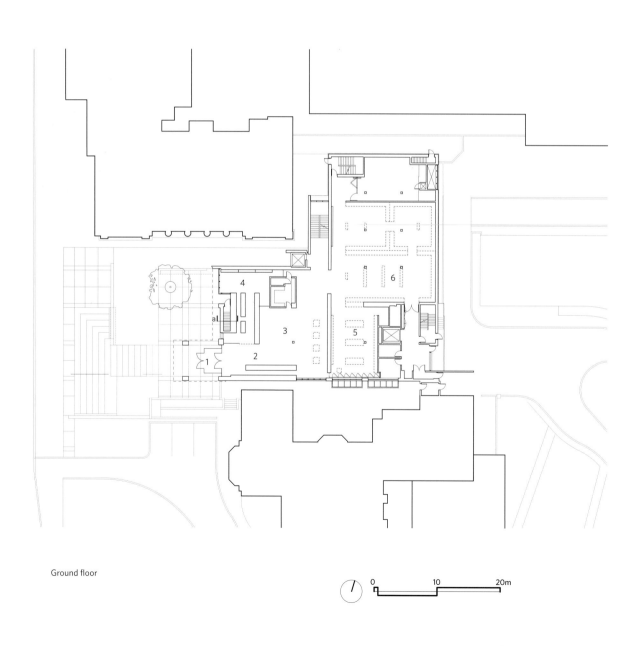

Ground floor

0   10   20m

Main entrance lobby with gift shop to left (top); contemporary
gallery (bottom left); detail of new stairwell (bottom right)

Third floor multi-purpose room (top); third floor exhibition gallery with inaugural exhibition *Jean-Pierre Larocque* (bottom right); view from third level terrace (opposite)

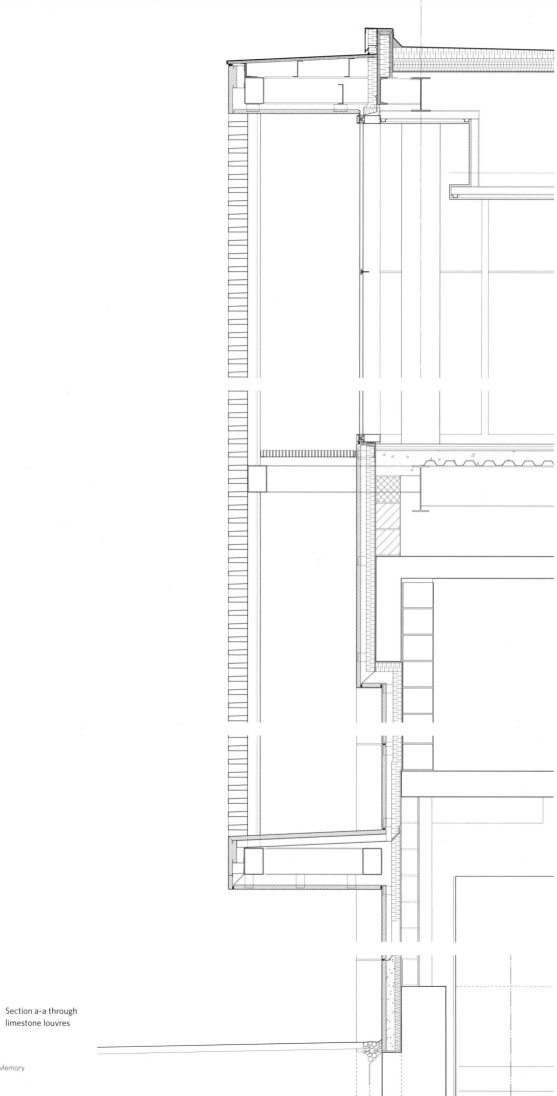

Section a-a through
limestone louvres

Views of main elevation (top); café/restaurant
(bottom); clay studio detail (opposite bottom)

Young Centre for the Performing Arts   TORONTO, ONTARIO 2006

The two clients for this project, the Soulpepper Theatre Company and the George Brown College Theatre School, partnered to create a hybrid centre combining teaching and performance in one public facility. In addition, it had to serve important civic and paedagogical functions to contribute to the growing vitality of the Distillery District as well as to provide a unique site for training, mentorship and hands-on practice programming in the dramatic arts. Moreover, it had to achieve these ambitions within a strict budget of $10 million (CAD).

Site The Young Centre is located within Toronto's Distillery District, an emerging retail and entertainment precinct east of downtown, housed in the revitalized industrial buildings of the former Gooderham and Worts Distillery, a 52,000-square-metre site founded in 1832. The Young Centre project occupies two existing brick warehouse buildings — Tankhouses 9 and 10 and the space between them — at the north-east end of the precinct.

Program The diverse program of 4,100 square metres includes a 400-seat flexible theatre, a 200-seat flexible format dance theatre, a 100-seat studio theatre, a cabaret stage, rehearsal/teaching studios, performance support spaces, workshop facilities, classrooms, lobby and ticketing facilities, and administrative offices for both organizations. The lobby and selected teaching spaces are designed to be easily converted into smaller performance venues.

Concept The concept was inspired by the anonymous architecture of the 19th century brick warehouse structures which were built by the same labourers who worked in the distillery. The masonry walls are treated as found objects and used as the backdrop to the program. Structural interventions are limited to massive Douglas fir beams which span the bearing walls of the two tank houses and enclose the space between to create a public lobby. Unlike traditional theatre lobbies that are designed for use before performances and during intermissions, the lobby of the Young Centre is accessible throughout the day and evening. A café and fireplace animates the space and a box office and large video screen promote the interactive and interconnected nature of the facility.

Materials The design is characterized by a warm industrial aesthetic to respect the historic fabric. Brick façades are left exposed, original windows are retained and the existing cobblestone pavements are conserved in their original states. New interior finishes are utilitarian, limited to concrete floors and painted walls. Ceilings are left exposed, and natural and artificial light reflected off the surfaces of the heritage fabric animates the space by day and night.

Outcome Within the Young Centre coexist layers of time and architecture, history and culture, teaching and performance. The flexible, utilitarian setting reinforces a commitment to theatre as an universal art form that transcends its setting. The playwright Thornton Wilder believed 'that theatre's ability to present the universal and the eternal made it the greatest of all arts.' The raw aesthetic of the Young Centre provided an apt backdrop for staging *Our Town* as the inaugural play to achieve Wilder's vision of foregoing scenery in order to foreground dialogue and action.

The intersection of a school and a professional drama company in one facility, with its array of multi-purpose and gathering spaces, has generated a lively culture of collaboration between students and actors and created a nexus for drama and performance for the city.

North elevation looking west (bottom); view of lobby (opposite)

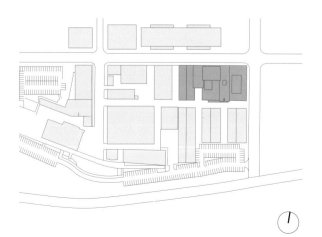

Typical rehearsal studio (top);
fireplace alcove in lobby (opposite)

SANDRA FAIRE AND IVAN FECAN ATRIUM

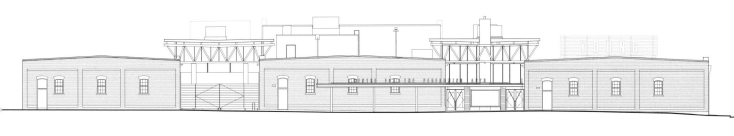

South elevation

0   5   10   20m

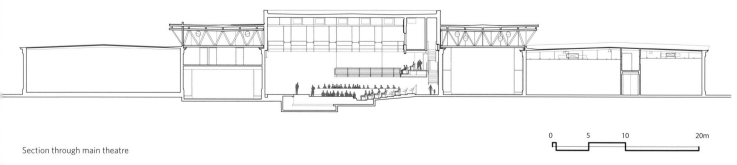

Section through main theatre

Canada's National Ballet School (NBS) is the only ballet academy in North America to provide dance training, academic instruction and residential care on one campus. Its emphasis on the physical and emotional well-being of the student has placed NBS as a leader in dance training. Since it was founded in 1959, its programs were distributed among a series of historic residences. The new purpose-built facility was conceived to match its rising international profile and to ensure the continued advancement and growth of its programs.

Site The project is located on two tight urban blocks (approximately 1 hectare) in the North Jarvis district, a former 19th century upper class neighbourhood in downtown Toronto that had been in a state of decline since the mid–20th century. It is sited to face Jarvis Street and integrates three Victorian era heritage buildings, Northfield House (1856), the former Havergal Ladies College (1889/1901) and the R.A. Laidlaw Centre (1988 restoration and renovation) which houses the Betty Oliphant Theatre.

Program The 16,700-square-metre project combines new construction and historic restoration to create an integrated campus containing 12 dance studios, a multi-purpose space, cafeteria, library/resource centre, teaching spaces, academic facilities and offices.

Concept The concept fuses architecture, dance, movement and spectacle within a series of horizontal stacked platforms to create a vertical campus. Three elevated transparent volumes — the six-storey North Tower, a horizontal five-storey 'bar' building and a four-storey pavilion building — are organized into an asymmetrical U-shaped configuration around Northfield House and connected to the Margaret McCain Academic Building (formerly Havergal Ladies College) and the R.A. Laidlaw Centre. The glazed curtain wall of the North Tower presents elevated views into the dance studios from the street and in turn allows the dancers to use the city as both backdrop and audience. The art of ballet as a form of storytelling is expressed on the façade of the Pavilion with a suspended plane of frit glass featuring an extract in Benesh Movement Notation of the opening scene from *The Nutcracker.*

Inside, the space between the heritage residence and the training centre is enclosed to create a three-storey Town Square. Here the major support programs — café, physiotherapy department and resource centre — converge. The café is encountered immediately upon entrance into the Town Square to manifest the school's stated mandate to nourish the mind, body and soul. Corridors and stairs are generously scaled to provide additional student warm-up and hang-out spaces. The second level, the piano nobile, is seamlessly linked via a bridge to classrooms in the Margaret McCain Academic Building and directly connected to the Betty Oliphant Theatre. Two-storey-high studios feature custom-designed sprung floors, ballet barres and lighting systems to optimize dance teaching and training.

Materials To achieve an economy of scale and enduring value the design maximizes innovative applications of pre-fabricated industrial systems. For example, the solid masonry walls that bookend the south and north buildings use pre-cast Shouldice Block in three colour tones laid out in a random pattern to modify the large surface areas while also making a subtle reference to French limestone and the fact that the creation of classical ballet occurred under Louis XIV.

Outcome The design has brought the art of dance to the street, stimulated community engagement and catalyzed urban revitalization. The thoughtful refinement of all elements, from the grand volumes of the dance studios to the ergonomics of the customized ballet barre, creates a supportive environment that inspires creativity and innovation. The design offers a model for harmonizing heritage and contemporary architecture and a metaphorical resolution to preserve and challenge the art of ballet.

Kuwabara Payne McKenna Blumberg Architects / Goldsmith Borgal & Company Ltd. Architects, Architects in Joint Venture

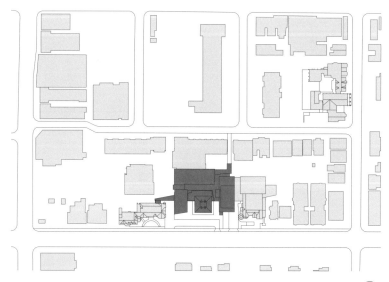

NATIONAL BALLET SCHOOL

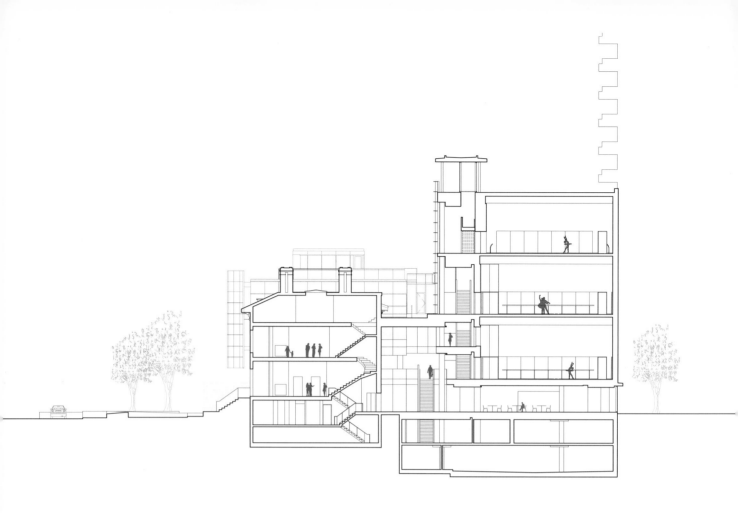

Section through east-west

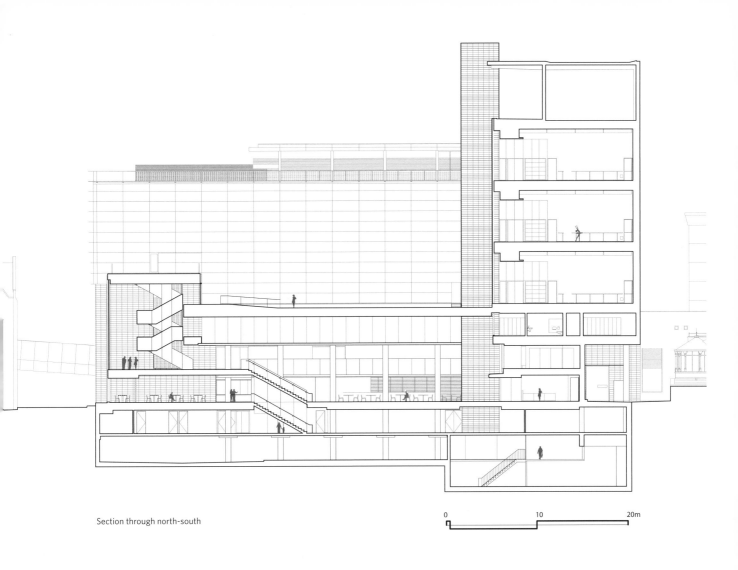

Section through north-south

0   10   20m

Student café/lounge off Town Square (top); bridge to Margaret McCain Academic Building (bottom); stair to level two; stair from Town Square (opposite bottom)

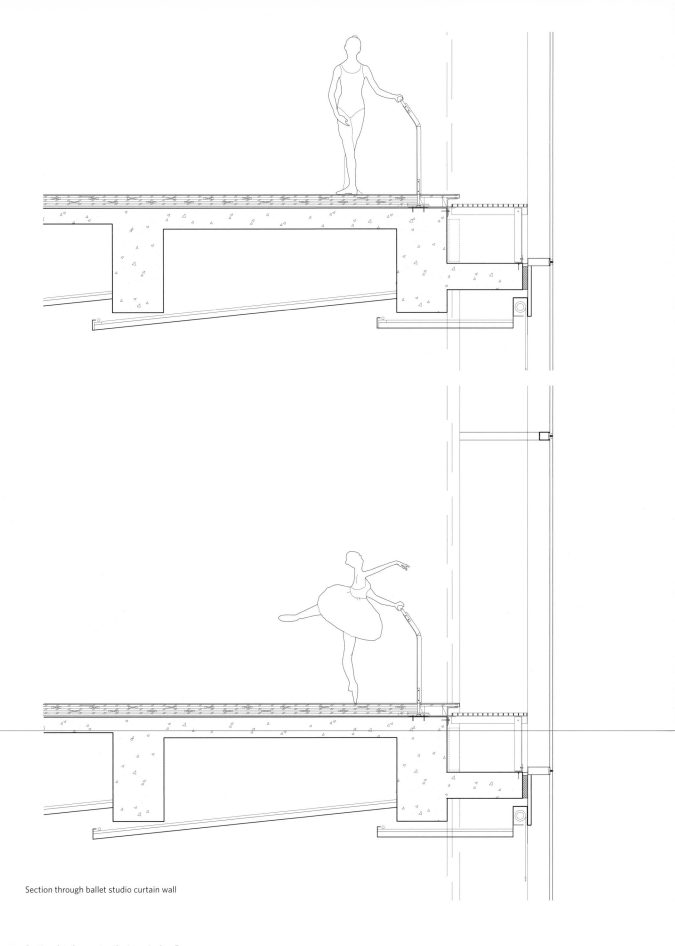

Section through ballet studio curtain wall

Section detail recreates the 'stage' edge. From
the interior of the studio, the exterior glazing
slides down past the edge of the floor (stage)
that is held back from the curtain wall and the
radiant heaters hidden below. From the exterior,
the ceiling is designed to read minimally and
monolithically like a three-dimensional blank
canvas with indirect lighting.

Dance studio overlooking Jarvis Street (top);
Jarvis Street studio (opposite bottom); detail of
custom-designed ballet barre (bottom)

City of Dance The Jarvis Street campus of Canada's National Ballet School is also part of a unique mixed-use development that aligns public and private interests to realize shared goals of urban revitalization. The dance training centre and full-time academic school is combined with the 32,500-square-metre Radio City high-density housing development (designed by architectsAlliance) comprising two point towers (25 and 30 storeys respectively) and a row of townhouses on the tight approximately 1-hectare site.

Massing strategies for the residential development and the low-density institutional building were conceived in tandem to conserve and integrate existing heritage structures and to configure shared public open space. Broadly recognized urban planning principles that link the vitality of street life and diversity of use to the level of safety in a neighbourhood, were also applied.

The Canadian Museum of Nature (CMN) opened in 1912 as the first purpose-built museum in Canada. The original building — known as the Victoria Memorial Museum Building (VMMB) — was designed by architect David Ewart in the Tudor-Gothic Style using Beaux-Arts planning principles. Shortly after its completion, the stone tower began to sink into the ground because of unstable soil conditions. In 1915, the upper part of the tower was removed, consequently disrupting the clarity of the plan order. During the course of the 20th century, the original park land that surrounded the museum was replaced with a concrete moat of parking. In 2001 the museum embarked on a renewal project to improve its public profile, functional performance, and exhibitions and programs as part of a vision of national service.

Site The project is located in Ottawa, Canada's national capital, at the south end of Metcalfe Street directly on axis with Parliament Hill in the Centretown neighbourhood. After Parliament Hill, this site is the largest green space in the downtown area.

Program The total program of 23,200 square metres involved 20,400 square metres of renovations to the existing heritage building and galleries and 2,800 square metres of new interventions.

Concept The design objectives were to cherish the heritage architecture as an artifact, restore the materials and craftsmanship of the Tudor-Gothic details and restate the axial clarity of the Beaux-Arts plan. To realize the museum's goals to raise its public profile, the architects also created a master plan for the redevelopment of the site. The former moat of parking that surrounded the building was relocated to the east, opening up space to consolidate back-of-house operational functions in a below-grade addition which is adapted as an elevated, outdoor South Terrace.

The terrace is set apart from the heritage walls and creates a platform from which to admire the robust sandstone walls laid and carved by 300 Scottish stonemasons over 100 years ago.

New interventions in the form of a Lantern Tower and Butterfly Stair revitalize the image of the museum while simultaneously restoring key elements of Ewart's original design. The glazed lantern element restates the original proportion of Ewart's entrance while the stair is inserted within the lantern to restore a continuous loop of movement through all four levels of the museum. The generously scaled stair contributes a series of new platforms from which to appreciate the craftsmanship of the historic building fabric up close.

Materials The majority of materials harmonize with the heritage building fabric. Danby Marble from Vermont is used for the Butterfly Stair and custom-coloured concrete pavers for the South Terrace match Sainte-Marc-Carrières limestone. Green roofs and the South Terrace landscaping feature native plants and grasses.

Outcome The renewal reinforces the value of preserving Canada's heritage artifacts for the enrichment of its social and cultural legacy. Since reopening, the museum has surpassed targeted attendance levels. Before the renewal, the museum was ranked fifth among the top destinations in Ottawa. It is now ranked second.

Padolsky, Kuwabara, Gagnon Joint Venture Architects (PKG): Barry Padolsky Associates Inc. Architects, Kuwabara Payne McKenna Blumberg Architects, Gagnon Letellier Cyr Ricard Mathieu Architectes

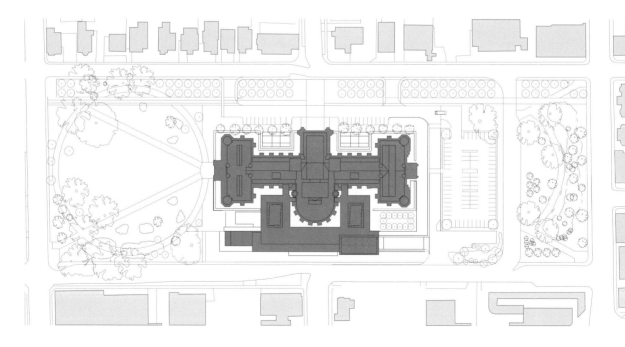

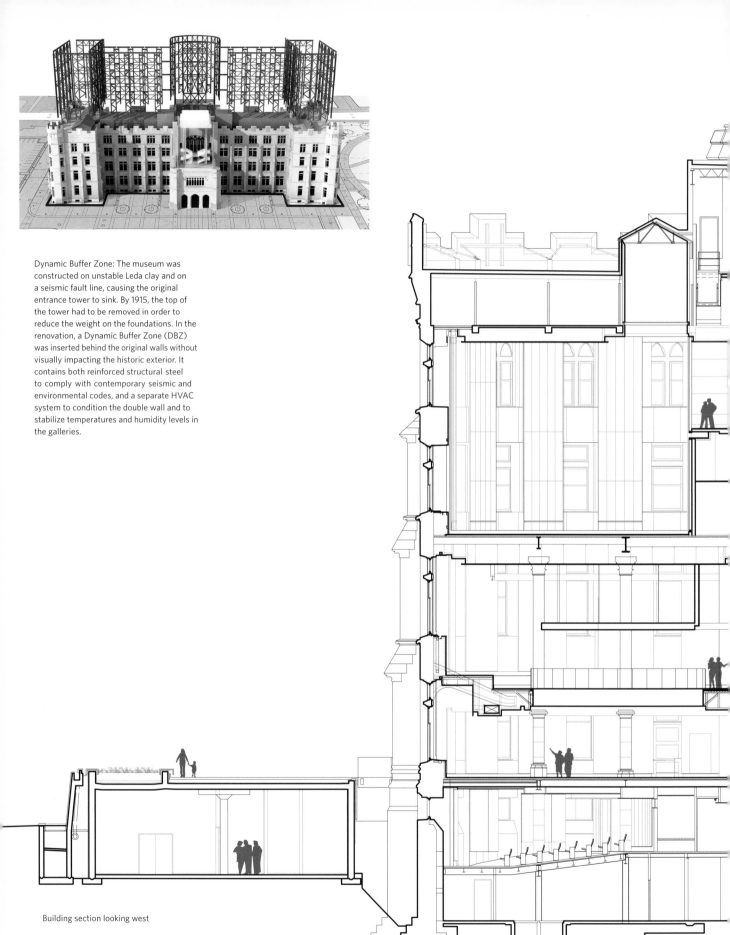

Dynamic Buffer Zone: The museum was constructed on unstable Leda clay and on a seismic fault line, causing the original entrance tower to sink. By 1915, the top of the tower had to be removed in order to reduce the weight on the foundations. In the renovation, a Dynamic Buffer Zone (DBZ) was inserted behind the original walls without visually impacting the historic exterior. It contains both reinforced structural steel to comply with contemporary seismic and environmental codes, and a separate HVAC system to condition the double wall and to stabilize temperatures and humidity levels in the galleries.

Building section looking west

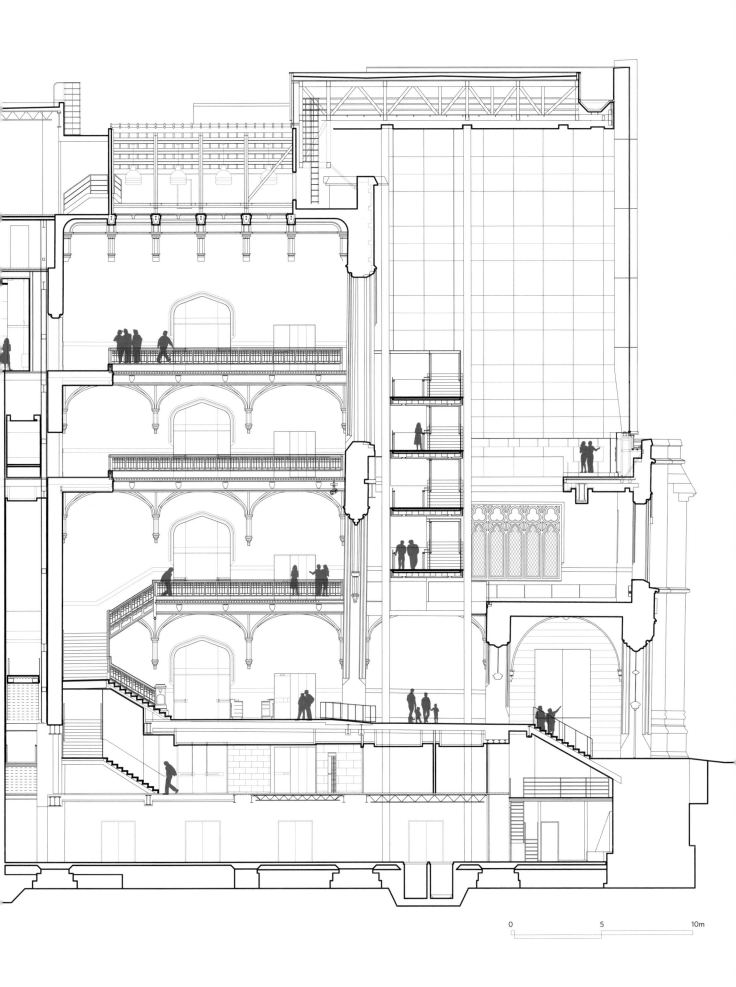

The Lantern is a structural glass fin assembly hung like a curtain from the cantilevered roof above the top of the existing stone parapet of the truncated original tower. Unlike the original heavy tower, it does not impose any weight on the existing masonry walls. The four columns supporting the roof truss are 35 metres tall and sit on new concrete piers supported by a 1.5-metre-thick concrete raft slab foundation. The Butterfly Stair ties the middle of these four columns together; the stair landings and flights structurally triangulate the assembly. The Lantern roof truss sits on the columns and is cantilevered from the two new concrete elevator core towers, located in the East and West Halls flanking the Atrium.

Since its opening in 1974, the Orchestra Hall has played a vibrant role in the cultural and civic life of Minneapolis. The original design by Hardy Holzman Pfeiffer focused on the auditorium, with a temporary lobby around the shell that was expected to be replaced after 15 years; it lasted more than 39 years. The renewal project focuses on improving the concert-going experience, contributing to the transformation and revitalization of the southern downtown district within the Twin Cities' cultural community and reinvigorating the outdoor public experience surrounding the Orchestra Hall.

Site The Orchestra Hall is located in the heart of Minneapolis's downtown core at Nicollet Mall, the southern end of the city's primary retail and commercial precinct and pedestrian and transit corridor. It is also the site of many buildings and public spaces designed by prominent 20th century architects including Gunnar Birkerts's Marquette Plaza (1972), Skidmore, Owings & Merrill's City Center (1983) and Philip Johnson's IDS Center (1972).

Program The 2,000-square-metre expansion of lobby and public spaces focuses on improving the overall concert-going experience and also adds 900 square metres for administrative offices.

Concept The architecture of the expanded lobby additions reasserts the presence of the Orchestra Hall as the south anchor of Nicollet Mall. Its crisp contemporary modernist aesthetic and emphasis on transparency were conceived to both harmonize with and act as a counterpoint to the existing Hardy Holzman Pfeiffer auditorium building. The main entrance is relocated to the building's west side, and marked with a wide canopy to create a generous arrival experience. A secondary entrance on Marquette Avenue welcomes patrons arriving by public transit. The expansion of the lobby to the west culminates in the City Room, a multi-purpose venue with a large fireplace, floor-to-ceiling windows and an outdoor terrace overlooking Peavey Plaza. Wood window mullions add warmth and complement the distinctive brick exterior of the original auditorium building. The total expansion of the new lobby will double the average floor area for each patron and provide a range of amenities including built-in benches, drink rails, bars and generous walkways which are woven through every level.

Materials The exterior is distinguished by Alabama Silver, honed light stone panels for the upper levels and Mesabi Black, honed dark stone for the base. Inside floors are finished in Champagne Mist, honed stone.

Outcome For the first time in its history, the Orchestra Hall will have a primary entrance. The design strategy ultimately ensures the long-term sustainability of the Orchestra Hall as a cultural beacon that will draw audiences from across the country and attract the world's great musicians.

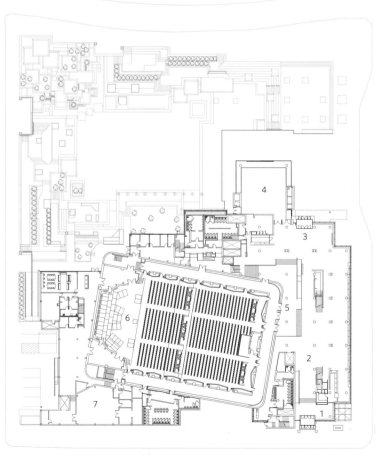

Ground floor

1   east entry
2   east lobby
3   west lobby
4   City Room
5   lower lobby
6   Orchestra Hall
7   rehearsal room

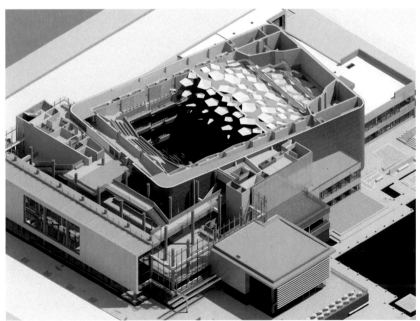

Remai Art Gallery of Saskatchewan

As part of one of western Canada's fastest growing urban centres and healthiest economies, the Remai Art Gallery of Saskatchewan is critical to the vitality of Saskatoon. It is conceived to participate in the realization of a 30-year plan to transform Saskatoon's south downtown into River Landing, an urban cultural and community redevelopment project between downtown Saskatoon and the South Saskatchewan River. There was also a requirement to build on the legacy of the Mendel Gallery, the city's primary cultural centre, which has served the citizens of Saskatoon with an engaging public space through all seasons and particularly during the long, cold months of the prairie winters, since 1964.

Site Located between downtown Saskatoon and the bank of the South Saskatchewan River, the gallery occupies the footprint of an L-shaped site located between First and Second Avenues.

Program The 11,500-square-metre, four-storey gallery includes a community gallery, studio classrooms, a film and lecture theatre, meeting rooms, spaces for receptions and other public events and ample storage space for the growing art collection.

Concept The massing strategy responds to the L-shaped site and faces south to the river and east to one of a series of roundabouts that connect the city to the river bank. The horizontal form evokes the topography of Saskatchewan's prairie landscape and its indigenous agrarian traditions of low-rising, rectilinear sheds and barns. Four cantilevered horizontal volumes engage the river edge to the south and the city skyline to the east. The south elevation spans the length of the site. The ground floor provides a continuous day-lit public space with entrances at each end to integrate the gallery into new pedestrian flows along the river bank.

Each of the four stacked horizontal volumes is designed as flexible loft space. The horizontal stratification maximizes south exposure for views to the river and access to natural light. Double-height areas and atria draw light deep into the floor plate, optimizing the low sun angles for passive solar heat gains during the colder seasons. Overhangs and screens block sunlight during warmer seasons.

Inside, a central atrium organizes the plan and is designed as a multi-purpose space for gathering and events. At the ground floor, a generously scaled connecting stair is conceived as a vertical community street.

Materials The exterior will be clad in a copper-coloured metal screen inspired by one of Saskatoon's historic architectural landmarks, the Bessborough Hotel, designed by the Canadian National Railway in 1932.

Outcome The design catalyzed a major donation from the Frank and Ellen Remai Foundation. The building will meet rigorous modern gallery standards, making it possible to host national and international touring exhibitions previously unavailable to the city, and to acquire new collections. The design will also achieve 50 percent lower energy consumption in a climate where temperatures drop to –40 degrees Celsius in winter months compared to gallery standards with a conventional climate concept. The design will reinforce the value of the arts for cultivating community while advancing Saskatoon's evolution as a creative city.

Kuwabara Payne McKenna Blumberg Architects,
Design Architect / Smith Carter Architects & Engineers,
Architect of Record

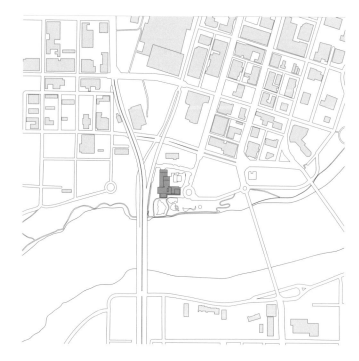

Artist rendering of south-west elevation (top);
main entrance view at south-east (bottom)

CAMPUS & COMMUNITY

**What makes life worthwhile and enables
civilizations to endure are all the elements and
qualities that have poor returns under commercial
metrics: universities, temples, poetry, choirs,
parks, literature, language, museums, terraced
fields, long marriages, line dancing and art.
Nearly everything humans hold valuable is slow
to develop and slow to change.**

Paul Hawken, *Blessed Unrest* (2007)

The City of Vaughan was originally part of an agriculturally oriented hinterland located at the northern edge of Metropolitan Toronto. Today it is one of Canada's fastest growing municipalities. In the latter half of the 20th century, Vaughan began to transition into an industrial-commercial epicentre. In the absence of a unifying urban plan, the pastoral landscape was rapidly replaced with disparate, generic big box retail outlets, subdivision housing and corporate headquarters. An invited competition was organized in 2003 to introduce environmentally responsible, civic-focused development. The competition terms required an architectural treatment for a new city hall building and a master plan for the entire Civic Centre site. The City Hall completes the first phase of development.

Site The 9.7-hectare site is bounded on the north and west by high-speed vehicular routes and on the east by the railway tracks of Metrolinx (GO Transit), Ontario's interregional public transit system; its GO station is also located to the north. On the south it backs onto a residential subdivision.

Program Phase 1 includes the 26,000-square-metre City Hall with Council Chamber, Civic Tower and civic administrative offices. Phase 2 will include a public library and Chamber of Commerce building as well the Civic Square, a reflecting pool/skating rink, public gardens and a naturalized park.

Concept The competition scheme is based on the idea of a civic campus assembled within a flexible infrastructure. Although the site was zoned for six storeys, no building is more than two storeys high to relate to the surrounding context of low-rise commercial and residential buildings. The organization of the civic campus into linear bands is conceived as an abstract trace of the dominant axes of the underlying concession grid pattern that characterizes Ontario's agrarian past. The plan order is also inspired by the clarity of town planning in Ontario, where city hall, civic square, market and cenotaph formally relate to define an identifiable civic precinct.

The City Hall and Civic Tower anchor the composition at the north-east. The program is organized into three wings and massed to step down in height from the north-east and to anticipate integration with future pavilions to be located to the west and south. Each wing is divided along its length at its mid-point by an atrium that rises to the uppermost roof level by one storey and allows daylight into the central floor plate. The ends of the atria are terminated by internal vertical circulation stairs.

Materials The material palette prioritizes natural, renewable and low-emission materials including chemical-free baked terracotta for exterior cladding, double- and triple-glazed glass curtain walls combined with thick slabs of Canadian Kodiak granite used both for exterior landscape and interior floor finishes. Interior spaces are finished in exposed concrete, perforated aluminum and oak wood with terrazzo and oak floors, and carpet tile.

Outcome Responding to the city's desire to demonstrate its leadership role in sustainability, the architecture is fully integrated with all facets of sustainable design — site, environment and human asset value. Every opportunity was sought out to reduce the building's operating dependence on natural resources. The design has also provided the people of Vaughan with a civic heart in which to gather and share the rich multicultural heritage and traditions of the city's diverse ethnic and immigrant population.

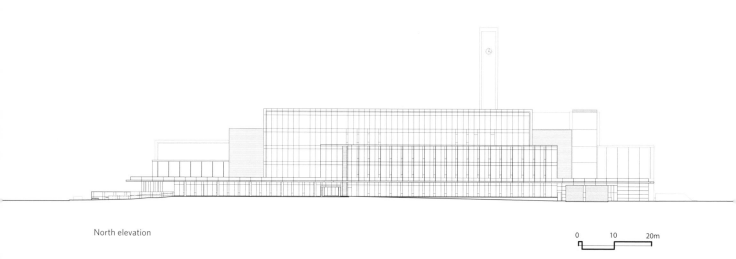

North elevation

0   10   20m

West elevation (top);
south-east elevation (bottom)

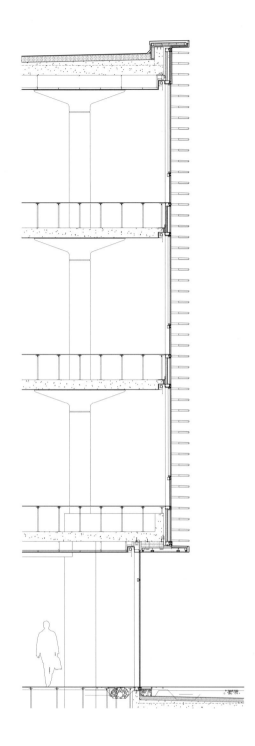

Wall section b showing terracotta louvres

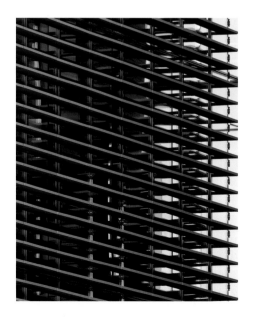

Views of central atrium (top and opposite top);
concrete form work during construction (bottom
and opposite bottom)

Vaughan City Hall   113

Work lofts adjacent to north atrium; detail
inside clock/stair tower (opposite)

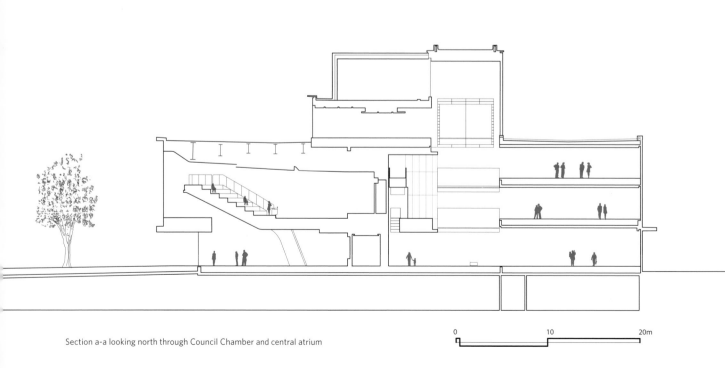

Section a-a looking north through Council Chamber and central atrium

0   10   20m

Council Chamber with views to Civic Square (bottom and opposite top); multi-purpose room beneath Council Chamber with access to Civic Square (top)

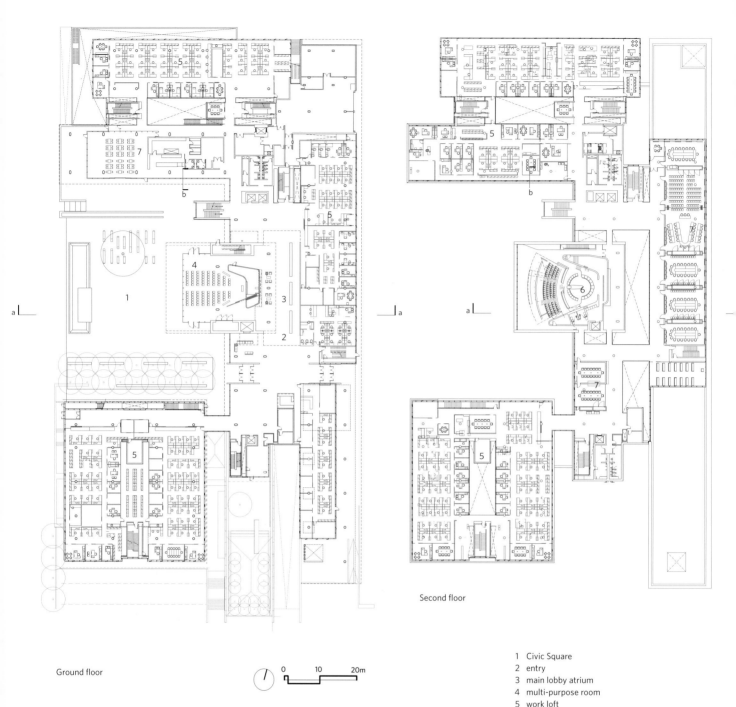

Ground floor

Second floor

1 Civic Square
2 entry
3 main lobby atrium
4 multi-purpose room
5 work loft
6 council chamber
7 committee/hearing rooms

0   10   20m

Civic Square looking towards south loft (top);
winning competition master model (bottom)

67

The Balsillie School of International Affairs completes the first phase of a master plan to transform the historic Seagram Distillery into a campus for the Centre for International Governance Innovation (CIGI). CIGI is an independent, non-partisan think tank located in downtown Waterloo. Waterloo is part of Canada's Technology Triangle delineated by the Waterloo Region which also includes the cities of Cambridge and Kitchener.

Since 2003, CIGI has been housed on the site of the distillery in the former Seagram Museum. The distillery was the city's economic force since 1857, until it closed in 1992 and was rezoned for commercial development. In 2007, CIGI partnered with the University of Waterloo and Wilfrid Laurier University to convert the historic site into an intellectual and social locus. The site was rezoned for institutional use to strategically contribute to the reurbanization of Waterloo.

Site The CIGI Campus is located on a 15,780-square-metre site in uptown Waterloo.

Program The three-storey, 10,700-square-metre building integrates public and teaching areas, faculty offices, student work spaces, administrative offices and service spaces as well as a bell tower and a 250-seat auditorium/lecture hall with an adjacent café. It is planned to accommodate 90 students, 60 affiliated faculty, 18 permanent faculty and director positions, visiting scholars, diplomats, senior civil servants and administrative staff.

Concept In response to the client's request for a courtyard building with a bell tower, the design offers a contemporary interpretation of the academic quadrangle in the 'Oxbridge' style with three interconnected bar buildings organized around a central courtyard.

A two-storey glass pavilion with a large-scale entrance canopy and bell tower marks the main entrance and is sited to create a publicly accessible pedestrian route between the new building and the historic barrel warehouse. The spaces facing onto the courtyard form a continuous glass-enclosed cloister with seating and fireplaces.

To achieve the goal to create a building that would last 100 years, the client chose not to pursue conventional LEED certification and instead invested in quality materials and construction to gain long-term value through durability and sustainable strategies that achieve 50 percent energy savings over the Model National Energy Building Code (MNEBC). The project was also planned to support the local economy by engaging local contractors and suppliers and optimizing the use of local materials.

Materials A limited palette of local limestone and brick masonry, Douglas fir, and glass is combined with a hybrid system providing in-slab radiant heating and cooling and structural slabs using the long-span composite slab BubbleDeck system to achieve high quality and reduce maintenance through durability.

Outcome The CIGI Campus demonstrates the tangible role architecture plays in mobilizing positive change and building civil societies. The integration of the new institution into the downtown community is directly contributing to the city's reurbanization efforts. The serene atmosphere supports focused research while the connected, transparent sequence of spaces catalyze face-to-face interaction between students, faculty and visitors in real time to generate transformative solutions to urgent global issues.

View over courtyard water feature into main
entrance pavilion (top); view across courtyard to
auditorium pavilion (opposite)

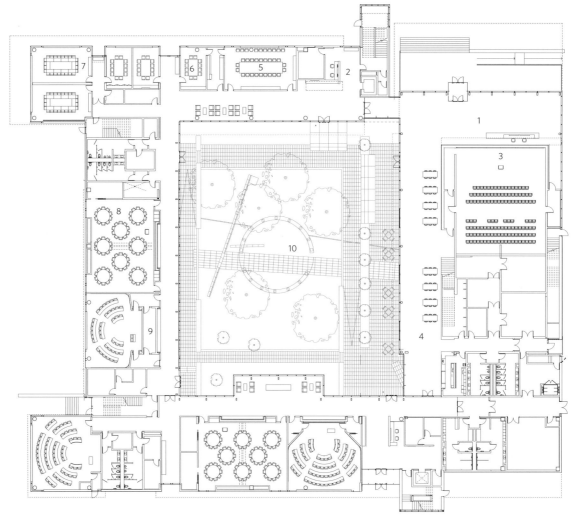

Ground floor

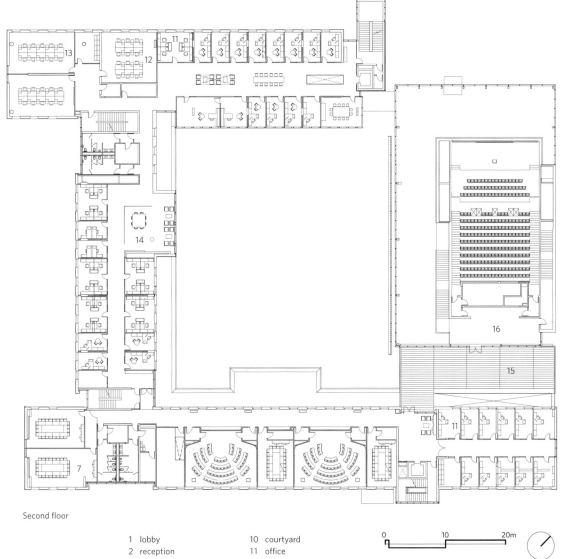

Second floor

1 lobby
2 reception
3 auditorium
4 café
5 boardroom
6 small seminar room
7 large seminar room
8 multi-purpose theatre
9 tiered classroom
10 courtyard
11 office
12 MA program area
13 seminar/study room
14 fireplace/lounge
15 exterior terrace
16 upper lobby

0   10   20m

Centennial College is one of the most culturally diverse post-secondary education institutions in Canada recognized for its emphasis on career-oriented programs. The Applied Research and Innovation Centre is a milestone in realizing the college's strategic objectives to forge stronger connections between university degree and college diploma programs and to meet demands for specialized and trained individuals in the labour market.

Site Located at the south-east corner of a major vehicular street within the watershed of the Highland Creek, the site slopes south to the ravine and Lake Ontario.

Program The overall program space of 23,000 square metres is designed to accommodate more than 2,700 day-time students and includes a full-service resource centre, six computer labs, 47 specialty labs, cafeteria, administrative offices and generous spaces for circulation, meeting and individual and group study.

Concept Historically, Centennial's facilities were modelled on the hermetic, locker-lined high school typology. The new building reflects substantial input by the student council to create a design that inspires accountability, self-discipline and independence.

The concept is based on the idea of creating a self-sufficient academic village. The four-storey, concrete-framed structure comprises two horizontal wings organized to form a broad V-shape that sits precisely within the contours of the triangular lot. It is organized as a flexible loft with a 6 by 12-metre structural grid with clear span raised floors, operable windows, high ceilings and internal partitions that can be shifted on a 1.5-metre grid.

The south-east entrance occurs where the two wings meet, forming a gateway that leads directly into the Town Square. The Town Square features a large wooden volume containing a lecture hall suspended above an indoor amphitheatre that is fully wired for informal study outside the classroom and flexible to accommodate formal assemblies. In each wing, light-filled interior streets run along both sides of central atria and provide generous circulation spaces culminating in lounges and views to the exterior.

Materials The ground levels of the south and west elevations are expressed as dark, charcoal brick retaining walls which follow the sloped topography. Frit and tinted glass and black corrugated steel siding distinguish the north elevations. Inside, with the exception of Douglas fir for the lecture hall, materials are characterized by low-cost, pre-fabricated industrial systems and painted drywall applied in broad expanses. Pre-cast raised floor tiles facilitate the integration of wireless technologies. MDF was routed and lacquered to add texture within the atrium spaces. Large expanses of south- and west-facing glazing are shaded by horizontal and vertical louvres.

Outcome The design has greatly improved the way Centennial trains its students, maximizing opportunities for practical applications with industry leaders while enhancing the intellectual rigour of its programs through new research programs with universities. Among its many benefits, the large common spaces and wide circulation systems provide an ideal setting for simulated hospital facilities for up to 700 participants and observers involved with patient triage and care in simulated disaster exercises.

Kuwabara Payne McKenna Blumberg Architects / Stone McQuire Vogt Architects, Associated Architects

West elevation (top); north-east elevation featuring a black sculpted pedestrian bridge that connects fourth level entrance to parking lot (opposite bottom and bottom)

Amphitheatre/stair beneath Douglas fir-clad lecture volume connects indoor Town Square to second level.

The Study at Yale Hotel converted and expanded the former Colony Inn (1962), a motor court hotel. As one of three hotel options for visitors to Yale University, it maintained a relatively privileged position, catering to visiting professors, parents of students attending Yale, researchers and foreign delegates. By the late 1990s its painted egg crate, concrete façade and interiors had devolved and it operated as a non-descript 'B' class city hotel. In 2006, the client and the architect developed a vision to redevelop the Colony Inn as a model for a future collection of well-serviced small hotels at accessible price points associated with North America's great university campuses.

Site Located in the Chapel West business district of downtown New Haven on the edge of Yale University's historic central campus, the building is just a few metres away from Yale's Art Museum and Centre for British Art and the Yale Repertory Theatre.

Program The original five-storey hotel was expanded to seven storeys to accommodate 120 rooms for a total of 6,500 square metres.

Concept The design was conceived as an urban infill project framed between two turn-of-the-century masonry-clad wall buildings and pushed forward by 3 metres to align with its neighbouring buildings and create a more harmonized street wall condition. The ground level features a 30-metre-long, one-storey glazed lobby raised above the sidewalk with a 'living room' lobby on the left, and a café/bar to the right of the centrally located entrance.

Two new steel frame floors were added to a reinforced frame of the existing building. An additional penthouse space above the seventh floor was developed to provide an exclusive rooftop lounge for guests, with panoramic views over the iconic skyline of Yale's campus. The new perimeter walls also provide maximum access to light and views, and are equipped with integral fan coils and operable windows as part of the hotel's green agenda.

Materials Wood and stone is used to echo the richness of Yale's architectural heritage. The canary-yellow façade was reskinned in a pewter-coloured curtain wall and animated with a random pattern of glass operating tiles, a subtle play on the popularity of stained glass in the collegiate Gothic architecture of Yale. A broad honed limestone frame stretches along the entire street elevation and is capped with a sleek metal and wood canopy.

Outcome Since opening in 2008, the Study has maintained a highly competitive price for accommodation and has been reviewed and recommended by the *New York Times*.

Eighth floor lounge overlooking Yale University campus (bottom); main entrance on Chapel Street (opposite top); view from Chapel Street looking into restaurant (opposite bottom)

The Joseph L. Rotman School of Management, part of the University of Toronto, is internationally recognized as one of the world's most innovative business schools because of its curriculum of Integrative Thinking™. The success of the program caused the school to rapidly outgrow its first purpose-built building. The expansion was conceived to create a global hub in which to evolve Rotman's core mission to promote the power of creativity, innovation and integrative thinking in 21st century business education. A design was selected through an invited competition held in 2007 to ensure the new architecture would establish the Rotman as a destination for the world of business to gather and mobilize solutions and initiatives that benefit the economy and society.

Site The project is located at the north-west precinct of the University of Toronto's downtown campus. It is surrounded by the original Rotman building (1995, Zeidler/Roberts Partnership) to the north, the John P. Roberts Research Library (1973, Warner Burns Toan & Lunde) across the street and Massey College (1963, Ron Thom architect) to the east. It also integrates a Victorian-era residence (1888–1889) as part of its St. George Street elevation.

Program The nine-storey expansion of 15,000 square metres doubles the size of the original Rotman facility. It includes the Desautels Centre for Integrative Thinking, the Lloyd and Delphine Martin Prosperity Institute, as well as other research programs and Institutes for Excellence, a 400-seat multi-purpose lecture/event hall, a diversity of tiered and flat floor classrooms, conference and multimedia rooms, student lounges, study rooms, offices and hospitality functions.

Concept The expansion is integrated with the existing building and the Victorian residence to form an integrated, vertical campus with connections at multiple levels. In scale and massing it responds to the variety of conditions presented by the surrounding context, mitigating between the residential scale of the Victorian residence and the massive scale of the Robarts Library across the street. It is sited to respect views and minimize shadow impact on Massey College to the east.

Two signature spaces epitomize the Rotman's commitment to integrative thinking and teamwork: the 400-seat Event Hall and the South Atrium. The Event Hall is expressed as a large-scale elevated glass box on St. George Street to broadcast the diversity and vibrancy of the Rotman's programs to the campus and the city. The South Atrium features a monumental serpentine stair with pink accents.

Materials The exterior cladding includes pre-cast concrete Ductal panels to resonate with the slate roofs of the historic campus fabric as well as tinted glazing in a range of subtle shades of grey to provide various degrees of reflection, shading and transparency. The interior palette employs white oak on both the atrium locker walls and on classroom walls and furnishings. The colour palette is limited to black glass and white drywall, with an accent of hot pink used in the atrium stair.

Outcome As the centrepiece of an ambitious capital, research and education project to enhance the global competitiveness of Ontario and Canada, the architecture has given the Rotman the necessary platform from which to embark on its next phase of growth; growth to establish the Rotman as one of the world's best business management schools.

1

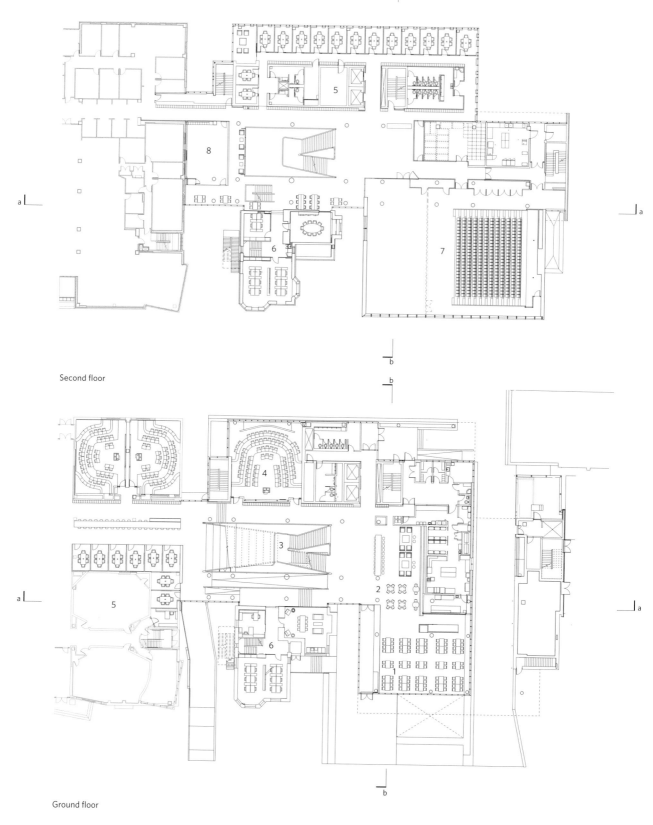

Second floor

Ground floor

1 café
2 fireplace lounge
3 atrium/stair
4 70-seat tiered classroom
5 study room
6 heritage house/Ph.D. offices
7 Event Hall
8 Venture Lab

0   10   20m

Entry foyer with fireplace lounge and café beyond
(top); second floor Event Hall with retractable
seating (bottom)

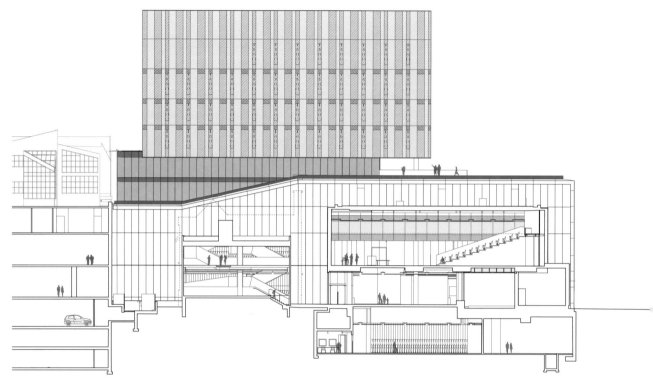

Section a-a looking east

Perimeter stairs and glazed corner offices optimize
views over the campus and the city beyond.

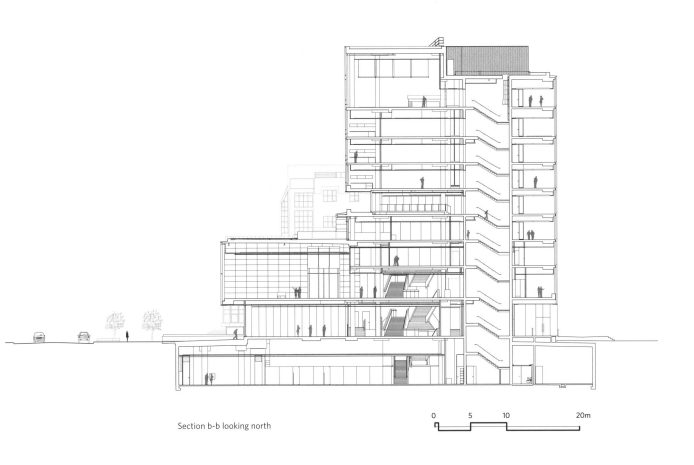

Section b-b looking north

0   5   10   20m

The fifth floor terrace features a polished
stainless steel ceiling and an ipê wood deck.

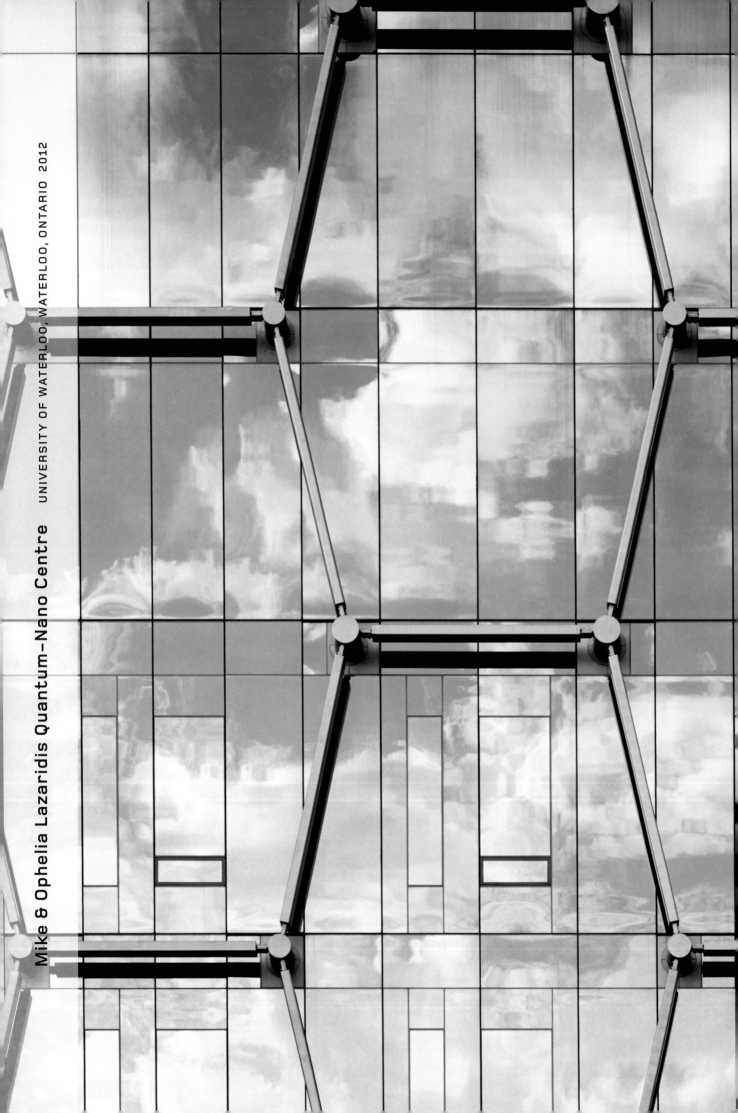

Mike & Ophelia Lazaridis Quantum–Nano Centre   UNIVERSITY OF WATERLOO, WATERLOO, ONTARIO 2012

The Quantum-Nano Centre (QNC) at the University of Waterloo is the first research facility of its kind in the world to bring together the disciplines of quantum computing and nanotechnology in one building. It was conceived to generate synergies between the respective fields of quantum computing and nanotechnology for groundbreaking research leading to innovative solutions and commercialization.

Site The building is located on the University of Waterloo's main campus in the Math/Computer/Science precinct and set within an existing network of routes and courtyards.

Program The five-storey, 26,500-square-metre facility houses the Institute for Quantum Computing (IQC), the Waterloo Institute for Nanotechnology and the University of Waterloo's undergraduate program in nanotechnology engineering for up to 400 academics. It includes a 929-square-metre cleanroom with fabrication facilities for quantum and nanodevices, an advanced metrology suite, extensive teaching and research laboratories, a multi-purpose space/auditorium, seminar rooms and offices.

Concept To provide the IQC and nanotechnology engineering each with its separate identity within the whole, the massing strategy combines two volumes joined by a common six-storey central atrium with two main entrances: one on the ring road to serve IQC and the other on the campus side for nanotechnology engineering. The atrium also provides a sheltered pedestrian route and informal gathering space.

The IQC is housed in a 'bar' building with an east-west orientation. The heart of the IQC is the six-storey atrium with suspended stairs. Conceptually inspired by the Newton Institute in Cambridge, England, it features 'mind spaces' — lounge, office and meeting rooms — organized around the atrium to promote interdisciplinary interaction. A series of back-painted glass whiteboards reflect light and provide writing surfaces for capturing spontaneous ideas.

The nanotechnology engineering research 'box' faces the campus. The plan is based on a traditional laboratory building layout while the exterior is distinguished by a hexagonal honeycomb structural steel lattice. The QNC is constructed to the most stringent scientific standards to reduce vibration, temperature fluctuations, electromagnetic fields and other sources of 'noise' that can disrupt quantum and nanoscale experiments.

In order to achieve an environment with low vibration, low electromagnetic interference (EMI) and minimal radio frequency interference, advanced structural, mechanical and electrical designs were employed and lab spaces were concentrated below grade where these effects are minimized.

Materials The podium is clad with burnished concrete block to relate to the primarily masonry campus fabric of the University of Waterloo. The IQC façade plays on the concept of 'superposition' (where a digital switch can be on, off or both simultaneously) through degrees of reflection, transparency and the play of light on its surfaces.

Outcome The QNC is a showcase for Canadian innovation and industry in the fields of quantum computing and nanotechnology. The social components of the facility in the form of atria, mind spaces and collaborative areas manifest the original goals to attract and inspire the brightest minds in the world. At the official opening, Stephen Hawking, world-renowned physicist and partner with the University of Waterloo since 1999, described the design as a work of 'architectural genius.'

Kuwabara Payne McKenna Blumberg Architects, with laboratory specialists HDR Architecture

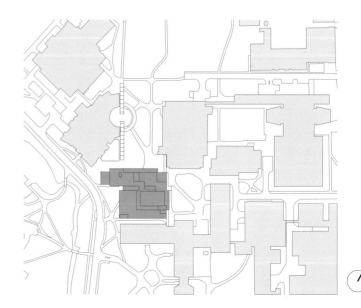

Orange glass is used to control the wavelength of light entering the cleanroom.

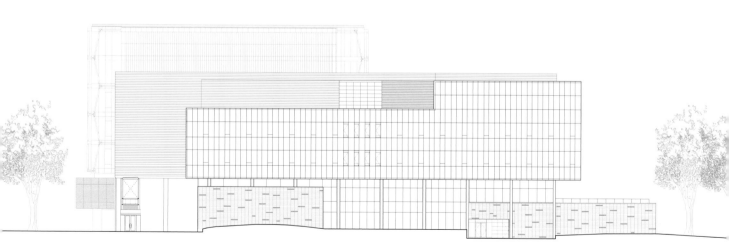

North elevation

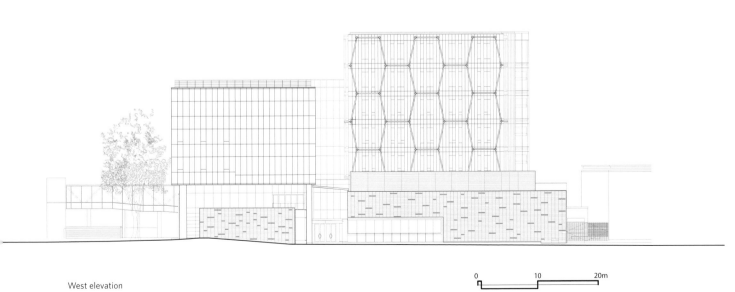

West elevation

0   10   20m

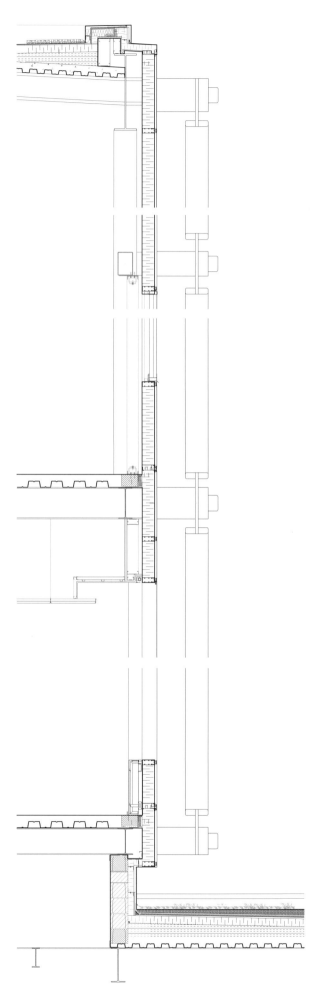

Nanotechnology wall section detail of honeycomb structural steel frame

Nanotechnology building east elevation (top):
the hexagonal honeycomb structural steel lattice
pattern refers to the intrinsically stable hexagonal
carbon structure of the nanotube and is structurally essential to support the cantilevered
perimeter office space and to mitigate column
interference in the cleanroom below.

Central atrium (opposite); café/lounge in IQC atrium (top); exit stair tower in nanotechnology engineering building (bottom)

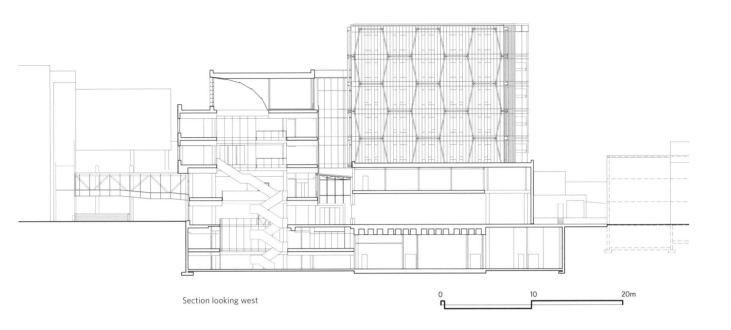

Section looking west

0   10   20m

IQC atrium with connecting stair (opposite); corridors
feature whiteboards and are generously proportioned to
encourage spontaneous interaction (bottom right)

As a premier global business school, the Kellogg School of Management at Northwestern University believes that business should be bravely led, passionately collaborative and world-changing. The design of its new building was selected through an invited international design competition. The primary goals were to create highly flexible and stimulating physical learning environments that transform the classroom experience, and to set the standard for how in-person learning will be physically structured and staged in the 21st century.

Site This new business campus will be the centrepiece of Kellogg's global network. Located on the shore of Lake Michigan, the project is sited to extend Northwestern's campus east to fully engage Lake Michigan and views of the Chicago skyline to the south.

Program The competition scheme organizes Kellogg's full-time MBA programs in a five-storey, 32,500-square-metre building. The design concept accommodates a variety of study, teaching, meeting and work spaces. Every space was planned to reflect Kellogg's unique team-based culture that supports collaboration amongst two and 20 individuals, and gatherings from 200 to 2,000.

Concept Kellogg's spirit of collaboration is manifested in the concept of a hybrid academic learning village/global hub. In the winning competition design, the plan order organized four five-storey loft structures, situated at the intersection of north-south and east-west cross axes, above a common two-storey-high base. The four loft structures are contained within a curvilinear framework of floor-to-ceiling transparent façades to optimize access to natural light, fresh air and views of Lake Michigan and the Chicago skyline.

Outcome The winning design responds directly to the campus framework, the natural and man-made history and geography of the site, and is reflective of Kellogg's 'Think Bravely' ethos.

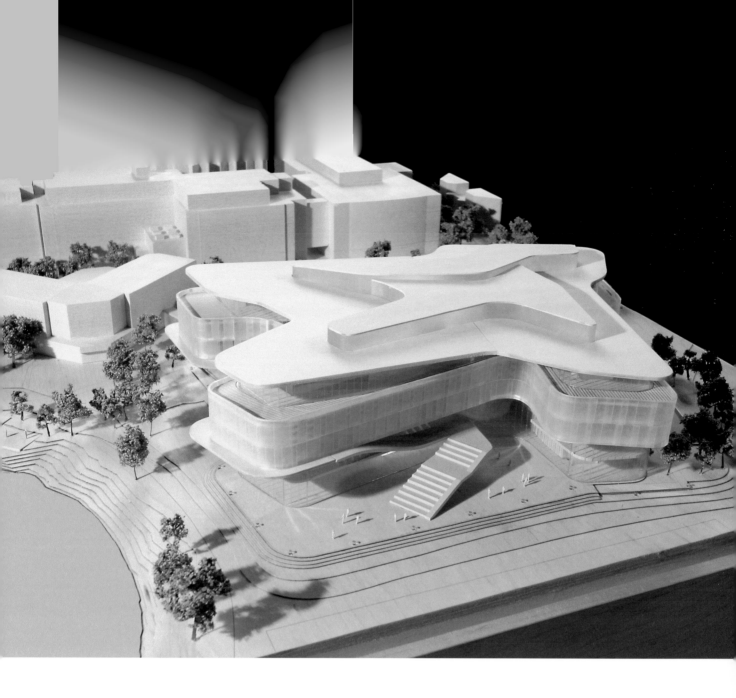

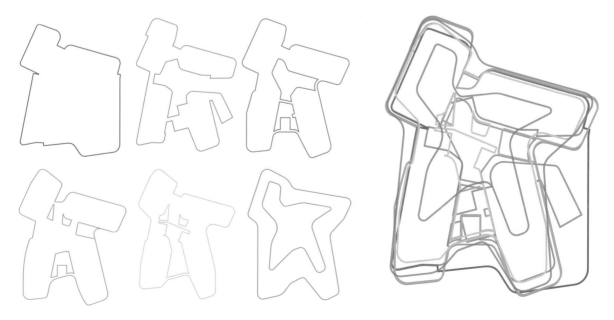

Winning competition rendering of south-west
elevation and model (top and opposite top);
diagrams of floor plates (bottom)

The re-purposing of the 20 Washington Road building from its former use as the Frick Chemistry building (1929) will participate in Princeton University's master plan vision to build academic neighbourhoods that have strong scholarly connections and provide much-needed space for expanded opportunities for teaching and research. The renovated building will be at the centre of the social sciences and humanities departments in the William Street neighbourhood and provide a new home for the economics department, several international offices and the Princeton Institute for International and Regional Studies (PIIRS).

Site The 20 Washington Road building is located in the north-east precinct of the campus and occupies a prominent position at the intersection of Washington Road and William Street. The site is situated on the seam where the historic west campus meets the more contemporary east campus. To the south, the building fronts on Scudder Plaza, a significant modern public space on the east campus.

Program The project has an area of 18,300 square metres and involves the adaptive reuse of the 20 Washington Road building to house Princeton's economics department and International Initiatives units. The building was built in 1929 and has had several additions over the years, containing large laboratory classrooms, offices and mechanical spaces.

Concept 20 Washington Road comprises a collegiate Gothic building and a 1964 extension completed in the same style. The existing building is monolithic in scale yet disconnected from the adjacent landscape. The building is clad in argylite stone with limestone-framed windows — the traditional palette of materials that characterizes the heritage campus buildings. The design concept focuses on an extensive transformation of the interior into a light-filled, accessible learning environment with a coherent system of corridors and public spaces while preserving the historic character of the exterior and key primary interior spaces, particularly the entry and the second floor library.

The economics department will be largely housed in the western 1929 part of the building. The historic entrance on Washington Road is on an axis with a newly constructed forum that functions as the heart of the academic community. Three glazed rooftop pavilion meeting rooms are added to the uppermost level affording spectacular views of the historic buildings to the west of Washington Road. International Initiatives will largely occupy the eastern part of the building, the 1964 addition. Their main entrance is a new three-storey atrium accessed from Scudder Plaza to the south, and a secondary entrance is provided from William Street to the north.

The surrounding campus areas also will be transformed to create a series of interlinking landscaped open spaces and courts that again are more in the tradition of the campus landscape.

Materials The new additions and the renovations of the existing building fabric will share a contemporary modern language that complements the heritage components of the buildings that are preserved. Traditional campus materials will be employed including bluestone paving inside and out, limestone and wood.

Outcome Currently, faculty members in the economics department have offices spread across the Princeton University campus. The adaptive reuse of 20 Washington Road will enable Princeton's goal to consolidate its economics department into a single location and provide a supportive, collegial platform on which to evolve and sustain a vibrant intellectual community. It will also centralize many international initiatives to improve the experience for those seeking international services.

VERTICAL NEIGHBOURHOODS

The soul of a city is about the finding of intimacy and stimulation in the streets that are a wardrobe and not just a place of business; on the shorelines that lyrically address the urban; in the residences that speak conviviality; under skylines that don't intimidate, but invite aspiration.

Pier Giorgio Di Cicco, *Municipal Mind: Manifesto for the Creative City* (2007)

Concordia University, founded in 1974, has grown to become one of Canada's largest universities located in a major urban centre. Unlike the gated campuses of traditional urban universities, Concordia comprises a collection of buildings integrated into the fabric of downtown Montreal. In 2001, Concordia held a design competition to initiate the first phase of its long-term vision to create a more cohesive identity for its urban campus: an integrated complex branded Le Quartier Concordia. The project was completed in two phases with the first phase comprising the Integrated Complex of Engineering and Computer Science (ENCS) and Visual Arts (VA), completed in 2005, and the purpose-built John Molson School of Business (JMSB), completed in 2009.

Site The project is located on two previously vacant urban blocks situated above an underground metro station and fronting onto Sainte-Catherine Street, Montreal's main retail street. Guy Street bisects the site into two parcels.

Program The 95,000-square-metre complex comprises three interconnected buildings: Engineering and Computer Science (46,000 square metres) and Visual Arts (14,000 square metres) and the John Molson School of Business (35,000 square metres).

Concept To accommodate the large multi-departmental program within the constraints of the site, the design is conceived as a vertical urban campus of three distinct yet interrelated buildings. Each building is organized into three vertical zones: base, middle and top. The base of each building is consistently three storeys high and scaled to relate to the streetscape and contribute to street animation. The middle zone contains multiple floors linked by stacked atria with interconnecting stairs. The top zones are distinguished by figurative canopies for the ENCS and JMSB and roof terraces for the Visual Arts building. Stairs, landings and lounges are consistently oriented to views of the city, Mont Royal and the St. Lawrence River.

A three-storey glass pavilion at the corner of Sainte-Catherine and Guy Streets forms a symbolic gateway and leads to the ground level concourses. The scale of the concourses is comparable to a major transit hub to accommodate the ebb and flow of students and the public arriving and departing from the underground metro station. Low ceilings, built-in benches and tables signify the public nature of the building and create an inviting, public atmosphere in which to linger throughout the day. The concourses of the ENCS and VA intersect to provide a sheltered route during Montreal's harsh winter and hot summer months.

Kuwabara Payne McKenna Blumberg Architects / Fichten Soiferman et Associés Architectes, Architects in Joint Venture

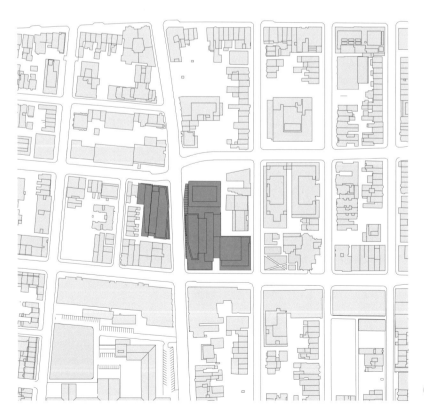

Materials Each building within the Le Quartier Concordia concept expresses the activity of the individual faculty both in its massing as well as the interior material palette. The materials also work in conjunction with the advancement of integrated building systems for sustainable design. The exteriors are primarily curtain walls using standard double-glazing systems with varying degree of ceramic frit patterns determined by the orientation to control the percentage of glass relative to the degree of sun exposure.

For the Engineering and Computer Science and Visual Arts integrated complex the selective use of stone wall tiles high-lights certain features within the public concourse. For both the John Molson School and the Engineering and Computer Science building, a copper-coloured, metal-panelled wall recurs inside and outside to weave the various program components together and to act as an architectural identifier for Concordia University on Montreal's skyline.

Outcome For the first time in its history, the downtown campus of Concordia University has a central hub. The integration of engineering, science, art and business has generated significant synergies between the faculties and attracted Hexagram, a multi-disciplinary institute for research and creativity in media and the arts, as a primary tenant. The new campus has provided Concordia with a platform on which to foster a critical mass of academics and to position Montreal as a showcase of academic excellence. By allowing the ground floor to be infiltrated by the public and the public transit system, the vertical campus creates an active interface between the university and the city.

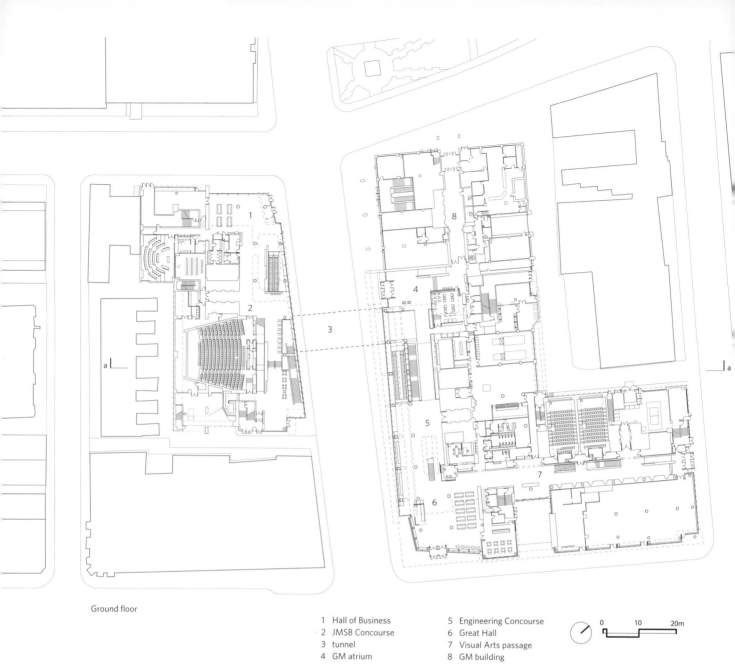

Ground floor

1 Hall of Business
2 JMSB Concourse
3 tunnel
4 GM atrium

5 Engineering Concourse
6 Great Hall
7 Visual Arts passage
8 GM building

View looking north to Mont Royal (bottom); ENCS main entrance pavilion; below-grade metro connection; lounge in atrium with connecting stair (opposite, left to right)

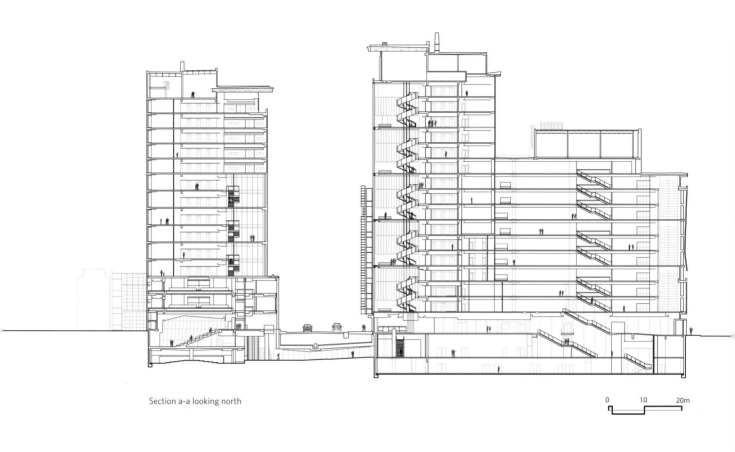

Section a-a looking north

0　　　10　　　20m

JMSB lecture volume with integrated artwork by Pierre Blanchette (top); ENCS entrance pavilion (opposite)

Spiral stair in ENCS stacked atria is crafted with
stainless steel, curved glass and granite treads
(top); escalator/stairs connecting ENCS to metro
below grade feature an LED wall (opposite)

View from Guy Street (top); detail of integrated art wall by Nicolas Baier in Visual Arts building (bottom); polished stainless steel sculptural relief on JMSB Maisonneuve Street elevation by Geneviève Cadieux (opposite bottom)

180 Queen Street West

The 180 Queen Street West site was initially zoned for a low-to-mid-scale hotel/commercial project. Over time, the site was recognized as an optimal location for the Federal Court, Canada's national trial court. The architects participated in the rezoning of the site for a high-rise office tower in order to anticipate expansion over a 20-year lease.

Site The tower is located at the confluence of Toronto's financial and legal precinct to the west and the trendy Queen Street West shopping precinct to the east, as well as in proximity to cultural landmarks to the north and south, including Gehry's expansion of the Art Gallery of Ontario, the Four Seasons Opera House, and the Toronto International Film Festival's Bell Lightbox. It is surrounded by a range of heritage buildings, including the Campbell House Museum (1822), the Canada Life Building (1831) and the Rex Hotel.

Program The 15-storey, 25,000-square-metre office tower houses the Federal Court Facilities, Health Canada Offices and Offices for the Public Health Agency of Canada. The base combines retail, restaurant and café services as well as a generous lobby space.

Concept A seven-storey-high podium is combined with a seven-storey-high tower to address the surrounding context of heritage and contemporary buildings. A double-height floor at the tower base is set back from the upper floors on the south and west sides to mitigate the impact of the overall mass at street level. The design incorporates an arcaded setback at grade along the east side of the building, and responds to a bylaw requirement for a through-block interior passage at mid-block. The eastern half of the base is articulated as a two-storey-high, fully glazed and publicly accessible lobby that acts as a showcase for a major art installation. The other half is occupied by Nota Bene, one of the city's best destination restaurants.

Materials To reflect core values of the Canadian justice system, the positive concept of transparency is reinforced in the choice of clear glass for all glazing systems. At the same time the enduring value of the judicial system is reflected in the robust solidity of the pre-cast concrete cladding and punched windows.

Outcome The concept balances an appropriate urban response to context and environmental objectives with a supportive work environment that is open yet secure, modern yet durable, dignified and calm. The project has been well-received by the community, bringing much-needed animation to a previously empty block of Queen Street West.

Kuwabara Payne McKenna Blumberg Architects with Webb Zerafa Menkes Housden Partnership, Consultants of Compliance

East elevation

0   10   20m

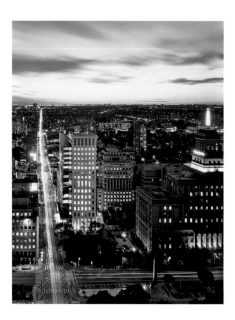

Queen Street elevation detail looking into Nota Bene restaurant (top); aerial view looking west (bottom left); office lobby (bottom right); Nota Bene bar interior (opposite bottom)

Torys LLP is a Toronto-based law practice founded in 1941. Recognizing that its existing interiors were no longer aligned with its reputation for leadership, innovation and advocacy of contemporary Canadian art and architecture, Torys LLP invested in transforming its offices into an environment that would underscore the creativity of critical thinking at the essence of its practice.

Site Since 1986, Torys LLP has occupied ten storeys of one of the five dark-painted steel and bronze-tinted glass towers comprising the Toronto Dominion Centre designed by Mies van der Rohe and completed between 1967 and 1991.

Program The 17,500-square-metre project focused on two key areas: client services and business practice.

Concept The former 1986-era interiors were stylistically undifferentiated and client spaces were distributed across ten floors. The renewed interior realigns its physical environment with the legacy of the Miesian grid and base-building conditions.

The centrepiece of the project is the client/conference centre. It is designed to showcase the firm's collection of contemporary Canadian art, including works by artists such as Edward Burtynsky, Rodney Graham and Yves Gaucher. The corridors are adapted as gallery halls, generously scaled and organized to form a continuous loop of movement around the building core.

The plan order is organized to frame a sequence of views north to the Financial District and south to Lake Ontario. This is reinforced by two art commissions for customized Skyfold walls in the north- and south-facing boardrooms. North-facing boardrooms feature Pascal Grandmaison's *With The Light (On My View)/False Reflection Become On Me*, a sequence of portraits of a colossal androgynous head which look onto the Cartesian grid of Mies's original north towers of the Toronto Dominion Centre. The south-facing boardrooms were created by artist Robert Fones; his work *Somewhere...* features a composite of individual panels covered with a short fragment of text from Miguel de Cervantes's *Don Quixote* in a custom-designed font interwoven with photographs of Lake Ontario.

Materials The material palette of marble, dark walnut, fumed oak and bronze, channels the essence of Mies's architecture. The bold dark mullions of the original tower are pushed into the foreground with the contrast of gallery-white walls and glass.

Outcome The client floor, when not in use for legal meetings, has become a cultural and civic venue. Events have ranged from dinners in honour of cultural leaders such as Phyllis Lambert, Founding Director of the Canadian Centre for Architecture in Montreal, to a memorial service for Detlef Mertins (1954–2011), pre-eminent historian and professor of modern architecture. Ultimately, the design creates a supportive platform for the practice of law while expanding the firm's contribution to the enrichment of cultural experience in the city.

For the customized Skyfold wall Toronto artist Robert Fones created *Somewhere ...*; the artist describes the panels as 'pages from a giant book, with its spine in Lake Ontario and its pages open to the city.'

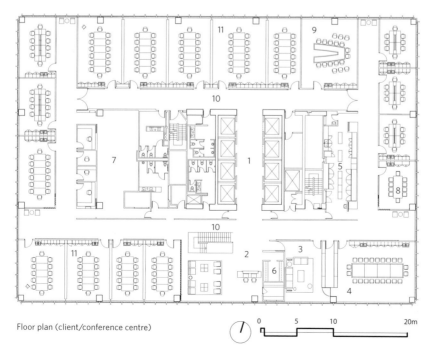

Floor plan (client/conference centre)

0   5   10   20m

1   elevator lobby
2   reception
3   caucus
4   boardroom
5   kitchen/servery
6   cloakroom
7   storage space
8   dining
9   dedicated video conferencing
10   gallery corridor
11   conference rooms with Skyfold partitions

North gallery corridor looking west (top);
south gallery corridor looking west (opposite)

The customized Skyfold walls along the north end of the floor are covered by *With The Light (On My View)/False Reflection Become On Me,* which the artist Pascal Grandmaison describes as a 'metaphor for the path (from broad to specific) of the decision-making process; how our inner powers of concentration can become an idea that can be communicated to others.'

Named after two adjacent buildings built in 1906 to house a co-op of sugar beet farmers, SugarCube is a mixed-use urban infill project designed to introduce contemporary design in Denver's historic Lower Downtown (LODO). The project participates in the revitalization of the district and responds to stringent urban design guidelines.

Site Located on a formerly vacant lot along Denver's 16th Street pedestrian mall and being the city's last significant urban infill opportunity, the project fell under the strict oversight of the LODO Design and Demolition Review Board.

Program The 15,400-square-metre, mixed-use development includes three decks of below-grade parking, retail at the ground floor, office space on the first three storeys and residential rental units on the upper six storeys.

Concept The massing strategy breaks the program down into three distinct volumes within the prescribed building envelope and setback requirements. A cubic element clad in dark brick with projecting balconies rises above two urban stone-clad wall buildings, one rising four storeys to address Blake Street and the other six storeys to address the 16th Street Mall. The stone-clad walls also make a contextual reference to the way in which the ornamented façade of the Sugar Building wraps the corner of the building against the laneway. Within the stone grid, the proportion of windows is high with deeply recessed side lights and operable units to add shadow and depth within the grid of stone.

Materials The central ten-storey volume is clad in manganese-coloured brick, and the two building volumes wrapping around its base, one rising four storeys and the other six storeys, are clad in buff brick.

Outcome The design simultaneously relates to and stands apart from its context. It provides a contemporary reinterpretation of the sense of permanence and comfort associated with buildings from the turn of the century and reinforces enduring value and quality for long-term sustainability. Completed after the 2008 world financial crisis, while other mixed-use projects were cutting rents to buoy occupancies, SugarCube experienced a steady increase in tenants.

Residential balconies (opposite); view on Blake Street; view at 16th Street Mall and Blake Street; detail of buff brick-clad wall building showing alignment with adjacent historic façade (top to bottom)

Gluskin Sheff + Associates is a Toronto-based investment company founded in 1984. Its original offices were designed by KPMB in the mid-1990s. By 2010, to accommodate its steady growth and rising profile in investment performance and client service, the firm re-commissioned the architects to create a supportive work environment to the same standards of quality and excellence that characterized the previous offices.

Site The new offices are located on the upper floors of the West Tower of the Bay Adelaide Centre.

Program The 4,600-square-metre program has room for 150 people and is planned to accommodate a projected total of 180 people and includes offices and support spaces for investment, client and business development, and accounting, as well as client, meeting and executive functions. Several meeting rooms of various sizes provide for two to 30 people.

Concept The serene background forms a counterpoint to the intensity of day-to-day investment activity. It is inspired by concepts of hospitality as well as requirements for functional performance and flexibility. A system of open and closed spaces was developed to support a balance of concentrated individual and teamwork.

The floor plate is treated as an urban plateau. The plan order prioritizes views of the city and the shoreline of Lake Ontario. Visitors enter through an expansive reception area located off the elevator core. Interconnecting stairs provide ease of circulation between floors to encourage interaction between departments. In anticipation of intensification and growth over time, all perimeter offices are proportioned and detailed to ultimately anticipate two people.

Generous corridors and ample wall space create a showcase for the firm's recognized contemporary art collection that includes works by established Canadian artists such as Lynne Cohen and Arnaud Maggs (1926–2012) as well as international artists such as Roni Horn.

Materials The central elevator core is clad in dark rift-cut walnut. The elevator lobby is framed by European beech also used in all client meeting rooms. Limestone paths in the reception zone transition to red elm hardwood floors in client zones. Glass and stainless steel screens frame the public circulation and interconnecting limestone staircases. Offices have etched glass fronts set within custom beech frames, white lacquer interiors and beech work surfaces.

Outcome The uncompromising attention to quality and detail reinforces the firm's values and reputation for pre-eminence in all its activities and services. The offices meet the original requirement to foster connections between departments while also providing a statement of common purpose. The emphasis on both comfort and elegance for staff and visitors alike has effectively enhanced the productivity and pleasure of the daily work experience.

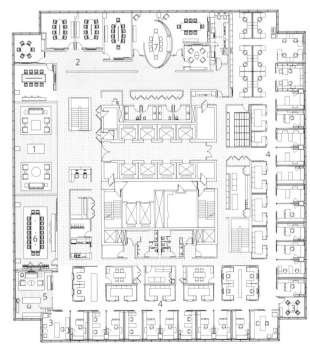

1 reception
2 client meeting area
3 meeting rooms
4 executive office area
5 CEO office
6 boardroom
7 private dining room

Floor plan

0   10   20m

18 York is one of three towers that form part of the South-core Financial Centre (SFC), a mixed-use, sustainable development initiative that participates in the City of Toronto's district planning strategy to establish a gateway to the Financial District from the waterfront and to increase density in the precinct.

Site Located between the Canadian National Railway Lands and the Gardiner Expressway on the north-west corner of York Street and Bremner Boulevard, the building is steps away from Toronto's Financial District, Union Station (a heritage landmark and regional transit node) and the waterfront. The project includes a new bridge over York Street that links into PATH, the city's underground pedestrian system.

Program The 26-storey, 83,000-square-metre tower includes three levels of parking below grade with 140 underground bicycle storage spaces and a two-storey base designed for mixed-use retail with access to a landscaped public terrace.

Concept The prismatic 26-storey complex combines a tower and podium condition. The tower was conceived at a time of transition from traditional compartmentalized approaches to office planning. It anticipates the workplace of the future by prioritizing universal access to daylight, vistas and good ventilation as fundamental criteria. The column-free floor plate between the core and the perimeter permits maximum latitude. Continuous floor-to-ceiling glazing maximizes views and permits daylight penetration deep into the floor plate.

The podium is designed as an active hub, featuring retail services and providing access to sheltered pedestrian routes leading to public transit. Vegetated roofs and terraces, including an 'urban forest' garden at the third floor, are planned to grow into a slice of St. Lawrence Lowland forest ecology and to provide green space as visual relief when viewed from the towers of the Financial District to the north.

Materials The minimalist building skin comprises a high-performance glazing system with maximum glass sizes to reduce the number of mullions and exterior metal elements. This also minimizes thermal bridging conditions and optimizes daylight transmission.

Interior finishes are consistent with the restrained elegance of the exterior. Lobbies and public spaces feature Algonquin limestone floor and wall finishes, walnut for panelling and doors, acid-etched mirror ceiling and wall features, and stainless steel accents.

Outcome The 18 York project achieved LEED CS Gold certification and the Bremner Tower is on track to achieve the same sustainability designation. The design fulfills the City's district planning strategy to use architecture as a gateway condition and to achieve a dense mix of commercial uses in this evolving precinct.

East view (bottom) and south-west view at Bremner Boulevard and York Street (opposite)

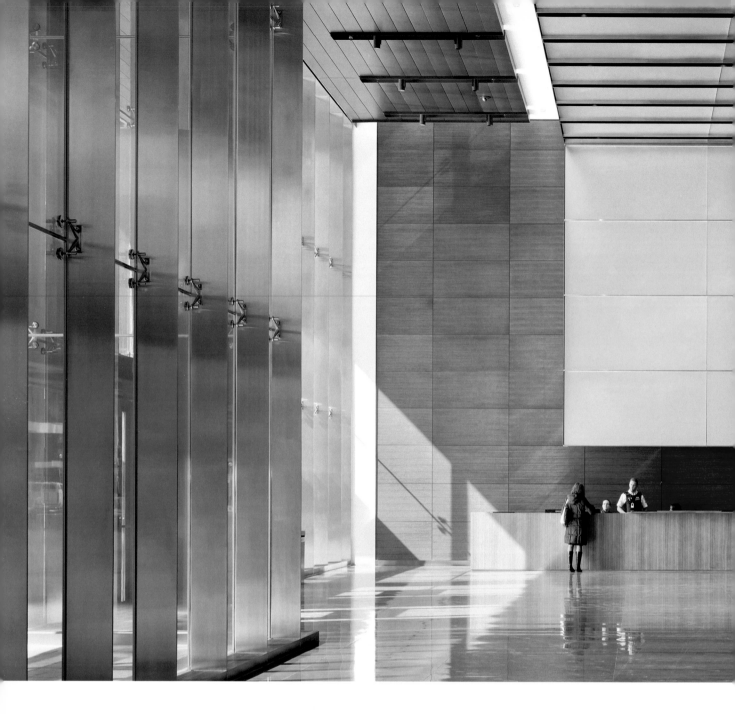

Interior lobby features Algonquin limestone and
walnut panels (top); lobby view looking east
with stainless steel fin supports for glazed walls
(bottom)

Toronto Community Housing (TCH) is the largest social housing provider in Canada and the second largest in North America. It provides homes for low- and moderate-income tenants, including seniors, families, singles, refugees, recent immigrants to Canada and people with special needs. TCH also plays a crucial role in maintaining a healthy mix of affordable residential opportunities in downtown Toronto. Block 32 was planned and designed to fill a need for family-centred affordable rental housing in the rapidly developing Railway Lands West precinct. The objective was to create a living environment that fosters social interaction and community building.

Site Block 32 is located immediately west of CityPlace, a large-scale residential development on former industrial rail lands, on a prime location along Fort York Boulevard. It is just two blocks east of Bathurst, one of the city's prime north-south arterials.

Program The 35-storey tower and eight-storey podium provide a total of 428 units and 45,500 square metres of social housing and amenity. The base of the tower includes an event space, a communal kitchen, playrooms and day-lit laundry facilities. The tower contains a range of one-, two- and three-bedroom flat floor units as well as completely barrier-free units. The podium accommodates two-, three-, four- and five-bedroom units. Two levels of parking and an internalized service area are located within the space below the elevated outdoor courtyard.

Concept To increase efficiency and create double-storey units, corridors and elevators are located on every second floor of the podium. Fully glazed corridors are selectively organized at the perimeter to form local neighbourhoods within the development. A multi-purpose pavilion at the south-east corner offers views into the park and is accessible both from the courtyard and the street.

The perimeter block contains a raised private courtyard. All units at the base of the courtyard have a private out-door space separated from the landscaped common area. The west podium roof is reserved for urban agriculture.

The street wall complies with urban design guidelines and is completed with an eight- to ten-storey perimeter block which includes a series of two-storey street-level townhouse units targeted to families. Accents of vibrant colours extend through all the public spaces of the project.

Materials Conventional exterior building systems are applied to create a two-storey white pre-cast 'wrapper' with supergraphics on the podium and the east side of the tower facing back to the city. The graphic pattern of the pre-cast 'wrapper' is referenced in the design of the window wall on the west side of the tower. The economies of window wall construction and modular pre-cast panels are maximized to achieve a distinct identity for the project.

Outcome Block 32 introduces a unique housing typology for families in a neighbourhood dominated by one- and two-bedroom units catering to singles and young couples. The stacking and interlocking of podium units reduces the number of common corridors to achieve increased amenity within the units. The emphasis on shared public spaces, glazed corridors and large two-storey units creates a secure and inviting living environment for families.

Kuwabara Payne McKenna Blumberg Architects in association with Page + Steele / IBI Group Architects

View from railway lands looking south (bottom)
and view from Portland Street looking south
(opposite)

Like every news business today, The Globe and Mail is faced with the challenges of radical and rapid transformation of news content generation and distribution. The new head-quarters for Canada's national newspaper was conceived to ensure The Globe and Mail sustains a leadership role in the content economy and continues to deliver reliable news reporting across Canada. The editor, John Stackhouse, stated: 'We envision a place to pull together ideas and inspiration, and to harness physical proximity and tap the human spirit.'

Site Located at the south-west corner of Spadina Avenue and Front Street at the eastern edge of Toronto's rapidly developing Downtown West Business District (DWBD), the project will bring a critical mass of employees and tenants into the precinct.

Program The 18-storey, 42,500-square-metre, multi-tenant office tower designates floors three to six for The Globe and Mail with a 5,574-square-metre newsroom on levels three and four. The ground floor features a restaurant café, kiosk and 300-seat venue with overflow for up to 500 people. A conference centre is located on the second floor. The seventh floor provides access to a roof terrace.

Concept The new building is conceived as a world stage for integrating content, creativity and technology. It is intentionally not a tall tower. The unusual geometric form is simultaneously an ode to the broad-sheet newspaper and a departure from the podium tower typology prevalent in Toronto's urban commercial office tower developments. The overall mass is set on a transparent ground plane and is sited to create a wider sidewalk and animate the corner of the two streets. The publicly accessible ground level is conceived as a cultural town square for 21st century Canadian media. Its sequence of public and social spaces will support and inspire new and expanded streams of projects and programs, including the 300-seat auditorium venue enclosed within a glass box. It also includes a landscaped route through the site.

On floors three to six, the typical floor plate is organized around a central atrium and provides an open plan concept to facilitate the reorganization of people (not desks) and to capitalize on innovation and productivity. The inherently flexible infrastructure provides maximum capacity to accommodate rapid change in reporting, distribution and powerful content technologies, and is structurally designed to allow future tenants to insert interconnecting stairs.

The building is being designed to LEED Gold standard. However, the principal goal is to prioritize the health and well-being of the people who inhabit it, and to contribute to building a vibrant urban community.

Materials The envelope is triple-glazed. The low-rise is highlighted with a grey-tinted glazing that makes its way across and up the south side and down the north. The east and west elevations are clad in high-performance clear glass. The entire ground floor including lobbies and amenities uses a structural glass cable system to create maximum expanses of unobstructed, column-free space. For durability, the public spaces use granite for floors and marble for the cores.

Outcome The architecture and enriched sidewalk experience is conceived to engage the city in content creation and facilitate goals to introduce a new business model aligned with the changing nature of news media and distribution. The new building will be highly transparent, accessible and collaborative, to allow The Globe and Mail to continue to attract and retain the most talented writers, thinkers and leaders in journalism and multi-media.

INTEGRATED DESIGN

... the collective knowledge, capability, and resources embodied within broad horizontal networks of participants can be mobilized to accomplish much more than one firm acting alone. Whether designing an airplane, assembling a motorcycle, or analyzing a human genome, the ability to integrate the talents of dispersed individuals and organizations is becoming the defining competency...

Don Tapscott and Anthony D. Williams, *Wikinomics: How Mass Collaboration is Changing Everything* (2006)

Manitoba Hydro is the Crown corporation and the primary energy utility for Manitoba. In 2002, as part of the negotiated purchase of Winnipeg Hydro, the City of Winnipeg required that Manitoba Hydro participate in the City's downtown urban revitalization strategy by consolidating 2,000+ employees from 15 leased suburban offices into one new building in the centre of the city. The building also had to be a symbol of Manitoba Hydro's commitment to energy efficiency and carbon emission reduction.

Site Manitoba Hydro Place is located in downtown Winnipeg, the capital of the Canadian province of Manitoba, in the centre of North America in an unprotected arctic trough that channels cold arctic air south across the Canadian Shield and the Prairies. This makes it one of the coldest cities with a population over 500,000 in the world. Temperatures drop to –35 degrees Celsius for almost half the year and can exceed +45 degrees Celsius with the humidex during the summer. It is also one of the sunniest and windiest places in Canada.

The building occupies a previously underutilized urban block in the centre of Winnipeg and faces onto Portage Avenue, the city's main street. Portage Avenue is typical of Winnipeg's wide thoroughfares which were planned to emulate the scale of Chicago's Michigan Avenue. The site was selected for its proximity to prominent downtown destinations, including The Forks (a historic aboriginal meeting place and green space at the confluence of the Red and Assiniboine Rivers), as well as to the city's sheltered pedestrian system. More than 95 percent of the bus routes pass this address, including routes to the suburbs where 80 percent of Manitoba Hydro employees live.

Program The 21-storey, 76,500-square-metre high-rise office tower accommodates 2,000 workstations and includes a three- to four-storey-high podium with an interior street and only one level of parking below grade to encourage employees to use public transit or park in one of the city's abundant parking lots.

Concept The design is the outcome of a formal Integrated Design Process (IDP). Form, orientation and massing are seamlessly integrated to capture maximum passive energy from Winnipeg's extreme climate. The form takes the shape of a capital A letter and consists of two glass office towers set on a stepped masonry-clad podium scaled to relate to the city's historic fabric.

The glass towers are set back to mitigate mass and shadow impact on Portage Avenue. The towers fuse at the north and splay open to the south for maximum exposure to the abundant sunlight and consistently robust southerly winds unique to Winnipeg's climate. At the north end a 115-metre-tall solar tower marks the main entrance on Portage Avenue.

By siting the building on a 45-degree angle to face due south, outdoor space was saved and converted into a new urban park. The overall orientation also optimizes visual connections to the city's legislative buildings and The Forks, Winnipeg's historic centre. Inside, a three-storey publicly accessible galleria bisects the solar axis of the podium and creates a sheltered route through the full city block. Instead of a conventional lobby, the galleria allows for the daily flow of 2,000 employees as well as creates a new indoor public gathering space for the city.

Materials The building's scale, geometry and material expression reference man-made and natural power sources as well as associations with Canada's northern landscape. Exposed architectural concrete and locally quarried Tyndall stone relate to Winnipeg's urban fabric of masonry buildings. Reclaimed Douglas fir from the former building that occupied the site is reused for soffits and benches. Large portions of the structure were left exposed to increase the conductivity of the radiant concrete mass.

Kuwabara Payne McKenna Blumberg Architects (Design Architect), Smith Carter Architects & Engineers (Executive Architect), Prairie Architects Inc. (Advocate Architect) with Transsolar (Climate Engineer)

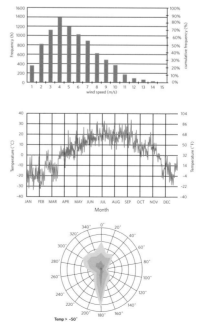

Climate profiles for Winnipeg, Canada: wind speed (top); temperature (middle); wind rose (bottom)

Integrated Design Process

Manitoba Hydro determined the new building would be realized through a formal Integrated Design Process (IDP) modeled on the successful C–2000 program developed by Natural Resources Canada (NRCan), a department of the Canadian Federal Government. One of the first tasks was to build the Integrated Design Team (IDT). In contrast to the conventional Request for Proposal (RFP) process where the architects are responsible for selecting the full team of consultants, the Design Architect was selected first and then worked with Manitoba Hydro to select all other major consultants for the IDT.

The first IDP Session was held off-site to clarify and agree on the core principle goals, which simultaneously defined the original design intentions. These were then summarized in a three-page project charter and signed by Manitoba Hydro's Executive and all IDT members.

Project Charter (Design Intentions)

1. Supportive workplace: healthy and effective contemporary office environment for 2,000 employees adaptable to changing technology and workplace environment for present and future needs.

2. World class energy efficiency: target 60 percent more energy efficiency than the MNECB (Model National Energy Code for Buildings), the Canadian minimum requirements for energy efficiency in buildings.

3. Sustainability: LEED Gold Level Certification.

4. Signature architecture: a design to celebrate the importance of Manitoba Hydro to the Province and to enhance downtown Winnipeg's image.

5. Urban regeneration: strengthen and contribute to sustainable future of Winnipeg's downtown.

6. Cost: Cost-effective and a sound financial investment.

The charter established identification and generated a sense of ownership by all.

The first year involved intensive monthly facilitated workshops and design charettes on the schematic design. Fifteen concepts were generated, three options were modelled and tested, and one preferred option was selected for development. Transsolar, the climate engineers, played a critical role in the conceptual development by converting the challenges of the extreme climate into an opportunity to harness passive wind and solar energies as well as optimize day lighting autonomy.

Year two involved facilitated bi-weekly meetings to design development, ensuring all architectural, structural, energy performance, cost and constructability goals were fully integrated in the final design solution.

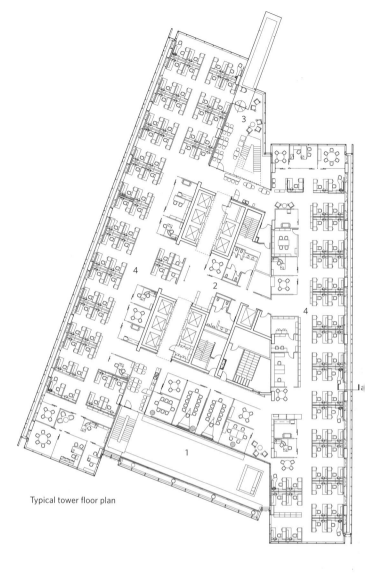

Typical tower floor plan

0   10   20m

1 south wintergardens
2 core
3 north atrium
4 column-free office lofts

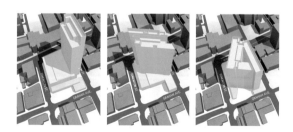

Three options from the original 15 selected for modelling (bottom); aerial view of north elevation showing Solar Chimney (opposite)

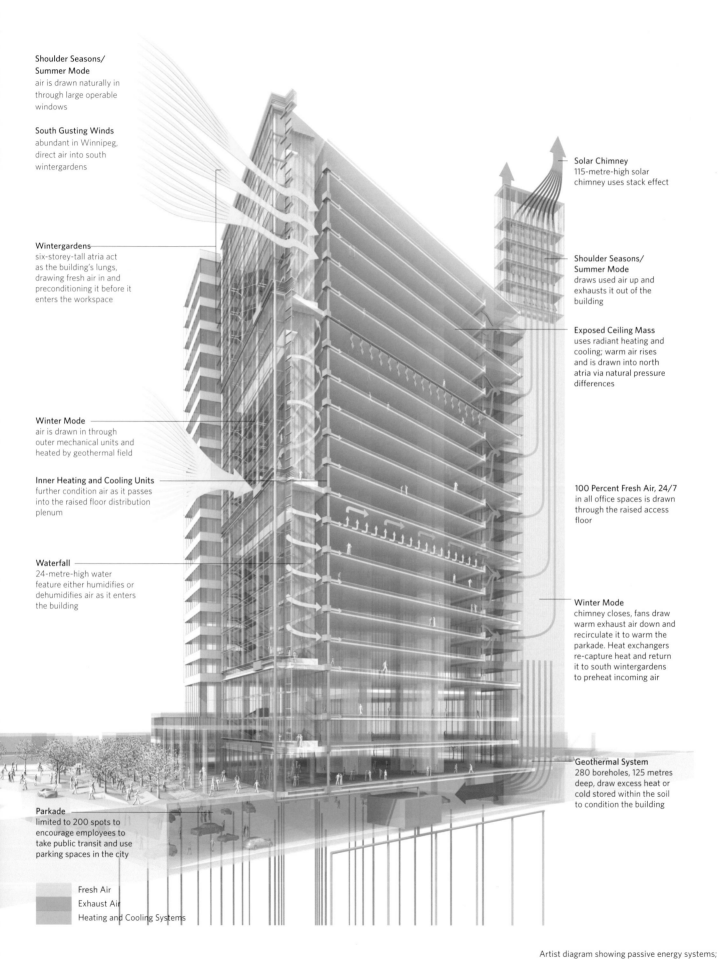

Shoulder Seasons/ Summer Mode
air is drawn naturally in through large operable windows

South Gusting Winds
abundant in Winnipeg, direct air into south wintergardens

Wintergardens
six-storey-tall atria act as the building's lungs, drawing fresh air in and preconditioning it before it enters the workspace

Winter Mode
air is drawn in through outer mechanical units and heated by geothermal field

Inner Heating and Cooling Units
further condition air as it passes into the raised floor distribution plenum

Waterfall
24-metre-high water feature either humidifies or dehumidifies air as it enters the building

Parkade
limited to 200 spots to encourage employees to take public transit and use parking spaces in the city

Solar Chimney
115-metre-high solar chimney uses stack effect

Shoulder Seasons/ Summer Mode
draws used air up and exhausts it out of the building

Exposed Ceiling Mass
uses radiant heating and cooling; warm air rises and is drawn into north atria via natural pressure differences

100 Percent Fresh Air, 24/7
in all office spaces is drawn through the raised access floor

Winter Mode
chimney closes, fans draw warm exhaust air down and recirculate it to warm the parkade. Heat exchangers re-capture heat and return it to south wintergardens to preheat incoming air

Geothermal System
280 boreholes, 125 metres deep, draw excess heat or cold stored within the soil to condition the building

Fresh Air
Exhaust Air
Heating and Cooling Systems

Artist diagram showing passive energy systems; view of south elevation (opposite)

Solar Chimney Typical North American buildings recirculate as much as 80 percent of the air. Manitoba Hydro Place provides 100 percent fresh air year round chiefly through three six-storey-high wintergardens that perform as the 'lungs' of the building. In the winter, exhaust air from the building is drawn to the bottom of the Solar Chimney by a fan. The heat from this exhaust air is used to pre-heat via heat exchange the incoming cold air in the south atria. During the shoulder seasons the majority of mechanical ventilation systems are turned off. The building is passively ventilated by fresh air that enters the building through occupant-controlled operable windows at the double-skin and wintergarden façades and is drawn through the building by the Solar Chimney.

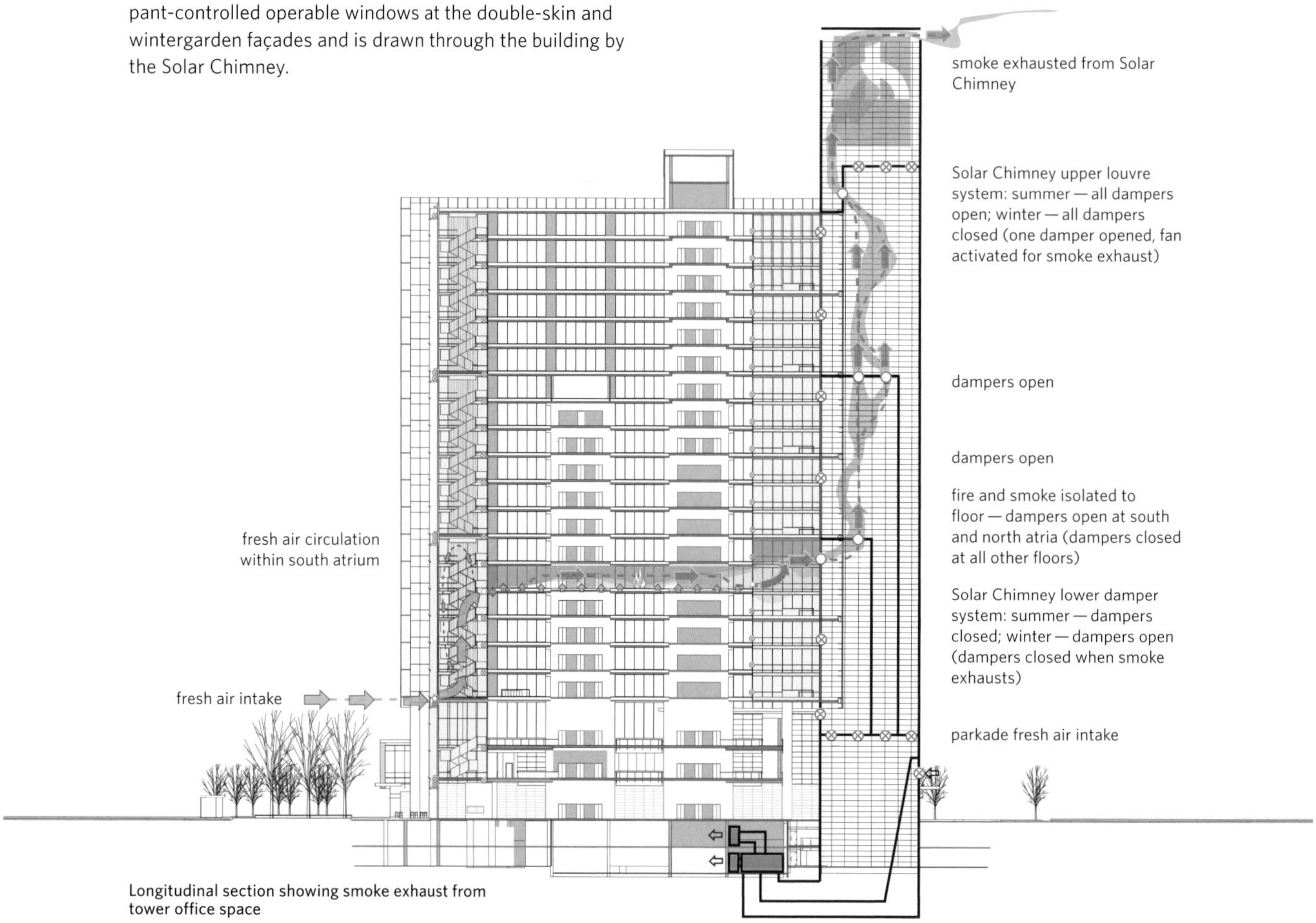

smoke exhausted from Solar Chimney

Solar Chimney upper louvre system: summer — all dampers open; winter — all dampers closed (one damper opened, fan activated for smoke exhaust)

dampers open

dampers open

fire and smoke isolated to floor — dampers open at south and north atria (dampers closed at all other floors)

Solar Chimney lower damper system: summer — dampers closed; winter — dampers open (dampers closed when smoke exhausts)

parkade fresh air intake

fresh air circulation within south atrium

fresh air intake

Longitudinal section showing smoke exhaust from tower office space

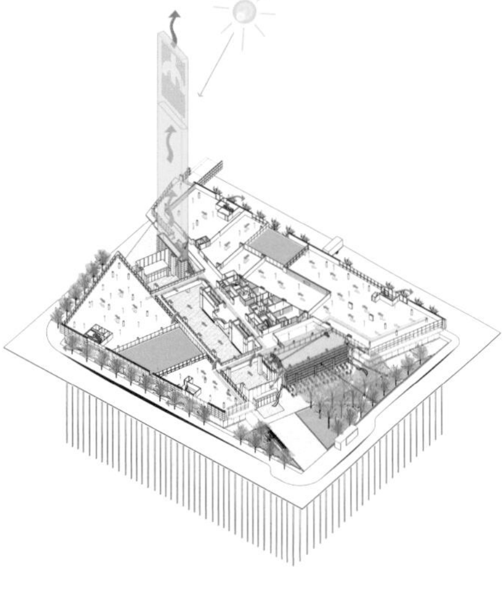

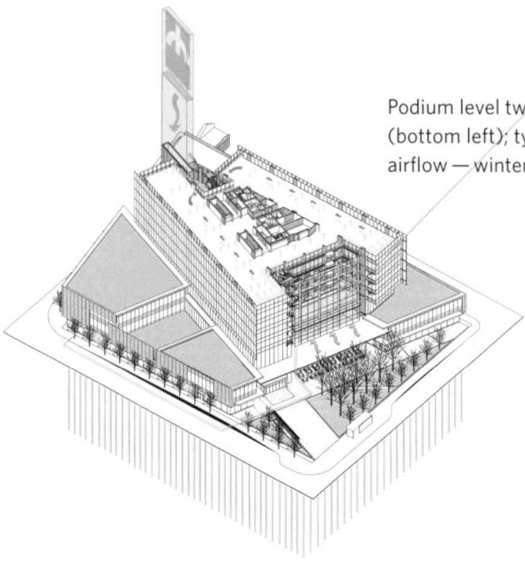

Podium level two airflow — summer operation (bottom left); typical office tower floor airflow — winter operation (bottom right)

Biodynamic Façade Ironically, a glass tower in the extreme climate proved the most effective solution. When it is extremely cold, it is also very sunny, ideal for solar gains. Triple glazing is used on all surfaces. The envelope is de-laminated into single- and double-glazed walls, with a buffer zone in between. Between the two walls temperatures fluctuate naturally for most of the winter months, maintaining the performance of a triple-glazed façade. While buffer zones are configured in the winter for thermal insulation and fresh air heating (in the case of the south atrium), their configuration changes with the seasons.

A biodynamic double façade on the west and east elevations creates a high-performance envelope that reduces heating/cooling loads by providing a tempered buffer to extreme outdoor temperatures. Operable windows on the inner and outer walls of the double façade permit natural ventilation at seasonally appropriate times of the year. The outer façade is motorized and centrally controlled, while the inner façade is manually operated.

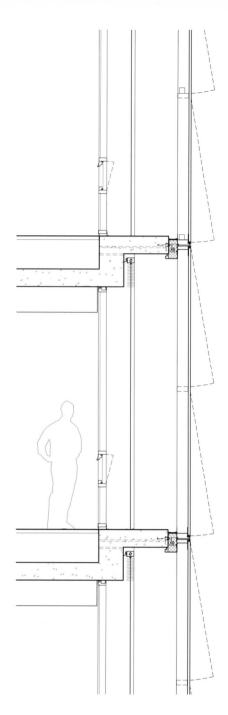

Section a-a through a typical east double-skin façade; west double-skin façade (opposite)

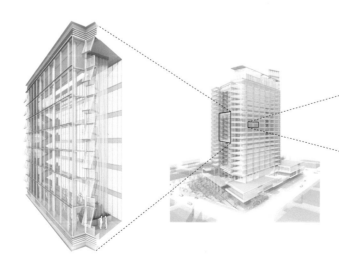

Passive venting and ventilation systems at wintergarden (bottom left) and typical office loft (bottom right)

Wintergardens — the Building's Lungs Three stacked, six-storey-high wintergardens face due south and are essentially large, unconditioned spatial volumes. Unique in the context of the conventional hermetically sealed North American office building, the wintergardens work in combination with the Solar Chimney to passively pre-treat fresh outdoor air regardless of temperatures to provide 100 percent fresh air year round.

Each wintergarden features a 24-metre-tall custom-designed curtain composed of 280 individual strands of 4-millimetre-wide mylar ribbons held in tension by bronze weights designed to humidify or dehumidify the air before it is distributed through the raised access floor plena. Placed end to end, the ribbons would extend over 23 kilometres. Small threaded valves at the top of each ribbon are carefully adjusted to control the flow of water down each ribbon. The aggregate surface area provided by the ribbons (measuring approximately 53 square metres) allows for a maximum amount of airflow through and around the water feature. Simultaneously sculptural and functionally kinetic, the water curtains encapsulate the fusion of performance and aesthetics at the heart of the project.

Wintergarden with functional water element (top and opposite)

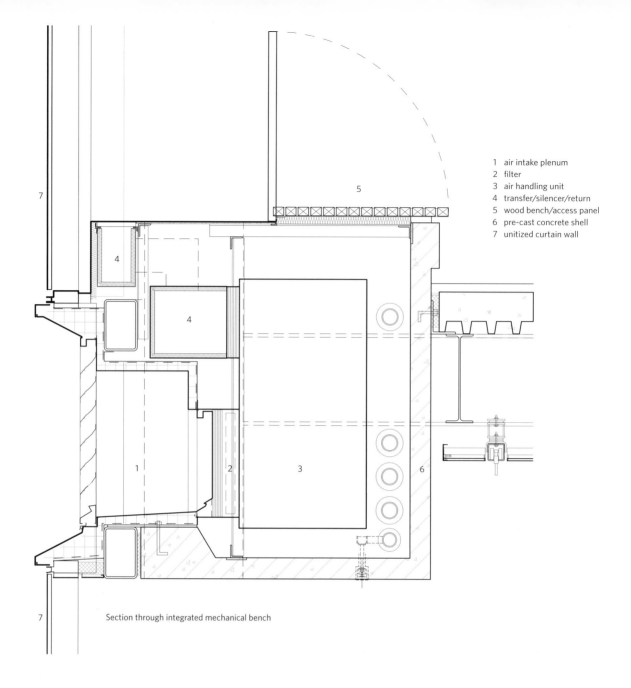

1 air intake plenum
2 filter
3 air handling unit
4 transfer/silencer/return
5 wood bench/access panel
6 pre-cast concrete shell
7 unitized curtain wall

Section through integrated mechanical bench

Mechanical bench and automated blind system
(bottom left); podium wintergarden in use (bottom
right); typical six-storey atrium (opposite)

Supportive workplace design The office program is divided between the two towers to result in a narrow column and grid-free floor plate depth for maximum views throughout. To catalyze interaction and teamwork, the plan organizes the symbiotic relationship between the building's respiratory system and a series of stacked vertical neighbourhoods around shared atria with interconnecting stairs.

Everyone receives natural lighting during 80 percent of normal office hours and 100 percent fresh air year round. Operable windows, task lighting and shading devices allow occupants to control their personal environments. The floor-to-ceiling windows offer previously unimagined views of Winnipeg's grand historic fabric, vast blue skies and the prairie horizon beyond.

Geothermal A closed-loop geothermal (ground source energy) system consisting of 280 boreholes, 125 metres deep, provides approximately 60 percent of the heating with highly energy-efficient condensing boilers providing the balance during the coldest months.

Typical north atrium and Solar Chimney (top); public galleria and entrance diagram (opposite top); public park space in front of south façade (opposite bottom)

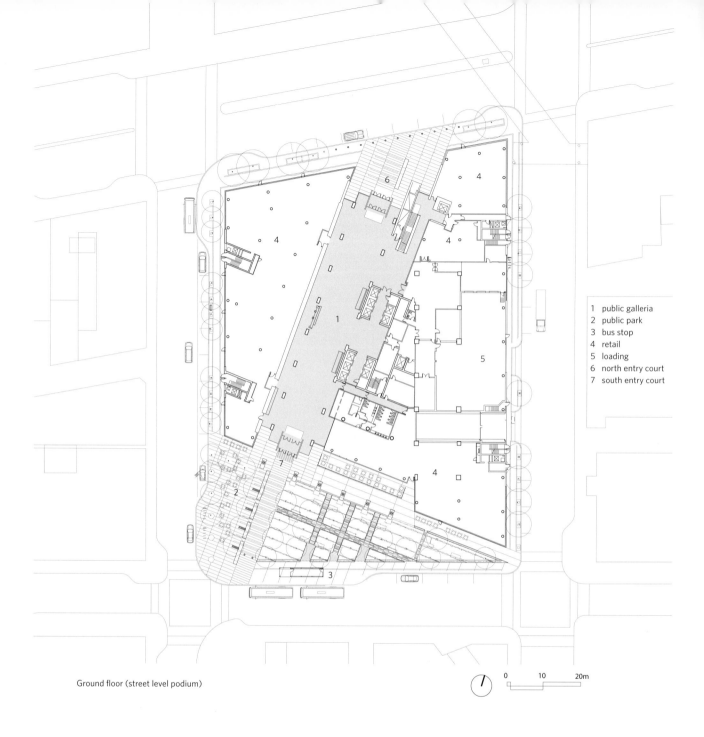

Ground floor (street level podium)

0   10   20m

1 public galleria
2 public park
3 bus stop
4 retail
5 loading
6 north entry court
7 south entry court

Outcome At first glance Manitoba Hydro looks like a classic, modern glass office tower. In actuality, it is a highly complex, energy-efficient large-scale building that offers a new paradigm for thinking about the design and delivery of low-carbon, energy-efficient contemporary architecture in a manner that simultaneously prioritizes the human experience and contributes to urban revitalization. Compared to the average office tower in North America, Manitoba Hydro Place at the time of this publication recorded more than 70 percent energy savings over the Model National Energy Building Code (MNEBC). Manitoba Hydro's usage is under 85 KWh/m²/a in an extreme climate, compared to conventional office towers in a moderate climate which typically use over 300 KWh/m²/a. In 2012, Manitoba Hydro Place became the most energy-efficient office tower in North America and the only office tower in Canada to receive the LEED Platinum rating.

In the previous suburban offices, 90 percent of the employees drove to work; now 70 percent are taking public transit. Partly because the building offers 100 percent fresh air year round, absenteeism due to illness is down by 1.5 days per employee and productivity has risen. The building is actively catalyzing the economic and civic revitalization of the downtown and a pride of place among citizens of Winnipeg.

Manitoba Hydro Place is a hybrid — between a living being and a machine. It breathes, stores, exhausts energy and fresh air and its systems are meticulously monitored and run like a highly sophisticated computer. Designed and delivered through a formal Integrated Design Process (IDP), this project introduces a new paradigm to a carbon-neutral future.

The galleria features two waterfall sculptures which are fully integrated into the humidification/dehumidification system and creates a public gathering place for special events and festivals (opposite).

George Brown College, Waterfront Campus   TORONTO, ONTARIO   2012

George Brown College is an urban community college with a series of campuses located throughout downtown Toronto. The Waterfront Campus, accommodating the Centre for Health Sciences, represents the college's fourth and newest campus. Recognizing that healthcare is shifting from isolated medical functions to an integrated model for the delivery of care and that changing the way healthcare providers are educated and trained is key to achieving this systemic change, George Brown College required that the design manifest the concept of Inter-Professional Education (IPE).

The goal of IPE is to transform healthcare education into a team-based learning method. Students from two or more professions learn about, from and with each other to enable effective collaboration and to prepare them for collaborative practice where multiple health workers from different professional backgrounds work together to deliver the highest quality of care.

The overall concept is the direct outcome of an integrated design process with co-leadership by George Brown College and the joint venture of Stantec Architecture/Kuwabara Payne McKenna Blumberg Architects to manifest IPE in the designed environment.

Site To reinforce themes of health and wellness, the building is strategically located in the East Bayfront precinct, one of the neighbourhoods within the large-scale urban redevelopment of Toronto's waterfront. The site faces south onto Lake Ontario and east onto Sherbourne Park designed by Phillips Farevaag Smallenberg.

Program The 47,100-square-metre project consolidates the Schools of Dental Health, Health and Wellness, Health Services Management and Nursing in a single, purpose-designed facility for 3,500 students, 500 faculty and continuing education and clinical programs. It includes retail, food services, clinics, student amenity space and an auditorium.

Concept The architectural section is organized as a continuous, vertical 'learning landscape' of three interconnected volumes and oriented to maximize views to the lake and the park.

A flexible academic loft bar building along the west anchors the scheme. A three-storey, transparent glass podium with views to the north, south and east houses the public functions. Above the podium at the south-east corner, a cantilevered two-storey element contains the library. Its roof is adapted as a wood-decked, landscaped terrace. Two stacked lecture hall volumes are suspended above the north-east corner above the podium.

Materials The materials were inspired by the maritime and industrial heritage of the site. For example, the exterior features corrugated 'galvalume'-coated steel siding as a reference to shipping containers while ipê wood soffits evoke wooden dock structures and warehouses.

Windows with lake views include glazing with ceramic frit pattern that is an abstraction of the reflection of light on the water. Orange glass entrance vestibules provide orientation and identity. Interior finishes were selected to maximize durability and include glass and steel plate guards, basalt stone flooring at the ground level and ceramic tile walls.

Wood is selectively woven through the interiors to inject warmth; an ipê wood ceiling at the ground floor extends the exterior soffit and is used for the learning landscape while Douglas fir cladding was chosen for the auditorium walls and doors.

Outcome The Waterfront Campus has been purpose-built to create a framework in which to support IPE and to ensure that graduates are collaborative-practice ready to deliver patient-centred team-based care. The facility supports a balanced program of academic instruction with hands-on experience that is increasingly essential to ensuring the relevance of future healthcare professionals and to the long-term sustainability of Canada's universally accessible healthcare program.

Stantec Architecture l Kuwabara Payne McKenna Blumberg Architects, Architects in Joint Venture

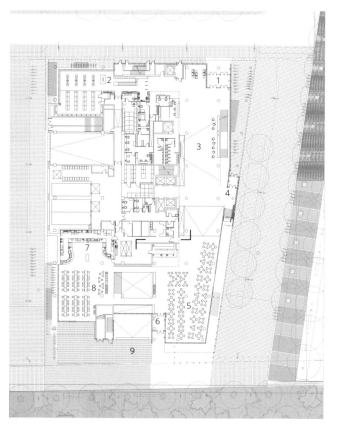

Ground floor

0   10   20m

1 main entrance
2 campus store
3 main atrium
4 Sherbourne Park entrance
5 student commons
6 waterfront entrance
7 cafeteria
8 dining hall
9 terrace

The 'learning landscape' comprises a series
of stacked stair/terraced seating.

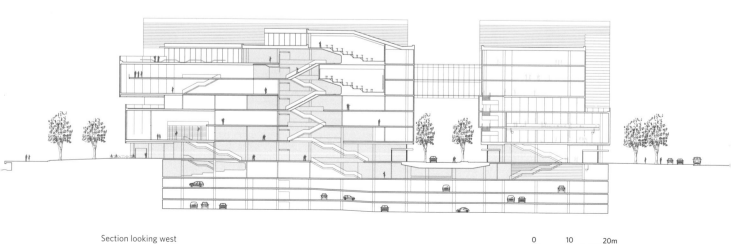

Section looking west

0   10   20m

One of the most important health issues of the 21st century is complex chronic disease. While the success of modern medicine has made it possible for people to live with multiple diseases, there was insufficient attention on improving their quality of life. The vision for Bridgepoint Health is to become Canada's leading centre dedicated to the treatment and research of complex chronic disease and an icon of accessible healthcare, one of the building blocks of Canada's national identity. The new purpose-built hospital and the restoration and adapative reuse of the Don Jail into a research centre for wellness and prevention represents the first phase in a ten-year master plan vision for the transformation of the existing site into a village of care.

In an integrated design process, two teams of architects were responsible for delivering the project under Infrastructure Ontario's Alternate Financing and Procurement, a two-tiered project design and delivery program. Stantec Architecture / KPMB Architect were the Planning, Design and Compliance Architect in charge of the project-specific outline specifications (PSOS) and the Design Exemplar. HDR Architecture / Diamond Schmitt Architects are the Architect of Record to the Design, Build, Finance and Maintain consortium responsible for the design as constructed.

Site The site is located on the eastern boundary of the City of Toronto and surrounded by the Don River Valley, Riverdale Park and Riverdale, one of the city's unique neighbourhoods. In the 19th century it was a site of isolation for people with communicable diseases as well as criminals sentenced to the Don Jail (1852). The redevelopment focuses on transforming the site from one of isolation to integration.

Program The ten-storey, 51,100-square-metre, 479-bed healthcare facility includes a podium and is integrated with the adaptive reuse of the historic Don Jail and designed to accommodate 20,000 annual visitors, 1,000 employees and

400 volunteers. Public components of the program include a café, auditorium, library and meditative labyrinth.

Concept The project balances goals for city building and community engagement with the vision for a village of care. The Design Exemplar builds on a previous master plan which located the historic jail at the centre of the project and the new hospital at the north-west edge. It extends the existing circulation systems and increases the number of pathways through the site to link to adjacent amenities.

The PSOS and Design Exemplar established five design criteria for the project: to create an environment of wellness, increase connection to community, provide a positive work environment, and maximize adaptability to change. It also reinforces the therapeutic benefits of nature for healing by maximizing visual and physical access to outdoors through the integration of the plan and fenestration patterns. The podium is conceived as a large-scale, communal urban porch to de-institutionalize the hospital environment and create a community resource. Within the tower, patient units are organized along the perimeter into communities of stacked 32-bed neighbourhoods. Each unit has horizontal windows with low sills.

Materials Exteriors combine local Ontario limestone, zinc cladding, ipê wood soffits with low-iron glazing. The low-iron glass blurs the boundaries between inside and outside. Public spaces feature glass screens, ipê wood ceilings and terrazzo flooring.

Outcome In 2008, the Design Exemplar earned Bridgepoint Health a *Canadian Architect* Award of Excellence. Since then, the Bridgepoint Collaboratory for Research and Innovation, Facility Design and Health was established to assess the effectiveness of the design on well-being and the delivery of healthcare in Canada.

Stantec Architecture / Kuwabara Payne McKenna Blumberg Architects, Planning, Design and Compliance Architect
HDR Architecture / Diamond Schmitt Architects, Design, Build, Finance and Maintain Architect

West elevation from Riverdale Park

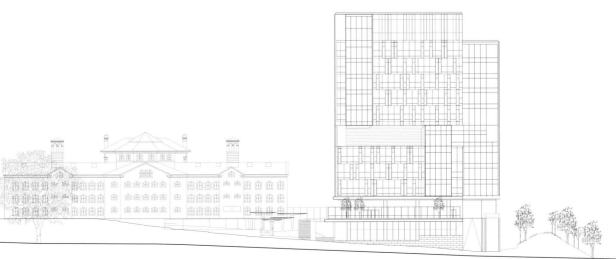

North elevation

0   10   20m

Elementary Teachers' Federation of Ontario

The Elementary Teachers' Federation of Ontario (ETFO) represents over 76,000 teachers and education workers in the province of Ontario. The ETFO headquarters was conceived to be a pinnacle of sustainable building practice with goals for a minimum 60 percent energy reduction over the MNECB (Model National Energy Code for Buildings), and LEED Platinum certification. The primary design goals were to provide a welcoming home for ETFO; create a highly sustainable and efficient green building; use architecture as an educational opportunity; and achieve effective neighbourhood integration and signature architecture. Two years were invested in developing the design and in consultations with the neighbourhood and the City, resulting in a successful rezoning of the site.

Site The project is located in the Upper Jarvis neighbourhood, a small enclave of Victorian homes in downtown Toronto designated as a community in transition. It is surrounded by high-rise commercial and condominium towers, a social housing complex, the massive Roger's Communication Headquarters, a nine-storey, 1970s-era rental apartment building and Casey House, Toronto's first AIDS hospice complex. Proximity to public transit and the downtown core made this an ideal location for ETFO.

Program The 11,250-square-metre owner-occupied office building includes training and conference facilities, flexible event space for owner and community use and a coffee bar.

Concept The design prioritizes a contextual response to knit together the divergent set of conditions that characterize the neighbourhood and its edge conditions. Siting strategies involved preserving the existing tree canopy to provide a natural shading device. The building is massed to respond to the rhythm and scale of Victorian residences to the west. A large black walnut tree was retained by creating a west-facing tree court cutting into the building. The varied landscape strategy, including transplanting mature trees to the site, a series of 'front yard' sized gardens addressing the sidewalk as well as a publicly accessible front porch and ground floor conference facilities harmonize the building into the residential neighbourhood. Large roof overhangs provide passive shade and allow winter light to penetrate deep into the floor plate.

Materials A façade of vision glazing, fibre-cement panels and vertical sunshade fins reduces solar gains. For south and west façades, late-day solar gains are countered by a fully automated exterior shading blind system — one of the only large-scale applications in Canada. Passive solar shading fins and panels are detailed to provide a finer grain and articulated façade. Large, brick-coloured fibre-cement panels and muted warm greys complement adjacent heritage buildings.

Outcome As the greenest, and most energy-efficient, purpose-built office building in the Toronto region, the new ETFO headquarters will be a model for other organizations to take action and confront energy-climate challenges. As a counterpoint to rapid high-rise urbanization, it reinforces the importance of designing buildings for the long term and as a strategy to manage urban growth.

1 atrium/reception
2 multi-purpose event/meeting room
3 training room
4 front porch
5 staff lounge
6 support
7 parkade entry

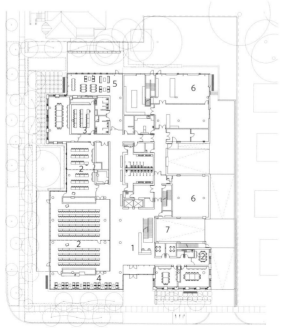

Ground floor

0   10   20m

Aerial view of building and neighbourhood (opposite top); south façade (opposite bottom)

Balcony/exterior event space (top); atrium
(bottom); training room detail (opposite
top); energy models for summer and winter
(opposite bottom)

Unlike many athletes' village projects that are purpose-built and then converted to other uses, Toronto's Athletes' Village for the 2015 Pan/Parapan American Games accelerates the build out of a development originally planned in three phases over a 12-year period to deliver a new neighbourhood for the city in five years. The project is part of a broader initiative by Waterfront Toronto in partnership with Infrastructure Ontario under a Design Build Finance model to revitalize Toronto's waterfront.

To achieve organic diversity and a distinct sense of place in one short phase, DundeeKilmer Developments, the preferred proponent developer for the athletes' village and the legacy community, assembled an integrated design team comprising four firms: architectsAlliance (aA) and Kuwabara Payne McKenna Blumberg Architects, Daoust Lestage Inc. and MacLennan Jaunkalns Miller Architects.

Site The new village will be located at the eastern edge of downtown Toronto and comprises 14.3 hectares of the 32-hectare West Don Lands development, a former industrial site undergoing transformation into a sustainable, mixed-use, pedestrian-friendly riverside community. It will be connected to the Distillery District to the west and Michael van Valkenberg's Don River Park to the east. Front Street, one of the city's major east-west arterials, will be extended through the site to terminate at Don River Park and act as the village's high street.

Program For July 2015, the project is designed to deliver 'a home away from home' for more than 10,000 athletes and officials participating in the 2015 Pan/Parapan American Games. Following the Games, the Village will be immediately converted into the Canary District, a sustainable mixed-use neighbourhood with a range of housing and services for people at all stages of life, health and at various income levels. It will include a YMCA recreation centre and a student residence for George Brown College.

Concept To achieve coherent diversity and to ensure every building contributes to the formation of a vibrant public realm, the team collectively developed a series of nine core design principles (outlined on the following page). Every building is designed by a different team according to these principles and within the parameters of Infrastructure Ontario's prescribed Precinct and Block Plans. The collective massing strategy was orchestrated to escalate the scale and geometry of expression of each building from east to west, maximize variety in scale and mass, and place every building in conversation with its adjacent and facing blocks. The ground floor spaces of all buildings are programmed for services and commercial uses to activate the wide pedestrian zone along the north side of Front Street, the main street of the neighbourhood.

Materials To establish contextual relationships with the masonry fabric of the adjacent Distillery District, brick, stone and wood add a finer grain to the ground floors of the buildings in the western precinct. From west to east amounts of glazing at the ground and upper levels increase and thus reduce the impact of the massing on the streetscape and foster an 'eyes on the street' condition.

Outcome The design celebrates the best qualities of Canada: open, inclusive and welcoming. In the short term it will give Pan/Parapan American athletes a unique experience of Toronto and Canada and create 15,000 jobs. In the long term it will strengthen the local economy and contribute another great neighbourhood to Toronto, the 'city of neighbourhoods.'

DundeeKilmer Integrated Design Team (IDT) comprising the joint venture of architectsAlliance (aA) and Kuwabara Payne McKenna Blumberg Architects (KPMB), working in association with Daoust Lestage Inc. and MacLennan Jaunkalns Miller Architects.

CORE PRINCIPLES FOR INTEGRATION

1. CITY AND NATURE CONNECTION
The massing and expression shifts from west to east, from unified, regular geometries to resonate with the historic masonry warehouses of the Distillery District to the south-west to increasingly unitized and deconstructed horizontal volumes east towards the park and the Don Valley.

2. GATEWAYS
Two historic buildings, the Canary and CNR buildings on Cherry Street, are restored and valorized as free-standing gateposts to mark the western entrance.

3. FRONT ST. CATALYST AND PROMENADE
Every block is developed to reinforce the extension of Front Street through to its terminus at Don River Park and its role as the main street and public promenade of the village. Every building base is transparent, and programmed with amenity to entice residents out of their units and into the street.

4. WALKABILITY
A sustainable city is a city that invites people to walk. A secondary system of pedestrian routes that follow the paths of two former rail lines are introduced through the mid-block courtyards north and south of Front Street. Mews and laneways, courtyards and paths are linked block to block to form continuous routes across the site.

5. GREENING THE BLOCK PLAN
The history of the site as a former parkland in the 19th century and proximity to the Don River Park inspires themes of health and wellness and the greening of courtyards, laneways, terraces and pedestrian routes.

6. EYES ON THE STREET
The Jane Jacobs thesis of 'eyes on the street' is optimized to create a safe, connected urban environment with an emphasis on transparency and views through every level of every building.

7. HORIZONTAL DATUM
Every building has a strong horizontal expression and the ground floors are consistently 6 metres high to establish connection to the industrial scale of the adjacent Distillery District and reinforce a pedestrian-scaled neighbourhood.

8. URBAN LIVABILITY
Simple gestures such as increasing the size and expanse of window openings and other features that contribute to the quality of daily life are optimized, including access to fresh air, the outdoors, sunlight, views, amenity, access to public transit as well as a balance of public and private space.

9. HOLISTIC SUSTAINABILITY
Social, economic and environmental sustainability touches on every aspect of the design to form a vibrant ecosystem of people, programs and place. The overall design meets LEED Gold criteria and honours Toronto's Mandatory Green Building Requirements to create a self-sufficient and diversified neighbourhood in which residents can live, work and play.

Historic buildings as western gateposts

Secondary paths trace former railway lines

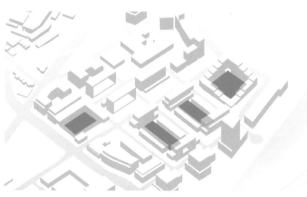

Courtyards as additional green spaces

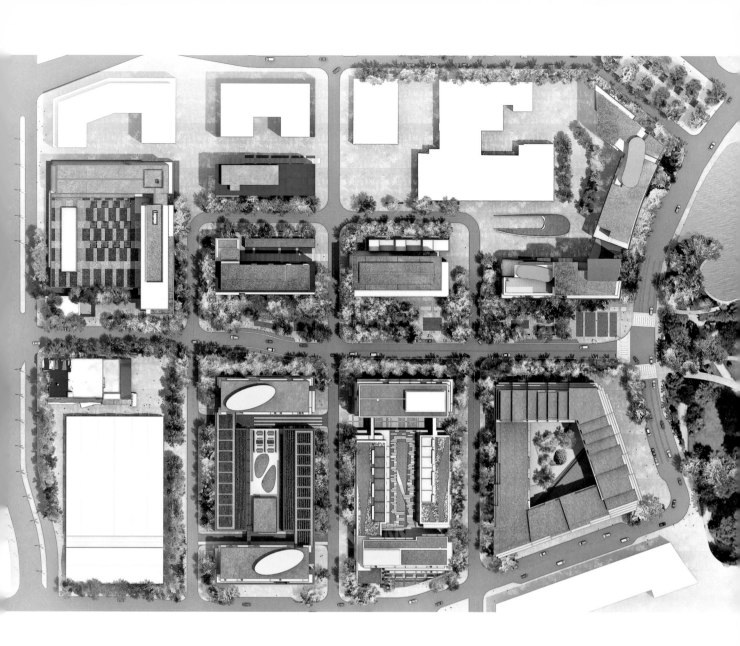

Competition rendering with CNR Office Building
(1923) on the left, Canary Restaurant (1920)
and historic Palace Street School (1859) on
the right, which are retained as gateposts to
the new neighbourhood. To the left of the CNR
Office Building is MJMA's YMCA recreation
centre and architects Alliance's George Brown
College student residence, and behind the Canary
Restaurant is KPMB's Block 11 condominium
(top); looking west along Mill Street (bottom);
winter scene on Front Street looking west
(opposite bottom)

Staff Since 1987

Safdar Abidi
Lauren Abrahams
John Agnidis
Afan Ahmed
Omar Aljebouri
John Allen
Pamela Allen
Fred Allin
Andrew Alzner
Kyle Anderson
John Armstrong
Michael Awad

Taymore Balbaa
Anna Baraness
Sebastian Bartnicki
Neil Bauman
Chris Beamer
Rejean Beaudin
Teddy Benedicto
Daniel Benson
Rob Beraldo
Mark Berest
George Bizios
Adrian Blackwell
Andrew Blackwood
Alexander Bodkin
Julie Bogdanowicz
Michael Bootsma
Alice Bowman
Justin Breg
Kevin Bridgman
François Brosseau
Jillian Brown
Kelly Buffey
Henry Burstyn
Andrew Butler

Jill Calvert
Franziska Cape
Nicolas Caron
Allison Carr
Byron Carter
Laura Carwardine
Steven Casey
Vince Catalli
Irene Chan
Clementine Chang
Rosa Chang
Jacalyn Chapel
Joy Charbonneau
Jeffrey Cheng
Natalie Cheng
Esther Cheung
Jessica Cheung
Lang Cheung
Heather Childs
Vivian Chin
Donald Chong
Kim Chong
Winston Chong
Olena Chorny
Kelly Chow
Larry Chow
Nicholas Choy
Coben Christiansen
Chester Chu
Dong-zhu Chu
Mark Cichy
Andrea Clark
Emily Clark
Krista Clark
Naomi Clarke
Kyra Clarkson
Bill Colaco
Donald Collins
David Constable
John Cook
Chris Couse
Maddie Couse
Margot Couse
Phyllis Crawford
Wendy Crolla
Ashley Curtis
Karen Cvornyek

Rachel Cyr
John Czechowski

Lisa d'Abbondanza
Jordan Darnell
Walter Daschko
Jennifer Davis
Matthew Dawson
Craig Deebank
Aurlien Delchet
Andre D'Elia
Nicholas Demers-Stoddart
Vincent Den
Deni DiFilippo
Elaine Didyk
Benny Domingos
Kelly Doran
Virginia Dos Reis
Heather Dubbeldam
Farhan Durrani
Andrew Dyke

Amin Ebrahim
Nicholas Elliott
Anila Elmas
Jose Emila
Jonathan Enns
Julie Epp
Michael Epp
Taewook Eum
Janine Ewart

Robert Faber
Deborah Fabricius
Gabriel Fain
Sharareh Farahani
Ali Fard
Shaun Fernandes
Virginia Fernandez
Graham Ferrier
Mary Jane Finlayson
Anne-Marie Fleming
Jaliya Fonseka
George Friedman

Dominic Gagnon
Rick Galezowski
Omar Gandhi
Hassan Gardezi
Collin Gardner
Joan Gardner
Victor Garzon
Rakshya Gauchan
Walter Gaudet
Alexandra Gaudreau
Meagan Gauthier
Colin Geary
Emad Ghattas
Maryam Ghayedikarimi
Razvan Ghilic Micu
Shay Gibson
Lyndon Giles
Shauna Gilles-Smith
Rob Gilvesey
Glenn Ginter
Kelvin Goddard
Valerie Gow
Bryce Gracey
Brian Graham
Meg Graham
Nardia Grant
Bill Greaves
Jill Greaves
Nicholas Green
Victoria Gregory
Sabine Grimes
Chanzy Gu
Greg Guerra
Don Gulay
Andrew Gunn

Mitchell Hall
Takuma Handa
Erin Hannon-Watkinson
Aisha Hassan

Siamak Hariri
Daphne Harris
Dirk Hartmann
Simon Haus
Courtney Henry
Alejandro Hernandez
Bettina Herz
Andrew Hill
Robert G. Hill
Zachary Hinchliffe
Bradley Hindson
Monica Hlozanek
Wai Cheong (Eric) Ho
David Holborn
Tina Hollinshead
Samer Hoot
Rick Hopkins
Beverly Horii
Stephanie Hosein
Christopher Hoyt
Fang Hsu
Lily Huang
Desmond Hui
Natalie Hui
Grant Hutchinson

Michael Isaac
Ian Izukawa

Mark Jaffar
Prish Jain
Ramon Janer
Erik Jensen
David Jesson
Eric Johnson
Forde Johnson
Andrew Jones

Wendy Kaiser
Joseph Kan
Vesna Kann
Rob Kastelic
Tanya Keigan
Lindsay Keir
Joo-Hwan (Terry) Kim
Jason King
Natalia Kirchteine
Rita Kiriakis
Alexandra Kiss
Tomislav Knezic
Artur Kobylanski
Tom Koehler
Lexi Kolt-Wagner
Stephen Kopp
Andrea Kordos
Tomislav Kraljevic
Matthew Krivosdusky
Michael Krus
Jennifer Kudlats
Claire Kurtin
Jennifer Kuwabara
Dace Kuze
Dan Kwak
Irene Kwong
Nelson Kwong

Frances Lago
Curtis Lai
Safira Lakhani
Alex Lam
Michelle Lam
Richard Lam
Noam Lamdan
Gerry Lang
Katherine LaRocca
Luigi LaRocca
Felix Larsen
Jeff Latto
Annette Lee
Brian Lee
Carolyn Lee
Jyh-Ling Lee
Kelly Lem
Clayton Lent
Aaron Letki

Alan Leung
Christine Levine
Norm Li
Thomas Li
Lilly Liaukus
Angela Lim
Jay Lim
Jason Lin
Skanda Lin
Diana Yun Liu
Leslie Livingston
Lisa Ljevaja
Mary Lou Lobsinger
Elizabeth Lofranco
Anne Lok
Aiden Loweth
Ken Lum
Sabina Luongo
Chris Lyle

Andrea Macaroun
Andrea MacElwee
James MacGillivray
Lara MacInnis
Caileigh MacKellar
Yvan MacKinnon
Glenn MacMullin
Todd Macyk
Marco Magarelli
Leah Maguire
Brian Main
Karen Mak
Glen Man
Drew Mandel
Elizabeth Mann
Phil Marjeram
Bryn Marler
Katya Marshall
Kevin Mast
Anita Matusevics
Michelle Mearns
Meika McCunn
Paul McDonnell
Shannon McGaw
Rob McKaye
Heidi McKenzie
Peter McMillan
Dan McNeil
Daniel McTavish
Gianni Meogrossi
John Mesitito
Robert Micacchi
Danielle Milburn
Devorah Miller
Goran Milosevic
Milda Miskinyte
Reena Mistry
Camille Mitchell
Katerina Mityuryayeva
Neil Morfitt
Sylvia Morgado
Joe Moro
Nariman Mousavi
Carla Munoz
Henry Murdock
Joanne Myers

Dan Nawrocki
Joseph Neuwirth
Vien Nguyen
Riki Nishimura
Maryam Nourmansouri

Yusuke Obuchi
Roy Oei
Meelena Oleksiuk-Baker
Mary O'Neill
Shane O'Neill
Kael Opie
Sean O'Reilly
Hayden Ormsby
Quinlan Osborne
Galina Oussatcheva
Graham Owen

Elizabeth Paden
Yekta Pakdaman-Hamedani
Nichola Pallotto
Lheila Palumbo
Miyako Panalaks
Katherine Pankratz
Mikyung Park
Glenn Parker
Lori Partenio
Juliette Patterson
Syliva Pawlowski
Karen Pawluk
Jason Pearson
Matthew Peddie
Annie Pelletier
Ioannis Peponoulas
Dmytriy Pereklita
Francesca Peruzzi
John Peterson
Lisa Peterson
Karen Petrachenko
Christopher Pfiffner
Sheryl Phillips
Lynn Pilon
Mike Poitras
David Poloway
Scott Pomeroy
David Pontarini
Lauren Poon
Frank Portelli
Suzanne Powadiuk
Andre Prefontaine
Andre Provencher
Anthony Provenzano
Olga Pushkar

Karine Quigley
Andres Quinlan

Ann Raback
Clare Radford
Johanna Radix
Shadi Rahbaran
Vis Ramasubramanian
Rabindra Ramcharan
Ron Renters
William Rhode
Corry Ricci
Howard Rideout
Steven Robinson
Paulo Rocha
Kristin Ross
Sara Rubenstein
Jerry Rubin

Shabbar Sagarwala
Ya'el Santopinto
Alexia Schliebener
Amanda Sebris
Thom Seto
Sheida Shahi
Amir Shahrokhi
Tyler Sharp
Leslie Shimotakahara
Sanaz Shirshekar
John Shnier
Birgit Siber
Mark A. Simone
Marc Simmons
Mark Simpson
Bob Sims
Jessica Sin
Andrew Sinclair
Danny Sinopoli
Lola Skytt
Cal Smith
David Smythe
Elyse Snyder
Mohammed Soroor
Jeanna South
Olesia Stefurak
Chris Stevens
Matthew Storus
Jeff Strauss
Rachel Strecker

Dawn Stremler
Tom Strickland
James Strong
Danya Sturgess
Danielle Sucher
Anna Sulikowska
Jimmy Sun
Howard Sutcliffe
Talbot Sweetapple

Armine Tadevosya
Antariksh Tandon
Myriam Tawadros
Sherene Tay
Judy Taylor
Michael Taylor
Simon Taylor
James Temos
Kevin Thomas
Lucy Timbers
Jennifer Ting
Elaine Tong
Janet Town
Dina Tranze-Drabir
Trisha Tremblay
Kathleen Triggs
Shih-Hua Tseng
Cameron Tudhope
Geoffry Turnbull
Jennifer Turner

Roland Ulfig
Charmaine Underw
Richard Unterthine
Brian Urbanik
Javier Uribe

Dustin Valen
Francesco Valente-G
Sonja Vangjeli
Vincent van den Br
Anna-Joy Veenstra
Catherine Venart
Claudio Venier
Alan Vihant

Brent Wagler
Jeff Wagner
John Wall
Deborah Wang
Bruno Weber
Evan Webber
Chris Wegner
David Weir
Emma Westley
Danielle Whitley
Marnie Williams
William Wilmotte
Matthew Wilson
Wendy Wisburn
Scott Wiseman
Janice Wong
Kenneth Wong
Michael Wong
Richard Wong
Rufina Wu
Ricardo Wulff

Ali Yarbakhti
Rick Yeates
Angela Yee
Arlene Yee
Gary Yen
Priscilla Yeung
Ryan Yeung
Gary Ying
Bo Yoon

Athos Zaghi
Paolo Zasso
Nick Zigomanis
Garth Zimmer

Project Credits

18 YORK AND SOUTHCORE FINANCIAL CENTRE

Location: 18 York Street, Toronto, Ontario
Completion Date: Fall 2011
Client: Great West Life Realty Advisors
Program: The 26-storey, 83,000-square-metre tower includes three levels of parking below grade and a two-storey base designed for mixed-use retail with access to a landscaped public terrace
Contract Value: Withheld at client's request
KPMB Architects: Thomas Payne (partner-in-charge), Chris Couse (principal in charge), Takuma Handa, Kevin Thomas, Thom Seto, Safdar Abidi, John Allen, Glenn MacMullin, Bill Colaco, Jose Emila, Victor Garzon, Ramon Janer, Rita Kiriakis, Carolyn Lee, Robin Ramcharan, Garth Zimmer, Razvan Ghilic Micu, Richard Lam
Engineers: Halcrow Yolles (structural), The Mitchell Partnership Inc. (mechanical), Mulvey + Banani (electrical)
Consultants: Urban Strategies Inc. (planning and development), Soberman Engineering (elevator), Corban and Goode (landscape), Leber | Rubes Inc. (building code), Extreme Measures Inc. (area measurements), Lea Consulting Ltd. (civil, traffic, parking), E.R.A (heritage), Halsall (sustainability), RWDI (wind), Aercoustics Engineering Ltd. (acoustics), Terraprobe Ltd. (geotechnical), Standard Parking of Canada (parking controls), Cini-Little (waste handling), Bhandari Plater/Entro Communications (signage), HydroSense (irrigation design), Turner & Townsend cm2r (cost), Brook Van Dalen & Associates Ltd. (façade consultant)
Project Manager: Pivotal Projects
Construction Manager: EllisDon
Photographs: Tom Arban, Tom Arban Photography, Toronto

180 QUEEN STREET WEST

Location: 180 Queen Street West, Toronto, Ontario
Completion Date: May 2007
Client: Great West Life Realty Advisors
Program: The 25,000-square-metre, 15-storey office tower includes fit-up projects for the Federal Judicial Centre (7,000 square metres), Health Canada Offices and Offices for the Public Health Agency of Canada
Contract Value: $52.2 million (CAD)
Architects: Kuwabara Payne McKenna Blumberg Architects with Stone McQuire Vogt Architects, consulting architects (base building); Kuwabara Payne McKenna Blumberg Architects [Webb Zerafa Menkes Housden Partnership, tenant's consultants of compliance for Federal Judicial Centre fit-up]
KPMB ARCHITECTS: Thomas Payne (partner-in-charge), Chris Couse (senior associate, all projects), Judy Taylor (associate in charge of Federal Judicial Centre fit-up, Health Canada and Public Health Agency fit-up); base building: Kevin Thomas (project architect), John Allen, Goran Milosevic, Luigi LaRocca, Clementine Chang, Rita Kiriakis, Katya Marshall, Thom Seto, Franziska Cape, John Agnidis; Federal Judicial Centre fit-up: Chris Wegner (project architect), David Poloway (project designer); Health Canada and Public Health Agency fit-up: Aaron Letki, Richard Wong.
STONE MCQUIRE VOGT ARCHITECTS: Heinz Vogt (partner in charge), Benny Domingos, Hassan Gardezi
Engineers: Halcrow Yolles (structural, building envelope), The Mitchell Partnership (mechanical), Mulvey + Banani (electrical)
Consultants: Urban Strategies (urban design), LEA Consulting (traffic), Leber | Rubes (building code), Solucore Elevator Solutions with Soberman Engineering (elevator), Extreme Measures (floor area analysis), RWDI (wind), Halsall Associates (LEED Federal Judicial Centre fit-up)
Construction Manager: EllisDon (base building); Govan Brown (tenant fit-up)

General Contractor: EllisDon
Photographs: Eduard Hueber, Arch Photo, New York; Tom Arban, Tom Arban Photography, Toronto
Selected Awards: 2008 Justice Facilities Review; 2007 Ontario Association of Architects Design Excellence Award

20 WASHINGTON ROAD, PRINCETON UNIVERSITY

Location: 20 Washington Road, Princeton University, Princeton, New Jersey
Completion Date: 2016
Client: Princeton University
Program: 15,600-square-metre renovation and 2.700-square-metre addition to provide offices and classrooms for Princeton's economics department, the International Initiative Programs and the Princeton Institute for International and Regional Studies.
Contract Value: Withheld at client's request
KPMB Architects: Bruce Kuwabara (design partner), Shirley Blumberg (partner-in-charge), David Jesson (senior associate), Mark Jaffar (associate), Lynn Pilon (project architect), Gabriel Fain, Annie Pelletier, Ya'el Santopinto, Elizabeth Paden, Victor Garzon, Clementine Chang, Carolyn Lee, Dina Sarhane, Rachel Cyr, Kristina Strecker
Engineers: Thornton Tomasetti (structural, building envelope), AltieriSeborWieber (mechanical, electrical, plumbing, fire protection), Van Note-Harvey and Associates (civil)
Consultants: Phil R. Sherman, P.E. (building code, fire and life safety), Vermeulens (cost), Brian Ballantyne Specifications (specifications), Cerami & Associates (acoustics, audio visual), Van Deusen (elevator), Tillotson Design Associates (lighting), Entro Communications (signage), Jablonski Building Conservation (heritage), Atelier Ten (sustainability), Michael Van Valkenburgh Associates (landscape)
Project Manager: William Zahn
Construction Manager: Barr & Barr

2015 PAN/PARAPAN AMERICAN GAMES ATHLETES' VILLAGE/CANARY DISTRICT, TORONTO

Location: West Don Lands, Toronto, Ontario
Completion Date: Spring 2015
Client: Infrastructure Ontario
Program: 14.3 hectare mixed-use neighbourhood development master plan. Phase 1 involves the Athletes' Village to house athletes and officials during 2015 Pan/Parapan American Games, designed for immediate conversion into a permanent mixed-use residential community: YMCA community centre (7,700 square metres) and student residence (17,500 square metres) for Block 1/14; market housing (31,500 square metres Block 4 and 28,900 square metres for Block 11); affordable rental housing (9,500 square metres for Block 3 and 12,900 square metres for Block 15)
Contract Value: $514 million (CAD)
Developer: Dundee Kilmer Developments Ltd.
Developer Architect Team: Dundee Kilmer Integrated Design Team: joint venture architectsAlliance (aA) and Kuwabara Payne McKenna Blumberg Architects (KPMB) in association with Daoust Lestage Inc. (DLi), MacLennan Jaunkalns Miller Architects (MJMA)
Proposal Team: Principal Team: Peter Clewes (aA), Bruce Kuwabara (KPMB), Renée Daoust (DLi), David Miller (MJMA); Adam Feldmann (aA), Andrew Dyke (KPMB), Rachel Stecker (DLi), Andrew Filarski (MJMA); Heather Rolleston (aA), Richard Unterthiner (KPMB); Supporting Team Members: Emerich Kaspar, Mariela de Felix, Shane Neill, Virginia Fernandez, Mary McIntyre, Rogelio Bayaton, Helen Tran (aA); Chris Pfiffner, Irene Chan, Taewook Eum, Gabriel Fain, Sanaz Shirshekar, Anna Sulikowska, Amanda Sebris, Johanna Radix, Dan Kwak (KPMB); Catherine St-Marseille, Hala Mehio, Carl Pineau, Stéphane Savoie (DLi); Viktors

Jaunkalns, Rick Galezowski, Chi Nguyen, Chen Cohen, Patrick Kniss, Jason Wah (MJMA)
Architects Phase 1:
ARCHITECTS ALLIANCE (Block 1/14 student residence): Peter Clewes (project leader), Adam Feldmann (proje design team leader), Blair Robinson, Emerich Kaspar, Jason Leblanc, Oliver Laumeyer, Clint Langevin, Mari De Felix, Evan Saskin, Nicolas Peters
KPMB ARCHITECTS (Blocks 4 and 11): Bruce Kuwabara (partner-in-charge), Luigi LaRocca (principal), Chris Couse (principal), Andrew Dyke (senior associate-in charge), Omar Aljebouri, Irene Chan, Dirk Hartmann, Claudio Venier, Chris Pfiffner, Taewook Eum, Joseph Kan, Julie Bogdanowicz, Aiden Loweth, Jose Emila, Ramon Janer, Francesca Peruzzi
DAOUST LESTAGE INC. (Blocks 3 and 15): Renée Daous (design principal), Rachel Stecker (project architect), Jean-Francois Bilodeau, Carl Pineau, Catherine St-Marseille, Stéphane Savoie, Marie-Josée Gagnon
MJMA ARCHITECTS (Block 1/14 YMCA community centre): David Miller, Andrew Filarski, Viktors Jaunkalns, Chen Cohen, Janouque LeRiche, Afsaneh Tafazzoli
Production Architects: Page + Steele/IBI Group Architects (Blocks 4 and 11, Blocks 3 and 15): Tim Gorley (Executive VP), Titka Seddighi (senior principal), Mar Genga, Jasna Burnazovic, Bini Saha, Meghna Bhambc Jerry Xu, Christina Chung
Engineers: Halsall Associates (structural, Blocks 1/14, 3 and 11), Adjeleian Allen Rubell Consulting Engineer (structural, Block 4), Hidi Rae Consulting Engineers (mechanical, electrical, communication systems, security systems)
Consultants: Munge Leung (interior design), NAK Design Group (landscape), Cole Engineering (civil, traffic), HH Angus & Associates (elevator), Leber | Rubes (building code), Terraprobe Environmental Services (environmental), Valcoustics Canada (acoustics), HF (commissioning), Brook Van Dalen & Associates Ltd. (building envelope)
Project Manager: EllisDon Ledcor PAAV Inc.
Construction Manager: EllisDon Ledcor PAAV Inc.
Photographs: Tom Arban, Tom Arban Photography, Toron
Selected Awards: 2012 Canadian Architect Award of Excellen

BRIDGEPOINT HEALTH

Location: 14 St. Matthews Road, Toronto, Ontario
Completion Date: 2013
Client: Bridgepoint Health
Program: Master plan site: 41,300 square metres comprising 51,100-square-metre purpose-built hospi and Don Jail: 7,100 square metres
Contract Value: Withheld at owner's request
Architects: Stantec Architecture/KPMB Architects, Planning, Design and Compliance Architects (PDC) in joint venture; HDR Architecture/Diamond Schmitt Architects, Design, Build, Finance and Maintain Architects (DBFM)
KPMB ARCHITECTS: Bruce Kuwabara (partner-in-charge), Mitchell Hall (principal, project architect), Judy Taylor, Kevin Thomas, Glenn MacMullin, Paulo Rocha, Lilly Liaukus
STANTEC ARCHITECTURE: Michael Moxam (principal-in-charge), Stuart Elgie (principal, project architect), Jane Wigle (healthcare planning lead), Deanna Brow Sylvia Kim, Norma Angel, Rich Hlava, Ko Van Klavere Tim Lee
HDR ARCHITECTURE ASSOCIATES INC.: Craig Ellis (proje principal), Rodel Misa (senior project manager), Tod Trigg (senior project manager), Stewart Earle (senior architect), Neil Sutton (senior project architect), Hyounjung Ahn, Ellen Rogojine, Jesus Santos, Andy Wong
DSAI ARCHITECTS: Jack Diamond (executive principal) Greg Colucci (principal-in charge), Antra Roze (associate and project architect), Jeong Choe, Kirste

Douglas, Gilda Giovane, Chris Hoyt, Brian McClean, Giuseppe Mandarino

Engineers: Stantec Consulting (structural, electrical), The Mitchell Partnership (mechanical)

Consultants: Phillips Farevaag Smallenberg (landscape), Stantec Consulting (sustainability, energy), Randal Brown & Associates (building code, fire and life safety), Soberman Engineering (elevators), Aercoustics Engineering Ltd. (vibration, noise, acoustics), CFMS Consulting (commissioning), McCarthy Tetrault (municipal legal advisor), Urban Strategies (urban planning), E.R.A. Architects (heritage), RV Anderson Associates (site servicing), BA Consulting Group (traffic, transportation), Agnew Peckham (functional programming), Golder Associates (environmental), Archeological Services (archeological), Bruce Tree Expert (arborist), Kaizen Foodservice Planning & Design (food services)

Photographs: Sam Javanrouh, Toronto

Design Build Finance Maintain Consortium: Plenary Health Bridgepoint (Plenary Health, Innisfree Health)

Constructor: PCL Constructors Canada

Selected Awards: 2008 Canadian Architect Award of Excellence

CANADA'S NATIONAL BALLET SCHOOL (PROJECT GRAND JETÉ STAGE 1: THE JARVIS STREET CAMPUS)

Location: 400 Jarvis Street, Toronto, Ontario
Completion Date: December 2005
Client: Canada's National Ballet School
Program: 16,700 square metres (13,200 square metres new construction, 3,500 square metres restoration/adaptive reuse) comprising new construction for dance studios and support spaces, the restoration of two heritage buildings, renovation of Betty Oliphant Theatre and underground parking
Contract Value: $75 million (CAD)
Architects: Kuwabara Payne McKenna Blumberg Architects and Goldsmith Borgal & Company Ltd. Architects, architects in joint venture
KPMB ARCHITECTS: Bruce Kuwabara (design partner), Shirley Blumberg (partner-in-charge), Mitchell Hall (design associate), Olga Pushkar (project architect), Myriam Tawadros, Krista Clark, Jill Greaves, Virginia Dos Reis, Ramon Janer, Maryam Nourmansouri, Jeff Strauss, Jimmy Sun
GOLDSMITH BORGAL & COMPANY LTD. ARCHITECTS: Phil Goldsmith (principal-in-charge), Paul Gagné (design associate), Allan D. Killin (associate architect), Mark Krapez, Darryl Fisher, Ida Seto, Gill Haley, Tanya Cazzin, Christopher Borgal
Engineers: Halcrow Yolles (structural), Crossey Engineering (mechanical, electrical, plumbing)
Consultants: The MBTW Group (landscape), Shady Lane Expert Tree Care (arborist), Scott Thornley + Company (branding), Bhandari & Plater (signage), Urban Strategies (urban planners), Marrack + Associates (food services), Engineering Harmonics (audio visual), Catherine Williams Fine Art Consultants (public art), Graycom Analysis (IT), MCD Design Group (furniture), Aercoustics Engineering Ltd. (acoustics), Soberman Engineering (elevator), iTRANS Consulting (traffic), Shaheen & Peaker (geotechnical), RWB Engineering (shoring), Rabideau & Czerwinski (land surveyor), A.W. Hooker Associates Ltd. (quantity surveyor), Clare Randall-Smith & Ass. (quantity surveyor, mechanical, electrical, plumbing), Larden Muniak Consulting (building code)
Project Manager: Sims Moelich Associates
Construction Manager: Eastern Construction
Photographs: Eduard Hueber, Arch Photo, New York; Tom Arban, Tom Arban Photography, Toronto; Maris Mezulis, Toronto
Selected Awards: 2009 Chicago Athenaeum International Architecture Award; 2009 American Institute of Architects/Committee on Architecture for Education,

Educational Facility Design Awards, Award of Merit; 2008 Urban Land Institute Global Award for Excellence; 2008 Governor General's Medal for Architecture; 2008 Urban Land Institute Award for Excellence; 2008 Royal Architectural Institute of Canada National Urban Design Award, Award of Excellence; 2007 Toronto Urban Design Awards, Award of Excellence; 2007 American Institute of Architects Honour Award for Architecture; 2006 Ontario Association of Architects Design Excellence Award; 2006 Canadian Interiors Best of Canada Design Competition, Project Winner; 2006 Pug Awards Best in Show; 2006 Heritage Toronto, Award of Excellence, Architectural Conservation & Craftsmanship Category

CANADIAN MUSEUM OF NATURE

Location: 240 McLeod Street, Ottawa, Ontario
Competition Date: November 2001
Completion Date: May 2010
Client: Canadian Museum of Nature
Program: 23,200 square metres total comprising 20,400 square metres existing; 2,800 square metres new construction
Contract Value: $162 million (CAD)
Architects: Padolsky, Kuwabara, Gagnon Joint Venture Architects (PKG): Barry Padolsky Associates Inc. Architects, Kuwabara Payne McKenna Blumberg Architects, and Gagnon Letellier Cyr Ricard Mathieu Architectes
KPMB ARCHITECTS: Bruce Kuwabara (partner-in-charge), Brent Wagler (project architect), Luigi LaRocca, John Allen, Bill Colaco, Yekta Pakdaman-Hamedani, Shabbar Sagarwala, Andrew Gunn, Brian Lee, Jose Emila, Jill Greaves, Bruno Weber, Walter Gaudet, Thom Seto, Tomislav Knezic, Virginia Dos Reis, Carolyn Lee, Lauren Abrahams, Lang Cheng, Bradley Hindson, Norm Li, Lilly Liaukus, Tyler Sharp, Esther Cheung, Meagan Gauthier, Francesco Valente-Gorjup, Anna Baraness, Taewook Eum
BARRY PADOLSKY ASSOCIATES INC. ARCHITECTS: Barry Padolsky (project manager), Louise McGugan (project and heritage architect), Mike Kelly, Eric Fruhauf, Elizabeth Saikali, Ursula Clarkson, Danica Lau, Mike Labine, Jason Lowe, Grant Stewart, Peter Elliott, Crystal Eryuzlu, Rene Mariaca
GAGNON LETELLIER CYR RICARD MATHIEU ARCHITECTES: Marc Letellier (partner-in-charge), Michel Gagnon (partner in charge of construction documents), Simon Brochu, François Paradis, Pierre Michaud, Suzanne Castonguay, Vincent Lavoie, Réal St-Pierre, Jean-Sébastien Laberge
RESIDENT SITE ARCHITECT: Paul Dolan
Engineers: Halsall Associates (structural), Genivar Consulting Group (mechanical, electrical, plumbing)
Consultants: Delcan Corporation (civil, transportation), McRostie Genest St. Louis (geotechnical), Dan Euser Water Architecture (water feature), Morrison Hershfield (building code), Gabriel Mackinnon (lighting), T. Harris Environmental Management (sustainability), GHE Greenhouse Engineering (greenhouse), Glaswal Systems (structural glazing), Hanscomb (cost, scheduling), Soberman Engineering (elevator), Marshall and Murray (quantity surveyor), Peeta Consultants (scheduler), IRC Sears Batten Group (roofing), Keller Engineering Associates (building conservation), Gruenwoldt-Copeland Landscape Planners (landscape), Yale Corbin (hardware), Leber | Rubes (security), A.J. Watts (food service), Engineering Harmonics (audio visual), JS Models (model design), Gottschalk + Ash (signage)
Construction Manager: PCL Constructors Canada
Photographs: Tom Arban, Tom Arban Photography, Toronto; Doublespace Photography, Ottawa

Selected Awards: 2011 Chicago Athenaeum International Architecture Award; 2011 Ontario Association of Architects Design Excellence Award

CENTENNIAL COLLEGE APPLIED RESEARCH AND INNOVATION CENTRE

Location: 755 Morningside Avenue, Scarborough, Ontario
Completion Date: August 2004
Client: Centennial College of Applied Arts and Technology
Program: 23,000 square metres accommodating 25 class-rooms, 47 specialty laboratories, six computer labs, lecture hall, full-service resource centre, faculty and administrative offices, and food court/café
Contract Value: $41 million (CAD)
Architects: Kuwabara Payne McKenna Blumberg Architects/Stone McQuire Vogt Architects, associated architects.
KPMB ARCHITECTS: Bruce Kuwabara (design partner), Shirley Blumberg (partner-in-charge), Luigi LaRocca (senior associate), Paulo Rocha (project architect), Steven Casey, Andre D'Elia, Ramon Janer, Shane O'Neill, Jimmy Sun
STONE MCQUIRE VOGT ARCHITECTS: Heinz Vogt (principal), Craig Bonham, Benny Domingos, Hassan Gardezi
Engineers: Read Jones Christoffersen (structural), Keen Engineering (mechanical), Mulvey + Banani (electrical), Halsall Associates (building envelope)
Consultants: IBI Group (IT consultants), Leber | Rubes (fire and life safety), NAK Design Group (landscape) iTRANS Consulting (traffic), Entro Communications (signage), Urban Watershed (stormwater management), Decommissioning Consulting Services (geotechnical)
Construction Manager: Vanbots Construction Corporation
Photographs: Tom Arban, Tom Arban Photography, Toronto; Eduard Hueber, Arch Photo, New York
Selected Awards: 2006 Chicago Athenaeum International Architecture Award; 2006 Canadian Interiors, Best of Canada Design Competition, Project Winner; 2006 American Institute of Architects/Committee on Architecture for Education, Educational Facility Design Awards, Award of Excellence

CENTRE FOR INTERNATIONAL GOVERNANCE INNOVATION (CIGI) CAMPUS

Location: 57 Erb Street West, Waterloo, Ontario
Completion Date: 2011
Client: Centre for International Governance Innovation (CIGI)
Program: 10,700-square-metre academic building
Contract Value: Withheld at client's request
KPMB Architects: Shirley Blumberg (partner in charge), Steven Casey (project architect), Bruce Kuwabara, Joy Charbonneau, Glenn MacMullin, George Bizios, Erik Jensen, Vivian Chin, Ramon Janer, Carolyn Lee, Danielle Sucher
Engineers: Blackwell Bowick Partnership (structural), Crossey Engineering (mechanical), HH Angus & Associates (electrical), Conestoga Rovers & Associates (civil)
Consultants: Transsolar (energy), Tillotson Design Associates (lighting), Aercoustics Engineering Ltd. (acoustics), Engineering Harmonics (audio visual), Phillips Farevaag Smallenberg (landscape), GSP Group (planning), Leber | Rubes (building code), Turner & Townsend cm2r (cost), Kaizen Foodservice Planning & Design (food services), Brian Ballantyne Specifications (specifications), Trillium Architectural Products (hardware)
Project Manager: Gregory J. Bewick and Associates
Construction Manager: Cooper Construction
General Contractor: Cooper Construction
Photographs: Tom Arban, Tom Arban Photography, Toronto; Maris Mezulis, Toronto
Selected Awards: 2013 Architectural Record, Good Design is Good Business Award; 2013 Ontario Association of

Architects Design Excellence Award; 2012 Canadian Interiors Best of Canada Award; 2012 Royal Institute of British Architects, International Award; 2012 Ontario Association of Architects Design Excellence Award

ELEMENTARY TEACHERS' FEDERATION OF ONTARIO

Location: 136 Isabella Street, Toronto, Ontario
Completion Date: Spring 2013
Client: Elementary Teachers' Federation of Ontario
Program: 11,250 square metres
Contract Value: Withheld at client's request
KPMB Architects: Bruce Kuwabara (design partner), Shirley Blumberg (partner-in-charge), Kael Opie (associate), Geoffrey Turnbull, Bruno Weber, David Constable, Zachary Hinchliffe, Christopher Pfiffner, Joseph Kan, Bryn Marler, Joy Charbonneau, Lynn Pilon, Carolyn Lee, Danielle Sucher, Bridget Freeman-Marsh, Lang Cheung
Engineers: Blackwell Bowick Partnership Ltd. (structural), Cobalt Engineering (mechanical), Smith & Andersen (electrical, security, communications), SCS Consulting Group (civil), Principle Water (irrigation), Halcrow Yolles (envelope)
Consultants: CDML (energy consultant/sustainability), NAK Design Group (landscape), Engineering Harmonics (audio visual), Leber | Rubes (code), CFMS (commissioning), N. Barry Lyon Consultants Ltd. (land use), Sorensen Gravely Lowes Planning Associates (planning), Davies Howe Partners (legal), Turner & Townsend cm2r (cost), LEA Consulting Ltd. (transportation), Kaizen Foodservice Planning & Design (food services), Cini Little (waste management), Soberman Engineering (elevator), Suzanne Powadiuk (lighting), Aercoustics Engineering Ltd. (acoustic), RWDI (wind study)
Project Manager: Turner & Townsend cm2r
Constructor: BIRD Construction
Photographs: Jesse Jackson, Toronto

GARDINER MUSEUM

Location: 111 Queen's Park, Toronto, Ontario
Completion Date: June 2006
Client: Gardiner Museum
Program: 4,300 square metres total (3,000 square metres renovation, 1,300 square metres new construction) renovation and expansion of an existing museum (1983)
Contract Value: $10 million (CAD)
KPMB Architects: Bruce Kuwabara (design partner), Shirley Blumberg (partner-in-charge), Paulo Rocha (design and project architect), John Allen, Kevin Bridgman, Steven Casey, Bill Colaco, Ramon Janer, Tom Knezic, Shane O'Neill, Thom Seto, Tyler Sharpe, Javier Uribe
Exhibition/Casework Design: PS Design in association with KPMB Architects. Exhibition design by PS Design: Debi Perna and Eric Siegrist; Casework design by KPMB Architects: Shirley Blumberg (partner in charge), Paulo Rocha (design and project architect) and Thom Seto. Casework executed by MCM 2001
Engineers: Halsall Associates* (structural), Crossey Engineering (mechanical, electrical)
Consultants: Leber | Rubes (fire and life safety), Vermeulens Cost Consultants (cost), Soberman Engineering (elevator), Suzanne Powadiuk (lighting), NAK Design Group (landscape), Marrack + Associates (food services)
Project Manager: Larry Kurtz
General Contractor: Urbacon
Photographs: Eduard Hueber, Arch Photo, New York; Tom Arban, Tom Arban Photography, Toronto; Shai Gil, Toronto
Selected Awards: 2008 Royal Institute of British Architects International Award; 2008 Chicago Athenaeum International Architecture Award; 2007 Ontario Association of Architects Design Excellence Award;

2007 Business Week/Architectural Record Citation for Excellence

GEORGE BROWN COLLEGE, WATERFRONT CAMPUS

Location: East Bayfront Precinct, Toronto Waterfront, Toronto, Ontario
Completion Date: September 2012
Client: George Brown College
Program: 47,100 square metres, comprising 15,000 square metres underground parking, 32,100 square metres Centre for Health Sciences program including classrooms, practice laboratories and offices
Contract Value: $140 million (CAD)
Architects: Stantec Architecture and Kuwabara Payne McKenna Blumberg Architects, architects in joint venture
KPMB ARCHITECTS: Bruce Kuwabara (partner-in-charge), Mitchell Hall (principal, project architect), Brent Wagler, William Rohde, Roland Ulfig, Elizabeth Paden, Fang Hsu, Lily Liaukus, Nariman Mousavi, Mohammed Soroor, Esther Cheung, Sabine Grimes
STANTEC ARCHITECTURE: Michael Moxam (design partner), Stuart Elgie (principal, project architect), Trish Piwowar (associate, health science team lead), Stephen Phillips, Rich Hlava, Gerard Dourado, Ko van Klaveren, Mick Dobbin, Stacy Fleming, Sarah O'Connor, Pani Eslami, John Ciarmela, Nancy Lindsay
Engineers: Stantec Consulting (structural, mechanical, electrical, civil, sustainability, energy)
Consultants: BA Consulting Group (transportation), Educational Consulting Services (functional programming), Hanscomb (cost), Leber | Rubes (building code), Kaizen Foodservice Planning & Design (food services), Phillips Farevaag Smallenberg (landscape), The Sextant Group (audio visual functional program), Soberman Engineering (elevator), SPH Planning and Consulting (accessibility), Isherwood Geostructural Engineers (geostructural), SHAL Consulting Engineers (marine engineer), Trow Associates (geotechnical, environmental)
Project Manager: Terry Comeau (executive director), Nerys Rau (project manager)
Construction Manager: EllisDon
Photographs: Tom Arban, Tom Arban Photography, Toronto; Maris Mezulis, Toronto
Selected Awards: 2013 SCUP/AIA-CAE Excellence in Architecture, Honor Award

THE GLOBE AND MAIL CENTRE

Location: 410 Front Street West, Toronto, Ontario
Completion Date: 2017
Client: The Woodbridge Company
Program: 42,500-square-metre 18-storey multi-tenant office tower
Contract Value: Withheld at client's request
KPMB Architects: Marianne McKenna (partner-in-charge), Steven Casey (associate), David Constable (project architect), Danielle Whitley, Vivian Chin, Joy Charbonneau, Glenn MacMullin, Ramon Janer, Dirk Hartmann, Thom Seto, Carolyn Lee, Jordan Evans
Engineers: Entuitive Corporation (structural, curtainwall), The Mitchell Partnership (mechanical), Mulvey + Banani (electrical, LEED), MMM Group (civil), Transsolar (climate)
Consultants: Turner & Townsend cm2r (cost), NAK Design (landscape), RWDI (wind), Aercoustics (acoustics), BA Group (parking), Savira Associates (program planning), Soberman Engineering (elevator), SPL Consultants (geotechnical), SVG (quantity surveyors), Theatre Consultants Collaborative (venue), Terraprobe (shoring), Tillotson (lighting), Brian Ballantyne Specifications (specifications), Kaizen Foodservice Planning & Design (food services), Leber | Rubes (building code)
Project Manager: PHA Project Management *Construction Manager:* EllisDon

GLUSKIN SHEFF + ASSOCIATES OFFICES

Location: Bay Adelaide Centre, 333 Bay Street, Suite 5100 Toronto, Ontario
Completion Date: September 2011
Client: Gluskin Sheff + Associates
Program: 4,600-square-metre office interior
Contract Value: Withheld at client's request
KPMB Architects: Bruce Kuwabara (partner-in-charge), Luigi LaRocca (principal), David Jesson (senior associate), David Poloway, Bryn Marler, Annie Pelletier, Carolyn Lee, Danielle Sucher, Rachel Cyr, Terry Kim
Engineers: Halcrow Yolles (structural), The Mitchell Partnership (mechanical), Mulvey + Banani (electrical)
Consultants: Tillotson Design Associates (lighting), Leber | Rubes (building code), Aercoustics Engineering Ltd. (acoustics)
Project Manager: PHA Project
Construction Manager: Govan Brown & Associates
Photographs: Maris Mezulis, Toronto

KELLOGG SCHOOL OF MANAGEMENT, NORTHWESTERN UNIVERSITY

Location: Northwestern University, Evanston, Illinois
Completion Date: 2016
Client: Northwestern University
Program: 32,500-square-metre purpose-built academic building
Contract Value: Withheld at client's request
Architects: Kuwabara Payne McKenna Blumberg Architects and FGM Architects, associated architects
COMPETITION TEAM: Bruce Kuwabara (design partner), Marianne McKenna (partner-in-charge), Luigi LaRocca (principal), John Peterson (associate), Brent Wagler (associate), Camille Mitchell, Joseph Kan, Geoffrey Turnbull, David Constable, Aidan Loweth, Kristina Strecker, Amanda Sebris (director of marketing), Dawn Stremler (marketing manager), Carolyn Lee (associate/interior designer), Danielle Sucher (interiors), Adrian Pfiffer, Office of Adrian Pfiffer (renderings), Anita Matusevics, Wonder Inc. (graphic design), Jack Szymoniak, JS Models (model)
KPMB ARCHITECTS: Bruce Kuwabara (design partner), Marianne McKenna (partner-in-charge), Luigi LaRocc (principal), Kevin Thomas (associate), John Peterson (associate), Camille Mitchell, Rita Kiriakis, Teddy Benedicto, Jonathan Enns, Vaughn Miller, Jennifer Davis, Andrew Hill, Carolyn Lee, Danielle Sucher, Mohammed Soroor, William Rhode
FGM ARCHITECTS: Joe Chronister
Engineers: Thornton Tomasetti (structural), AEI Affiliated Engineers (mechanical, electrical, plumbing), Eriksson Engineering (civil, geotechnical), Transsolar (energy, climate)
Consultants: Hoerr Schaudt (landscape), HJ Kessler Associates (LEED), Tillotson Design Associates (lighting), Construction Cost Systems (cost), CM Architects (accessibility), Threshold (acoustic, audio visual), Soberman Engineering (elevator), S20 (food services), Desman (parking, traffic), Brian Ballantyne Specifications (specifications), Cini Little (waste management)
Project Manager: Northwestern University

LE QUARTIER CONCORDIA, CONCORDIA UNIVERSITY, ENGINEERING AND COMPUTER SCIENCE AND VISUAL ARTS INTEGRATED COMPLEX

Location: 1515 Sainte-Catherine Street West, Montreal, Quebec
Competition Date: November/December 2000
Completion Date: September 2005
Client: Concordia University
Program: Engineering and Computer Science: 46,000 square metres faculty and graduate offices, classrooms, retail, heavy engineering labs (including

vibration pit), wet labs, white labs, computer labs, workshops and fitness centre; Visual Arts: 14,000 square metres faculty and graduate offices, design art studios, photography dark rooms, electronic and experimental arts studios, black box theatre, galleries, art store and teaching amphitheatres

Contract Value: $134 million (CAD)

Competition Team: Bruce Kuwabara, Marianne McKenna, Andrew Dyke, Paulo Rocha, Julie Dionne, Catherine Venart, Jacob Fichten, Gerald Soiferman, Stephan Tremblay

Architects: Kuwabara Payne McKenna Blumberg Architects and Fichten Soiferman et Associés Architectes, architects in joint venture

KPMB ARCHITECTS: Bruce Kuwabara (design partner), Marianne McKenna (partner-in-charge), Andrew Dyke (associate), Glenn MacMullin (project architect), Anne-Marie Fleming (project architect), John Peterson, Lucy Timbers, Chris Wegner, Bill Colaco, Paolo Zasso, Andre Prefontaine, Rita Kiriakis, Meika McCunn, Eric Ho, Deborah Wang, Dan Nawrocki, Jill Greaves, Lilly Liaukus, Henry Burstyn

FICHTEN SOIFERMAN ET ASSOCIÉS ARCHITECTES: Jacob Fichten (partner-in-charge), Gerald Soiferman (partner, administration), Andrij Serbyn (partner, production, contract administration), Michael Conway, Julie Dionne, Victor Garzon, Ngae Chi Wong, Michael Hall, Bernard Jacques, Serge Labossière, Sandrine Zanbo, Nicolas-Malik Paquin, Benoît Picard, Andre Tremblay, Xin Wu

Engineers: Nicolet Chartrand Knoll Ltée (structural), Pageau Morel et Associés, Dupras Ledoux Ingénieurs, Keen Engineering (mechanical, electrical, sustainability)

Consultants: Brook Van Dalen & Associates Ltd. and Chiovitti Consultants (building envelope), Exim (elevator), Curran McCabe Ravindran Ross Inc. (cost), Technorm (building code, life safety), Leber | Rubes (building code, life safety), Moureaux Hauspy Design (furniture and wayfinding), Trizart Alliance (audio visual), Doucet et Associés (IT, security)

Project Manager: Gespro Sst

General Contractor: L.A. Hébert Ltée, EBC, Hervé Pomerleau

Public Art Installation: Nicolas Baier in conjunction with Bruno Braën and Hans Brown designers

Campus Master Plan: Groupe Cardinal Hardy

Photographs: Eduard Hueber, Arch Photo, New York; Tom Arban, Tom Arban Photography, Toronto; Marc Cramer, Montreal; James Brittain, Montreal

Selected Awards: 2006 Royal Architectural Institute of Canada National Urban Design Award

LE QUARTIER CONCORDIA, CONCORDIA UNIVERSITY, JOHN MOLSON SCHOOL OF BUSINESS

Location: 1455 de Maisonneuve Blvd West, Montreal, Quebec

Competition Date: November/December 2000

Completion Date: August 2009

Client: John Molson School of Business, Concordia University

Program: 35,000 square metres; 17 storeys, 45 state-of-the-art classrooms, 3,000 classroom seats ranging from 'the Harvard' to the 'breakout' for 8,000 undergraduate and graduate students; 300-seat auditorium, two 150-seat amphitheatres, four 120-seat amphitheatres, 22 conference rooms, 289 offices, 44 private study rooms, three designated open study areas, eight open relaxation/study areas, seven waiting areas

Contract Value: $90 million (CAD)

Architects: Kuwabara Payne McKenna Blumberg Architects and Fichten Soiferman et Associés Architectes, architects in joint venture

COMPETITION TEAM: Bruce Kuwabara, Marianne McKenna, Andrew Dyke, Paulo Rocha, Julie Dionne,

Catherine Venart, Jacob Fichten, Gerald Soiferman, Stephan Tremblay

KPMB ARCHITECTS: Bruce Kuwabara (design partner), Marianne McKenna (partner-in-charge), Andrew Dyke (associate), John Peterson (project architect, design and documentation), Rob Kastelic (project architect, design and documentation), Glenn MacMullin (project architect, contract administration), Lucy Timbers, Eric Ho, Paulo Zasso, Andre Prefontaine, Jill Greaves Osiowy, Omar Gandhi, Esther Cheung, Virginia Dos Reis, Lilly Liaukus, Olesia Stefurak, Deborah Wang.

FICHTEN SOIFERMAN ET ASSOCIÉS ARCHITECTES: Jacob Fichten (partner-in-charge), Gerald Soiferman (partner, administration), Andrij Serbyn, Benoit Lamoureux, Julie Dionne, Victor Garzon, Artur Kobylanski, Etienne Gibeault, Jessica Cuevas, Patrick Tiernan, Dimitri Koubatis, Martine Lacombe, Eric Jofrient, Marie-Hélène Trudeau, Bertrand Marais, Lheila Palumbo

Engineers: Nicolet Chartrand Knoll Ltée (structural), Groupe HBA Experts-Conseils (mechanical, electrical)

Consultants: Curran McCabe Ravindran Ross Inc. (cost), Technorm (building code, life safety), Exim (elevator), Trizart Alliance (audio visual), Doucet et Associés (IT, security)

Project Manager: Genivar

General Contractor: Verreault

Public Art Installation: Geneviève Cadieux, Pierre Blanchette

Campus Master Plan: Groupe Cardinal Hardy

Photographs: Eduard Hueber, Arch Photo, New York; Tom Arban, Tom Arban Photography, Toronto; Marc Cramer, Montreal; James Brittain, Montreal

MANITOBA HYDRO PLACE

Location: 360 Portage Avenue, Winnipeg, Manitoba

Completion Date: September 2009

Client: Manitoba Hydro

Program: 76,500 square metres, 21-storey high-rise office building to house 2,000 workstations for 2,000 employees. Three-storey podium base contains retail and interior street; one level of parking below grade and an 18-storey office tower and a three-storey mechanical penthouse above

Contract Value: $283 million (CAD)

Architects: Kuwabara Payne McKenna Blumberg Architects (Design Architect), Smith Carter Architects & Engineers (Executive Architect), Transsolar (Specialist Energy/Climate Engineer), Prairie Architects (Advocate Architect)

INTEGRATED DESIGN PROCESS (IDP) DESIGN CHARETTE TEAM: Manitoba Hydro (Tom Gouldsborough, Doug McKay, Tom Akerstream, Kevin Leung, Colleen Johnson, Julie Gervino; KPMB (Bruce Kuwabara, Luigi LaRocca, John Peterson, Kael Opie, Lucy Timbers, Eric Johnson, Javier Uribe, Taymoore Balbaa); Smith Carter (Jim Yamashita, Rick Linley, Glen Klym, Al Coppinger, John Crocker, Colin Reed, Ron Pidwerbesky, Kirk McLean, Brad Cove, Sheila Reenders); Specialist Engineers/Consultants on IDP Team: Transsolar (Thomas Auer, Alex Knirsch); AECOM (John Munroe, Chris Saunders, Mike Shewchuck, Alan Aftanas, Steve Ruel); Brook Van Dalen & Associates Ltd. (Mark Brook); Halcrow Yolles (Barry Charnish, David Gray); Crosier Kilgour & Partners (Tom Malkiewicz, Joel Smith); Soberman Engineering (Jon Soberman); Aercoustics Engineering Ltd. (John O'Keefe); Prairie Architects (Dudley Thompson); Integrated Designs/Commissioning Agents (Ken Coutu, Jamie MacPherson, Kevin Thurston, Murray Guy) Pivotal Lighting Design (Jeff Miller, Blythe von Reckers); Phillips Farevaag Smallenberg (Greg Smallenberg, Jeff Staates); Hilderman Thomas (Frank Cram, Glen Manning); PCL Constructors Canada (Alfred Schlier, Randy Storoschuk, Monique Buckberger, Steve Bioletti,

Brian Hine); Hanscomb (Isaac Gwendo, Arthur Maw, David Crane)

CLIENT TEAM (MANITOBA HYDRO): Tom Gouldsborough, Tom Akerstream, Dave Little, Doug McKay, Kevin Leung, Colleen Johnson, Julie Gervino, Leah Rensfelt, Susan Aird, Darren Sachvie, Mark Pauls, Carmen Hebert, Roberta Radons, Joan Anderson, Dan Beaudoin, Gary Rossol, Dan Zelich

KPMB ARCHITECTS (Design Architect): Bruce Kuwabara (partner-in-charge), Luigi LaRocca (senior associate), John Peterson (project architect), Kael Opie (project architect), Lucy Timbers, Glenn MacMullin, Ramon Janer, Javier Uribe, Taymoore Balbaa, Steven Casey, Clementine Chang, Chu Dongzhu, Virginia Dos Reis, Andrew Dyke, Omar Gandhi, Bettina Herz, Eric Ho, Tanya Keigan, Steven Kopp, John Lee, Norm Li, Eric Johnson, Andrea Macaroun, Rob Micacchi, Lauren Poon, Rachel Stecker, Matt Storus, Richard Unterthiner, Dustin Valen, Francesco Valente-Gorjup, Marnie Williams, William Wilmotte, Paulo Zasso

SMITH CARTER ARCHITECTS & ENGINEERS (Executive Architect): Jim Yamashita (partner-in-charge), Rick Linley (project director), Glen Klym (project manager), Al Coppinger, John Crocker, Colin Reed, Ron Pidwerbesky, Kirk McLean, Matt Baker, Neil Hulme, Phil Harmes, Stephane Chappellaz, Richard Chan, Dallas Ptosnick, Brad Cove, Stephen Londrey, Ron Martin, Charlene Kroll, Daryl Hnylycia, Sheila Reenders, Lynne Richardson

TRANSSOLAR (Climate Engineers): Thomas Auer, Alex Knirsch, Helmut Meyer, Nicole Kuhnert, David White

PRAIRIE ARCHITECTS (Advocate Architects): Dudley Thompson, Crystal Bornais, Dennis Kwan, Teresa da Costa Neubauer

Engineers: Crosier Kilgour & Partners (structural), Halcrow Yolles (structural), AECOM (mechanical, electrical)

Consultants: Integrated Designs (commissioning), Groundsolar Energy Technologies (geothermal), Omicron Consulting Group (geothermal), Pivotal Lighting Design (lighting), Hilderman Thomas Frank Cram (landscape), Phillips Farevaag Smallenberg (landscape), Leber | Rubes (life safety), Brook Van Dalen & Associates Ltd. (building envelope), Soberman Engineering (elevator), Aercoustics Engineering Ltd. (acoustics), RWDI (microclimate), Hanscomb (quantity surveyor), Wardrop Engineering (municipal and site services), ND Lea Engineers & Planners (traffic, access and parking), UMA Engineering in partnership with Dyregrov Consultants (geotechnical, hydrogeologist), Dan Euser Water architecture (water feature)

Project Manager: Tom Gouldsborough (Manitoba Hydro)

Construction Manager and General Contractor: PCL Constructors Canada

Photographs: Eduard Hueber, Arch Photo, New York; Tom Arban, Tom Arban Photography, Toronto; Gerry Kopelow, Photographics, Winnipeg; Maris Mezulis, Toronto

Selected Awards: 2012 Urban Land Institute Global Award for Excellence; 2012 Chicago Athenaeum: Green GOOD DESIGN™ Award; 2011 The Outstanding Building of the Year (TOBY) Award BOMA Manitoba; 2011 Royal Architectural Institute of Canada Innovation in Architecture, Honourable Mention; 2010 ACEC Canadian Consulting Engineering Award — Buildings; 2010 Engineers Canada Award; 2010 Sustainable Architecture & Building Magazine Awards, Project Winner; 2010 Royal Architectural Institute of Canada National Urban Design Award; 2010 American Institute of Architects/Committee on the Environment Top Ten Green Projects Award; 2009 Council on Tall Buildings and Urban Habitat, Best Tall Building Award Americas; 2009 ArchDaily Building of the Year Award, Offices Category; 2008 International Building Skin-Technology (IBS) Awards, Highly

Commended; 2006 Canadian Architect Award of
Excellence; 2006 MIPIM/Architectural Review Future
Projects Awards, Award of Merit for Innovation

MIKE & OPHELIA LAZARIDIS QUANTUM-NANO CENTRE, UNIVERSITY OF WATERLOO

Location: 200 University Avenue West, Waterloo, Ontario
Completion Date: Summer 2012
Client: University of Waterloo
Program: 26,500-square-metre facility for quantum
   computing and nanotechnology; accommodates
   400 academics and includes a 929-square-metre
   cleanroom, metrology suite, teaching and research
   laboratories, multi-purpose space/auditorium, seminar
   rooms and offices
Contract Value: $160 million (CAD)
KPMB Architects: Marianne McKenna (partner-in-charge),
   Mitchell Hall (principal-in-charge/design architect),
   Glenn MacMullin (project architect), Lucy Timbers
   (project architect), Nic Green, Sebastian Bartnicki,
   Jacki Chapel, Krista Clark, Virginia Fernandez, Omar
   Ghandi, Collin Gardner, Alexandra Gaudreau, Sabine
   Grimes, Takuma Handa, Fang Hsu, Ramon Janer, Lilly
   Liaukus, Bryn Marler, Elizabeth Paden, Olga Pushkar,
   Thom Seto, Roland Ulfig, Deborah Wang, Wendy
   Wisbrun, Garth Zimmer, François Brosseau, Alice
   Bowman
Engineers: Halsall Associates (structural), H.H. Angus &
   Associates (mechanical, electrical), Conestoga-Rovers
   & Associates (civil)
Consultants: HDR Architecture (laboratory consultants),
   Chung & Vander Doelen Engineering (geotechnical),
   NAK Design Group (landscape), Martin Conboy
   Lighting Design (lighting), Leber | Rubes (fire and life
   safety), Aercoustics Engineering Ltd. (acoustics), Colin
   Gordon Associates (vibration), RWDI (microclimate),
   Vitatech Electromagnetics (EMI, RFI), Engineering
   Harmonics (audio visual), Curran McCabe Ravindran
   Ross Inc. (cost, quantity surveyor)
General Contractor: Aecon Buildings
Photographs: Tom Arban, Tom Arban Photography,
   Toronto; Maris Mezulis, Toronto

NOTA BENE RESTAURANT

Location: 180 Queen Street West, Toronto, Ontario
Completion Date: August 2008
Client: Franco Prevedello, Yannick Bigourdan, David Lee
Program: 700-square-metre destination bar and
   restaurant
Contract Value: Withheld at client's request
KPMB Architects: Thomas Payne (partner-in-charge),
   David Jesson (associate-in-charge), Brad Hindson
   (project architect), Carolyn Lee, Frances Lago
Engineers: AVAM Mechanical Design (mechanical),
   Kyneta Group (electrical)
Consultants: Anjinnov Management (kitchen), Suzanne
   Powadiuk Design (lighting)
Project Manager and Construction Manager: Anjinnov
   Management
Photographs: Tom Arban, Tom Arban Photography,
   Toronto

ORCHESTRA HALL RENEWAL

Location: 1111 Nicollet Mall, Minneapolis, Minnesota
Completion Date: September 2013
Client: Minnesota Orchestral Association
Program: 2,000-square-metre expansion of lobby and
   public spaces and 900-square-metre renovation of
   administrative offices
Contract Value: $38.6 million (USD)
KPMB Architects: Marianne McKenna (partner-in-
   charge), Chris Couse (principal), Robert Sims
   (senior associate), Bruce Kuwabara, Meika McCunn
   (associate), Ramon Janer, Janice Wong, Farhan
   Durrani, Razvan Ghilic Micu, Sharareh Borzabadi

Farahani, Carolyn Lee, Sheida Shahi, Danielle Sucher,
   Olena Chorny, Katerina Mityuryayeva
Engineers: Meyer Borgman Johnson (structural), Dunham
   (mechanical, electrical)
Consultants: Sound Space Design (acoustics), Schuler
   Shook (theatre lighting), Summit Fire Protection
   (building code)
Project Manager: Nelson Tietz & Hoye
Construction Manager: Mortenson Construction

REMAI ART GALLERY OF SASKATCHEWAN

Location: 102 Spadina Crescent East, Saskatoon,
   Saskatchewan
Completion Date: Construction documents completed in
   July 2012; project completion scheduled for spring
   2015
Client: City of Saskatoon
Program: 11,500-square-metre purpose-built art gallery
Contract Value: $84 million (CAD)
Architects: Kuwabara Payne McKenna Blumberg
   Architects (Design Architect); Smith Carter Architects
   & Engineers (Architect of Record)
KPMB ARCHITECTS: Bruce Kuwabara (design partner),
   Shirley Blumberg (partner-in-charge), Matthew
   Wilson (associate), Paulo Rocha (associate),
   Matthew Krivosudsky, Terry Kim, Marcus Colonna,
   David Poloway.
SMITH CARTER ARCHITECTS & ENGINEERS: Grant Van
   Iderstine (principal-in-charge, project architect), Brad
   Cove (project coordinator), Neil Hulme
Engineers: Entuitive (structural), Crossey Engineering
   (mechanical), Mulvey + Banani (electrical)
Consultants: Lundholm Associates Architects (museum
   planning), Transsolar (climate), Turner & Townsend
   cm2r (cost), Daniel Lyzun & Associates (acoustics),
   Aercoustics Engineering Ltd. (vibration), Mulvey +
   Banani (security, IT, audio visual), Enermodal (LEED),
   MMM Group (civil and transportation), Leber | Rubes
   (building code), Enro/Creative Fire (signage); Tillotson
   Design Associates (lighting), Kaizen Foodservice
   Planning & Design (food services)
Selected Awards: 2011 Canadian Architect Award of
   Excellence

ROYAL CONSERVATORY TELUS CENTRE FOR PERFORMANCE AND LEARNING

Location: 273 Bloor Street West, Toronto, Ontario
Completion Date: September 2009
Client: The Royal Conservatory
Program: 17,280 square metres, including 1,135-seat
   concert hall, 280-square-metre rehearsal room and
   60 practice studios ranging in size from 6 to 22 square
   metres; 5,000 square metres of renovation
Contract Value: $110 million (CAD)
KPMB Architects: Marianne McKenna (partner-in-charge),
   Robert Sims (associate-in-charge), David Smythe
   (project architect), Meika McCunn (project architect),
   Carolyn Lee, Frances Lago, Dan Benson, Krista Clark,
   Bill Colaco, George Friedman, Ramon Janer, Erik
   Jensen, David Jesson (2006–2007), John Mestito,
   Gary Yen, Robin Ramcharan, Rita Kiriakis, Lexi Kolt-
   Wagner, Scott Pomeroy, Olga Pushkar, Mark Simpson,
   Jimmy Sun, Deborah Wang, Chris Wegner, Norm Li,
   Clare Radford
Engineers: Halcrow Yolles (structural), Crossey
   Engineering (electrical), Merber Corporation
   (mechanical)
Consultants: Sound Space Design with Aercoustics
   Engineering Ltd. (acoustics), Anne Minors
   Performance Consultants (theatre), Janet Rosenberg
   + Associates (landscape), Turner & Townsend cm2r
   (cost), Martin Conboy Lighting Design (lighting),
   Engineering Harmonics (audio visual), Goldsmith
   Borgal & Company Ltd. Architects (heritage), Bhandari
   and Plater (signage)
Project Manager: Chris Dineley, Anjinnov Management

General Contractor: PCL Constructors Canada
Photographs: Eduard Hueber, Arch Photo, New York; Tom
   Arban, Tom Arban Photography, Toronto
Selected Awards: 2012 Civic Trust Award; 2011 American
   Institute of Architects/Committee on Architecture
   for Education, Educational Facility Design Awards,
   Award of Excellence; 2010 Heritage Toronto Award of
   Excellence; 2010 Chicago Athenaeum International
   Architecture Award; 2010 Governor General's Medal
   in Architecture; 2010 Royal Architectural Institute of
   Canada National Urban Design Award; 2010 Ontario
   Association of Architects Design Excellence Award;
   2010 United States Institute for Theatre Technology
   (USITT) Honour Award; 2010 Canadian Interiors
   Best of Canada, Project of the Year; 2005 Canadian
   Architect Award of Excellence

JOSEPH L. ROTMAN SCHOOL OF MANAGEMENT EXPANSION, UNIVERSITY OF TORONTO

Location: 91–97 St. George Street, Toronto, Ontario
Completion Date: June 2012
Client: University of Toronto
Program: 15,000-square-metre academic building
   expansion
Contract Value: $65.6 million (CAD)
KPMB Architects: Bruce Kuwabara (design partner),
   Marianne McKenna (partner-in-charge), Luigi LaRocca
   (principal-in-charge), Paulo Rocha (associate, design
   and project architect, all phases), Dave Smythe
   (associate, project architect, contract administration),
   Myriam Tawadros (project architect), Bruno Weber,
   John Peterson, Janice Wong, Richard Wong, Victor
   Garzon, Lilly Liaukus, Bryn Marler, Rachel Stecker,
   Maryam Karimi, Carolyn Lee, Danielle Sucher, Laura
   Carwardine
Engineers: Halcrow Yolles (structural), Smith & Andersen
   (mechanical, electrical)
Consultants: Turner & Townsend cm2r (cost), BVDA
   Group (building envelope), Transsolar, Halsall
   Associates (energy, LEED), E.R.A. Architects
   (heritage), Leber | Rubes (life safety), Janet
   Rosenberg + Associates (landscape), ACSI
   (elevator), Engineering Harmonics (audio visual),
   Aercoustics Engineering Ltd. (acoustics), Kaizen
   Foodservice Planning & Design (food services), Brian
   Ballantyne Specifications (specifications), Entro
   Communications/G+A (signage), Cole Engineering
   (civil)
Project Manager: Capital Project, University of Toronto
Construction Manager: Eastern Construction Company
General Contractor: Eastern Construction Company
Photographs: Tom Arban, Tom Arban Photography,
   Toronto; Maris Mezulis, Toronto
Selected Awards: 2013 Ontario Association of Architects
   Design Excellence Award

SUGARCUBE

Location: 1555 Blake Street, Denver, Colorado
Completion Date: August 2008
Client: Urban Villages
Program: 15,400-square-metre, ten-storey mixed-use
   development including ground floor retail, offices and
   residential units and below-grade parking
Contract Value: Withheld at client's request
KPMB Architects: Bruce Kuwabara (design partner),
   Shirley Blumberg (partner-in-charge), Bruno Weber
   (project architect), Myriam Tawadros, Javier Uribe, Bill
   Colaco, Jose Emila, Richard Wong, Roland Ulfig
Engineers: Halcrow Yolles (structural), ABS Consultants
   (mechanical, electrical, plumbing), MB Consulting
   (civil)
Consultants: Wiss, Janney, Elstner Associates (building
   envelope), Soberman Engineering (elevator), MB
   Consulting (landscape), D.L. Adams Associates
   (acoustics), Specifications by Design (specifications),

JeHN Engineering (dewatering), BCER Engineering (building code)
Project Manager: Urban Villages
General Contractor: JE Dunn Construction Group
Photographs: Tom Arban, Tom Arban Photography, Toronto
Selected Awards: 2008 Rocky Mountain Commercial Real Estate/DU School of Real Estate Project of the Year

THE STUDY AT YALE HOTEL

Location: 1157 Chapel Street, New Haven, Connecticut
Completion Date: September 2008
Client: Hospitality 3
Program: 6,500-square-metre expansion of existing to accommodate 120 rooms, lobby, lounge and restaurant
Contract Value: Withheld at owner's request
KPMB Architects: Thomas Payne (partner-in-charge), David Poloway (project architect), Marianne McKenna, Dan Benson, Jill Greaves, Mark Jaffar, Rita Kiriakis, Lilly Liaukus, Amir Sharokhi
Engineers: DeSimone (structural), Natcomm (mechanical, electrical), VHB — Vanasse Hangen Brustlin (civil), Langan Engineering (geotechnical), Godfrey-Hoffman Associates LLC (quantity surveyor)
Consultants: Bruce J. Spiewak, AIA (building code, fire and life safety), Suzanne Powadiuk Design (lighting), Brian Ballantyne Specifications (specifications), Romano Gatland (food services), SKS Design (audio visual), Lerch Bates (elevator)
Construction Manager: Enterprise Builders
Photographs: Tom Arban, Tom Arban Photography, Toronto

TIFF BELL LIGHTBOX AND FESTIVAL TOWER

Location: Reitman Square, 350 King Street West, Toronto, Ontario
Competition Date: 2003
Completion Date: September 2010
Client: Toronto International Film Festival and King + John Festival Corporation (c/o The Daniels Corporation)
Program: 42-storey mixed-use development including five-storey base comprising 17,570 square metres of flexible, multi-use space, including three cinemas and two flexible screening spaces for a total of 1,300 cinema seats; 37,550-square-metre, 38-storey residential condominium tower
Contract Value: Withheld at client's request
Architects: Kuwabara Payne McKenna Blumberg Architects (Design Architect); Kirkor Architects & Planners (Architect of Record)
COMPETITION TEAM: Bruce Kuwabara, Shirley Blumberg, Bruno Weber, Brent Wagler, Tyler Sharp, Esther Cheung, Norm Li
KPMB ARCHITECTS: Bruce Kuwabara (design partner), Shirley Blumberg (partner-in-charge), Luigi LaRocca (senior associate), Matthew Wilson (project architect), Matt Krivosudsky, Bruno Weber, Brent Wagler, Glenn MacMullin, Andrea Macaroun, Rita Kiriakis, Lilly Liaukus, Carolyn Lee, David Poloway, Tyler Sharp, Debra Fabricus, Claudio Venier, Thom Seto, Walter Gaudet, Krista Clark, Clementine Chang, Winston Chong, Carla Munoz, Elizabeth Paden, Bill Colaco, Nicko Elliot, Norm Li, Robin Ramcharan, Jill Greaves
KIRKOR ARCHITECTS & PLANNERS: Clifford Korman (partner), Steven Kirshenblatt (partner), Mario Gumushdjian (architect, partner), Richard Golab (associate), Mike Nonis, Brent Whitby
Engineers: Jablonsky, Ast and Partners (structural), SNC Lavalin – LKM (mechanical, electrical)
Consultants: Leber | Rubes (life safety), NAK Design Group (landscape), Helyar & Associates (cost), Aercoustics Engineering Ltd. (acoustics), Westbury National Show Systems & Azcar Technologies (audio visual), Peter Smith Architect (theatre), RWDI (wind), Marshall Macklin Monaghan (transportation), Kaizen

Foodservice Planning & Design (food services), Pivotal Lighting Affiliated Engineers (lighting), Mulvey + Banani (security), Ehvert Engineering (IT), Gottschalk + Ash (signage)
Project Manager: Nexus PM
General Contractor: PCL Constructors Canada
Photographs: Tom Arban, Tom Arban Photography, Toronto; Maris Mezulis, Toronto
Selected Awards: 2012 Ontario Association of Architects Design Excellence Award; 2011 Pug Awards, Best Commercial/Institutional Building

TORONTO COMMUNITY HOUSING, BLOCK 32

Location: 155 Dan Leckie Way, Toronto, Ontario
Completion Date: 2012
Client: Toronto Community Housing Corporation
Program: 45,500-square-metre 35-storey tower with eight-storey podium for a total of 428 units
Contract Value: $90 million (CAD)
Architects: Kuwabara Payne McKenna Blumberg Architects in association with Page + Steele/IBI Group Architects.
KPMB ARCHITECTS: Shirley Blumberg (partner-in-charge), Andrew Dyke (senior associate), Richard Unterthiner (project architect), Bryce Gracey, Ryan Yeung, Suzanna Rizzo, Carolyn Lee, Danielle Sucher.
PAGE + STEELE/IBI GROUP ARCHITECTS: Mansoor Kazerouni (P+S IBI design lead), Tim Gorley (P+S IBI project manager), Claudia Stodt (P+S intermediate architect), Nebojsa Miloradovic (P+S intermediate architect), Koathy Hariharan (P+S unit designer), Titka Seddighi (P+S IBI project manager, contract documents phase), Louie Alati (P+S IBI job captain, contract docs phase), Terry Ruscak (P+S IBI contract administrator)
Engineers: Read Jones Christoffersen (structural), Smith & Andersen (mechanical, electrical)
Consultants: Janet Rosenberg + Associates (landscape), BA Consulting Group (traffic), Leber | Rubes (building code)
Development Manager: Context Developments
Construction Manager: Bluescape Construction Management
Photographs: Maris Mezulis, Toronto; Tom Arban, Tom Arban Photography, Toronto

TORYS LLP OFFICES

Location: 79 Wellington Street West, Suite 3000, Toronto, Ontario
Completion Date: August 2008
Client: Torys LLP
Program: 17,500-square-metre office interior
Contract Value: Withheld at client's request
KPMB Architects: Marianne McKenna (partner-in-charge), Steven Casey (design/project architect), George Bizios, Rita Kiriakis, Gary Yen, Thom Seto, Jose Emila, Lilly Liaukus, Jill Greaves
Engineers: Halcrow Yolles (structural), Andronowski & Associates (mechanical), Carinci Burt Rogers Engineering (electrical)
Consultants: Aercoustics Engineering Ltd. (acoustics), Curran McCabe Ravindran Ross Inc. (cost), Spectech (communications, IT), Intercon (security), Westbury (audio visual), Trillium Architectural Products (hardware), Suzanne Powadiuk Design (lighting), Fela Grunwald, Fine Arts (art), Leber | Rubes (fire and life safety, access), Brian Ballantyne Specifications (specifications)
Project Manager: Royal LePage Commercial (Phase I), PHA Project Management (Phase II)
Construction Manager: Rae Brothers
Photographs: Tom Arban, Tom Arban Photography, Toronto; Maris Mezulis, Toronto; Pascal Grandmaison, Toronto
Selected Awards: 2009 Ontario Association of Architects Design Excellence Award; 2008 Interior Design Magazine Best of Year Award, Finalist

VAUGHAN CITY HALL

Location: 241 Major Mackenzie Drive, Vaughan, Ontario
Competition Date: 2003
Completion Date: 2011
Client: City of Vaughan
Program: 26,000-square-metre city hall comprising civic tower, council chambers and civic administration offices
Contract Value: $84.3 million (CAD)
Competition Team: Bruce Kuwabara, Kevin Bridgman, Tyler Sharp, Javier Uribe, Andrea Macaroun
KPMB Architects: Bruce Kuwabara (design partner), Shirley Blumberg (partner-in-charge), Goran Milosevic (principal-in-charge), Kevin Bridgman (design associate/project architect), Garth Zimmer (project architect), Walter Gaudet, Andrea Macaroun, Artur Kobylanski, George Bizios, Shane O'Neil, Carla Munoz, Bill Colaco, Richard Wong, Safdar Abidi, Ramon Janer, Dave Smythe, Lilly Liaukus, Jacki Chapel, Armine Tadevosyan
Engineers: Halcrow Yolles (structural), Stantec Architecture (mechanical), Mulvey + Banani (electrical)
Consultants: Phillips Farevaag Smallenberg (landscape), LEA Consulting (traffic, municipal), Stantec Mechanical (LEED, sustainability), Leber | Rubes (building code), Brook Van Dalen & Associates Ltd. (building envelope), Connestoga Rovers (civil)
General Contractor: Maystar General Contractors
Photographs: Tom Arban, Tom Arban Photography, Toronto; Maris Mezulis, Toronto
Selected Awards: 2012 World Architecture Festival Finalist; 2012 Ontario Association of Architects Design Excellence Award; 2012 Governor General's Medal in Architecture; 2004 Canadian Architect Award of Excellence

YOUNG CENTRE FOR THE PERFORMING ARTS

Location: The Distillery District, Tank Houses 9 and 10, Toronto, Ontario
Completion Date: January 2006
Client: George Brown College, Soulpepper Theatre Company
Program: 4,100 square metres; performing arts, training and youth outreach centre
Contract Value: $10 million (CAD)
KPMB Architects: Thomas Payne (partner-in-charge), Chris Couse (senior associate), Mark Jaffar (project architect); Goran Milosevic, Kevin Thomas, Anne Lok, Andrea Macaroun, Thom Seto, Krista Clark, Ramon Janer, Clementine Chang, Stephen Kopp, Andrew Sinclair, Carolyn Lee, Virginia Dos Reis
Engineers: Read Jones Christoffersen (structural), Crossey Engineering (mechanical, electrical)
Consultants: Theatre Projects Consultants (theatre), Aercoustics Engineering Ltd.(acoustics), E.R.A. Architects (heritage), The Beggarstaff Sisters (signage), Engineering Harmonics (performance sound)
Project Manager: PHA Project Management
General Contractor: Dalton Engineering
Photographs: Tom Arban, Tom Arban Photography, Toronto
Selected Awards: 2007 Business Week/Architectural Record Award of Excellence; 2007 Ontario Association of Architects Design Excellence Award; 2007 United States Institute for Theatre Technology (USITT), Honour Award for Architecture; 2006 Canadian Interiors Best of Canada Design Competition, Project Winner

Office History

Bruce Kuwabara, Thomas Payne, Marianne McKenna and Shirley Blumberg have been leading figures on Canada's architecture scene for more than two decades since founding the practice in 1987. They conceived a hybrid studio model merging individual creativity, collaborative teamwork and professional practice. The ethnic and gender diversity of the practice, unusual among North American firms at the time, also distinguishes it as a uniquely Canadian practice and this continues to be one of its signature strengths.

In the first five years of practice, the firm won significant design competitions for Kitchener City Hall and the Joseph S. Stauffer Library. This work, along with a number of smaller-scaled interiors and contemporary interventions to existing structures, rapidly established the firm's reputation for design excellence and high-quality production standards. Since then, it has created a diverse portfolio of award-winning work for educational, cultural, healthcare, civic and corporate clients throughout North America and Europe and has earned 12 Governor General's Medals for Architecture, Canada's highest honour, as well as distinguished international awards from the American Institute of Architects and the Royal Institute of British Architects, among others.

KPMB has built a body of work over time that is stylistically diverse yet identifiable and coherent in its ideas about city building and enduring value. The firm also shares a commitment to conceiving architecture as a sustainable platform that directly supports the growth and viability of an organization or institution over the long term.

KPMB is also unique in having a core staff of 30 individuals who have been with the studio since the early days of practice, and who have played leading roles in delivering consistency of quality and architectural excellence working in collaboration with stakeholders and experts.

This book documents KPMB's major projects from 2004 to the present and represents the firm's contribution to raising the international profile of Canadian architecture and urbanism.

Partners

BRUCE KUWABARA was born in Hamilton, Ontario, in 1949. He studied architecture at the University of Toronto. Upon graduating in 1972, he joined the teaching office of architect and critic George Baird. In 1975 he joined Barton Myers Associates and was an associate there until 1987. He held the position of Visiting Adjunct Professor at Harvard University (1990-1991) and has acted as visiting critic and lecturer at universities across North America. He is the Honorary Co-Chair for Fundraising responsible for establishing the Frank Gehry International Visiting Chair in Architectural Design at the John H. Daniels Faculty of Architecture, Landscape and Design at the University of Toronto. He serves on the Board of the Directors for the Canadian Centre for Architecture in Montreal and has been the Chair of Waterfront Toronto's Design Review Panel since 2005. He holds an Honorary Degree from McMaster University in Hamilton. He is the recipient of the Royal Architectural Institute of Canada (RAIC) Gold Medal (2006) and was invested as an Officer of the Order of Canada in 2012.

THOMAS PAYNE was born in Chatham, Ontario, in 1949. He studied architecture at Princeton University, École nationale supérieure des beaux-arts, Paris and Yale University where he completed his Master's degree in 1974. Thomas Payne worked for John Andrews International Architects, Sydney, before moving to Toronto in 1979. There he worked first for George Baird before joining Barton Myers Associates in Toronto for eight years. He was a studio critic at Harvard University's Graduate School of Design in 1981 and a thesis advisor at the University of Toronto from 1986-1989.

MARIANNE MCKENNA was born in Montreal, Quebec, in 1950. She studied at Swarthmore College Philadelphia, B.A., 1972 and Yale University, Master of Architecture (1976). She worked for Bobrow & Fieldman, Architects in Montreal from 1976-1978 and for Denys Lasdun, Redhouse & Softley in London from 1978-1979. In 1980, she joined Barton Myers Associates in Toronto and from 1981-1987 was an associate of the firm. Marianne McKenna has served various academic and design critic functions at McGill University (1979-1980, 1997), the Université de Montréal (1991-1993, 1994) and Yale University (1994-1995). She established and taught the Professional Practice Course at the School of Architecture at the University of Toronto (1993-1995), She served as a member of the Board of Directors of the Institute for Contemporary Culture at the Royal Ontario Museum (2010-2013) and currently is a member of the Board of Metrolinx. She has an honorary fellowship from the Royal Conservatory, and was invested as an Officer of the Order of Canada in 2012.

SHIRLEY BLUMBERG was born in Cape Town, South Africa, in 1952. She began her architectural studies at the University of Cape Town and completed her Bachelor of Architecture, Honours, at the University of Toronto (1976). Shirley Blumberg joined the Toronto office of Barton Myers Associates in 1977 and was an associate of the firm until 1987. She has lectured and acted as visiting critic at several universities in Canada and the United States, including the University of Toronto as adjunct professor (1987, 1989-1990) and as thesis tutor (1997-1998, 2001). In 1994, she became the first woman appointee to the Hyde Chair for Excellence in Architecture at the University of Nebraska-Lincoln. Shirley served as a member of the City of Toronto's Design Review Panel and is currently a member of the Toronto Community Housing Design Review Panel and the Presidential Advisory Council for the Ontario College of Art & Design.

Principals

Chris Couse was born in Toronto, Ontario, in 1957. Bachelor of Architecture from Carleton University in Ottawa (1982). During his studies he spent a term abroad at the Architectural Association, London, with Zaha Hadid's Unit 9. In 1984, he joined Barton Myers Associates in Toronto until KPMB's formation in 1987. Promoted to associate in 1989, senior associate in 1994 and principal in 2011. LEED Accredited Professional.

Luigi LaRocca was born in Toronto, Ontario, in 1954. Studied at the University of Toronto, Bachelor of Architecture (1979). Worked for Hamilton Kemp Architects in Toronto from 1980–1981, Arthur Erickson Architects and Webb Zerafa Menkes Housden Partnership in Toronto (architects in joint venture) in 1982, and Barton Myers Associates from 1983–1987. In 1987, he joined KPMB, was promoted to associate in 1989, senior associate in 1995 and principal in 2011. LEED Accredited Professional.

Mitchell Hall was born in Montreal, Quebec, in 1960. Graduate of Carleton University in Ottawa, Bachelor of Architecture (1988). Worked for Young & Wright Architects in Toronto before joining KPMB in 1989. Promoted to associate in 1995, senior associate in 2005 and principal in 2011. Visiting critic and guest lecturer at various Canadian and American universities.

Goran Milosevic was born in Windsor, Ontario, in 1959. Studied at the University of Toronto, Bachelor of Architecture (1985). Worked for Miller Bobaljik Peel Architects in Toronto from 1986–1987 and Anthony Kemp Architects in Toronto from 1988–1989. Joined KPMB in 1989, leaving in 1991 to work for Ruth Cawker, Architect. Returned to KPMB in 1993 and became an associate in 1995, senior associate in 2005 and principal in 2011. LEED Accredited Professional.

Directors

Phyllis Crawford was born in Glasgow, Scotland, in 1969. She obtained her Certified General Accountant designation in 2000. Previously, she was an accountant at IBI Group, the controller for Brisbin Brook Beynon Architects and a consultant for firms including Amec and 20th Century Fox before joining KPMB in 2008 as the Director of Finance.

Phil Marjeram was born in Horsham, England, in 1968. He studied at the School of Industrial Design, Carleton University, and graduated in 1992. He worked for O'Hara Technologies as IT/QA Manager until he joined KPMB in 1997 as IT Manager and was promoted to Director of Information Technology in 2011. He is also a founding member of the Ontario Revit Users Group and a member of the Balmy Beach Club.

Amanda Sebris was born in Toronto, Ontario, in 1964. She studied at the University of Toronto and graduated with a Master's degree in art history in 1993. She joined KPMB in 1988, leaving in 1997 to work at Bruce Mau Design in Toronto until 2002. Rejoined KPMB in 2003 and was promoted to Director of Marketing in 2011.

Senior Associates

Andrew Dyke was born in Toronto, Ontario, in 1966. Graduate of the University of Toronto, Bachelor of Architecture (1990). Joined KPMB after graduation and was promoted to associate in 1997 and senior associate in 2011.

David Jesson was born in Toronto, Ontario, in 1961. Graduate of Carleton University in Ottawa, Bachelor of Architecture (1990). Joined KPMB in 1990 and became an associate in 1997 and senior associate in 2011.

Robert Sims was born in Toronto, Ontario, in 1963. Graduate of the University of Waterloo, Bachelor of Architecture (1990). Joined KPMB after graduation and was promoted to associate in 1995 and senior associate in 2011.

Judith Taylor was born in Sudbury, Ontario, in 1963. Graduate of Carleton University in Ottawa, Bachelor of Architecture (1987). Worked for Au & Chan Architects, Moriyama & Teshima Architects, Aki International in Tokyo and Webb Zerafa Menkes Housden Partnership in Toronto. Joined KPMB in 1990. Promoted to associate in 1995 and senior associate in 2011. LEED Accredited Professional.

Associates

Kevin Bridgman was born in Toronto, Ontario, in 1970. Graduate of the University of Toronto, Bachelor of Architecture (1994). Worked for Terence Van Elsander Architect in Toronto for two years before joining KPMB in 1996. Promoted to associate in 2011.

Steven Casey was born in Montreal, Quebec, in 1972. He was educated at Queen's University, Bachelor of Arts, Honours in Sociology (1996), and the University of British Columbia, Master of Architecture (2000). Moved to Toronto after graduation to work on a number of independent design projects. Joined KPMB in 2002 and was promoted to associate in 2011.

Mark Jaffar was born in Colombo, Sri Lanka, in 1966. Graduate of the University of Toronto, Bachelor of Architecture (1991). Worked for Baird Sampson Architects in Toronto and Shin Takamatsu Architect & Associates in Berlin before joining KPMB in 1994. Promoted to associate in 2011.

Carolyn Lee was born in Ottawa, Ontario, in 1971. Graduate of the University of Manitoba, Bachelor of Interior Design (1999). Joined KPMB after graduation and was promoted to associate in 2011.

Meika McCunn was born in Pictou County, Nova Scotia, in 1972. Studied at the Technical University of Nova Scotia (Dalhousie University), Bachelor of Environmental Design (1995) and Master of Architecture (1998). Worked for Edberg Christiansen Heidenreich Architecture in Seattle and Roesling Nakamura Terada Architects in San Diego before moving to Toronto in 2002. Joined KPMB and was promoted to associate in 2011.

Glenn MacMullin was born in New Waterford, Nova Scotia, in 1965. Graduate of Holland College in Prince Edward Island, Building Technology Degree (1987), Technical University of Nova Scotia, Bachelor of Environmental Design (1995) and Dalhousie University, Master of Architecture (1997). Joined KPMB in 1992, leaving in 1993 to continue studies. Returned to KPMB in 1997 and was promoted to associate in 2011.

Kael Opie was born in Toronto, Ontario, in 1971. Graduated from the University of Toronto, Bachelor of Architecture (1996). Worked for Teeple Architects in Toronto before joining KPMB in 2005 and being promoted to associate in 2011. LEED Accredited Professional.

John Peterson was born in Richmond, British Columbia, in 1966. Studied at the University of British Columbia, B.Sc. (Physics, 1990), and the Technical University of Nova Scotia in Halifax, Bachelor of Environmental Design (1992) and Master of Architecture (1995). Moved to Toronto in 1997 and worked for Baird Sampson Neuert Architects, Mackay & Wong Design and Teeple Architects. Joined KPMB in 2001 and was promoted to associate in 2011. LEED Accredited Professional and founding member of the Ontario Revit Users Group.

Paulo Rocha was born in Porto, Portugal, in 1972. Graduated in 1996 with a Bachelor of Architecture from the University of Toronto. Joined KPMB in 1996 and was promoted to associate in 2011.

David Smythe was born in London, England, in 1961. Studied at the University of Western Ontario, Bachelor of Engineering (1984), and McGill University, Bachelor of Architecture (1992). Worked for Saia Barbarese architectes in Montreal and Montgomery Sisam Architects in Toronto before joining KPMB in 2000. Promoted to associate in 2011. He is a recipient of the Toronto Construction Association's Certificate of Excellence in 2010.

Kevin Thomas was born in London, Ontario. Graduated from Carleton University in Ottawa with a Bachelor of Architecture (2001). Recipient of the American Association of Architects (AIA) Henry Adams Graduation Medal and the Ontario Association of Architects Scholarship. Joined KPMB in 2001 and was promoted to associate in 2011.

Brent Wagler was born in Stratford, Ontario, in 1965. Studied architecture at Carleton University, Bachelor of Architecture (1991), and McGill University, Master of Architecture in History and Theory (1995). Worked for Nicolas Hare Architects in London, Peter Rose + Partners in Montreal and E.R.A. Architects in Toronto. Joined KPMB in 1997 and was promoted to associate in 2011. He taught at McGill University School of Architecture, lectured at the Ontario College of Art and was a visiting critic at Carleton University and the University of Kentucky. LEED Accredited Professional.

Bruno Weber was born in Montreal, Quebec, in 1968. Educated at the Ringling School of Art and Design in Sarasota, Florida, Bachelor of Interior Design (1990), and Dalhousie University in Halifax, Bachelor of Environmental Design (1998) and Master of Architecture (2000). Worked for The Folsum Group in Sarasota, Florida, Bas Smith Architect in Victoria, British Columbia, and spent three years with Brian McKay-Lyons Architecture + Urban Design before joining KPMB in 2000. Named an associate in 2011.

Matthew Wilson was born in Bristol, England, in 1962. Graduate of the University of Toronto, Bachelor of Architecture (1987). After graduation, he joined KPMB and worked there for three years before joining the Kirkland Partnership. Returned to KPMB in 1994 and was promoted to associate in 2011.

Clients, Collaborators, Projects Since 1987

CLIENTS
Air Canada Corporate
  Real Estate
Alliance Communications Corporation
Ammirati Puris Lintas
Art Gallery of Hamilton
Art Gallery of Ontario
Assiniboine Park Conservancy
Berkshire Theatre Festival
Branksome Hall
Bridgepoint Health
Brookfield Properties
Build Toronto
Canada's National
  Ballet School
Canadian Museum of Nature
Centennial College
Centre for Addiction and Mental Health
Centre for International Governance
  Innovation (CIGI)
CIBC Wood Gundy
City of Kitchener
City of Ottawa
City of Richmond
City of Toronto
City of Vaughan
Concord Adex Developments
Context
Daniels Corporation
Concordia University
Conrad Hotel
Corporation of Massey Hall
  & Roy Thomson Hall
Correctional Services Canada
CTV
Design Exchange
Disney Animation Studios
Dundee Realty
Elementary Teachers' Federation of
  Ontario
Foreign Affairs and International Trade
  Canada
Gardiner Museum
George Brown College
Goodman Theatre
The Globe and Mail
Gluskin Sheff & Associates
GWL Realty Advisors
Hasbro Inc.
Health Canada
Hospitality 3
Hilton Hotel
H&R Developments
Indigo Books and Music Inc.
Infrastructure Ontario
Italinteriors
Japanese Canadian
  Cultural Centre
Kilmer Group
Lanterra
McGill University
McMaster University
Manitoba Hydro
Maple Leaf Sports
  and Entertainment
Marc Laurent
Massachusetts Institute
  of Technology
Minnesota Orchestra
National Arts Centre
National Ballet of Canada
National Defence Canada
Nicolas Stores
Northwestern University
Nota Bene Restaurant
Oliver + Bonacini
Ontario College of Art
  and Design
The Power Plant
Princeton University
Providence Healthcare
Public Health Agency
  of Canada
Public Works and Government Services
  Canada
Queen's University

Remai Art Gallery
  of Saskatchewan
Royal Conservatory
Ryerson University
Soulpepper Theatre Company
St. Andrew's College
Star Alliance
Stratford Festival
Toronto Community
  Housing Corp.
Toronto International
  Film Festival
Toronto Public Library
Toronto Waterfront Revitalization Corp.
Torys LLP
Trinity College (Hartford)
University of British Columbia
University of Michigan
University of Ottawa
University of Toronto
University of Waterloo
Urban Villages LLC
Vincor International
Walt Disney
  Animation Canada
Wilfrid Laurier University
Woodbridge Co. Ltd.
Woodcliffe Developments
Yale University
York Bremner Developments
York University

ENGINEERS, SPECIALTY CONSULTANTS, PROJECT MANAGERS
AECOM
  (formerly Earth Tech)
Aercoustics Engineering Ltd.
Alpine EBan
AltieriSeborWieber
Anjinnov Management
Brian Arnott Associates
Artec Consultants Inc.
A.W. Hooker Associates Ltd.
BA Consulting Group Ltd.
Bhandari & Plater Inc.
Blackwell
Brook Van Dalen
  & Associates Ltd.
Bush Bohlman & Partners
Carinci Burt Rogers
Carruthers & Wallace Ltd.
Century Group Inc.
Cobalt Engineering
Martin Conboy
  Lighting Design
Crossey Engineering Ltd.
Curran McCabe Ravindran Ross Inc.
James Donaldson Architects
Donnell Consultants
Alan Dudek
Educational Consulting Services
Enermodal
Engineering Harmonics
Entuitive Co.
E.R.A. Architects
George Sexton Associates
Gespro Sst
Gottschalk & Ash
Govan Brown & Associates
Groupe HBA Experts
  Conseils Inc.
Cornelia Hahn Oberlander
Halsall Associates
Hanscomb Ltd.
HDR Architecture Associates Inc.
HH Angus Consulting Engineers
Hilderman Thomas Frank Cram
Kaizen Foodservice Planning & Design Inc.
Kirkegaard Associates
Larden Muniak
LEA Consulting Ltd.
Leber/Rubes Inc.
NAK Design Group
O.P. McCarthy & Associates
Le Messurier Consultants

Merber Corporation
Anne Minors Performance Consultants
The Mitchell Partnership Inc.
Mulvey+Banani
  International Inc.
MMM Group
Nicolet Chartrand Knoll Ltée.
Novita Design Services
Pellemon Inc.
PHA Project Management
Philip R. Sherman, P.E.
Pivotal Lighting Design
Suzanne Powadiuk Design
Read Jones Christoffersen Consulting
  Engineers
Janet Rosenberg + Associates
RWDI Inc.
Rybka, Smith & Ginsler Ltd.
Sasaki Associates Inc.
SDK Associates LLC
Schuler Shook
The Sextant Group
Smith + Andersen
  Consulting Engineers
Soberman Engineering
Sound Space Design
Stantec Consulting
The Talaske Group
Theatre Projects Consultants
Theatre Consultants Collaborative
Scott Thornley + Company
Thornton Tomasetti Inc.
Tillotson Design Associates
Towers|Golde LLC
Transsolar Climate Engineering
Neil Turnbull Landscape Architect
Turner & Townsend cm2r
Valcoustics Canada Ltd.
Van Zelm Heywood
  & Shadford Inc.
Vermeulens Cost Consultants
Yolles (C2MH Hill)

BUILDERS
Alberici Constructors Inc.
Barr & Barr Inc.
Bluescape Construction
Bondfield Construction
Boszko and Verity Inc.
Dalton Construction Inc.
Dominion Construction
Eastern Construction Ltd.
EllisDon
Gilbane Inc.
Jaltas Inc.
Ledcor Construction Ltd.
Le Groupe Decarel Inc.
Merit Contractors
Mortenson Construction
Pomerleau Inc.
SNC-Lavalin Construction (Ontario) Inc.
Trammell Crow Co.
Turner Construction Co.
Vanbots Construction Corp.
Verreault

OTHER SIGNIFICANT COLLABORATORS
Art Magic Carpentry
Brian Ballantyne Specifications
D2S Lighting
Eliile
Herman Miller
Holly Hunt
Interior Elements
Italinteriors
Italinteriors Contract
JS Models
Kiosk
Klaus
Knoll
Louis Interiors
Maharam
MCM: 2001/Gregory Rybak
Plan b
Wesbury

ARCHITECTS IN JOINT VENTURE OR ASSOCIATION
Adamson Associates
architectsAlliance
Barry Padolsky
  Associates Inc. Architects
Barton Myers Associates
Daoust Lestage Inc.
FGM Architects
Fichten Soiferman et Associés Architectes
Gagnon Letellier Cyr Ricard Mathieu
  Architectes
Goldsmith Borgal & Company Ltd.
  Architects
Greenberg Consultants
Groupe Cardinale Hardy
Hotson Bakker Architects
Hughes Condon Marler Architects
MacLennan Jaunkalns
  Miller Architects
McClier Corporation
Moffat Kinoshita Architects
Montgomery Sisam Architects
Page + Steele/IBI Group Architects
Patrick T.Y. Chan Architect
Phillips Farevaag Smallenberg Landscape
  Architects
Prairie Architects
Pysall Ruge Von Matt Architekten
Rave Architekten
Smith Carter
  Architects + Engineers
Stantec Architecture
Stone Kohn McQuire
  Vogt Architects
Urban Strategies
II BY IV Design Associates

PHOTOGRAPHERS
Peter Aaron/ESTO
Tom Arban Photography
Michael Awad
James Brittain
Michel Brunelle
Robert Burley Design Archive
Steven Evans
Ted Fahn
Al Ferreira, Photography
Peter Gill
Shai Gil Fotography
Jeff Goldberg/ESTO
Dan Harper
Robert Hill
Wolfgang Hoyt/ESTO
Eduard Hueber,
  Arch Photo Inc.
Gerry Kopelow
Walter Mair
Maris Mezulis
Chris Phillips
Ben Rahn/A-Frame
Peter Sellar/KLIK
Volker Seding
Martin Tessler
Peter Wagner, Skylab Media
David Whittaker

PROJECT CHRONOLOGY

1991   Marc Laurent, Toronto

1989   Dome Productions, Toronto
Tudhope Associates Graphic Design Studios, Toronto

1990   35 East Wacker Drive, Chicago, IL
Creed's, Toronto

1991   Nicolas, Toronto
Reisman-Jenkinson Residence, Richmond Hill
King James Place, Toronto
Woodsworth College, University of Toronto

1992   Creative Copy & Design, Toronto
Oasis, Oakville

1993   Kitchener City Hall, Kitchener
Ammirati Puris Lintas, Toronto
Hasbro Headquarters, Pawtucket, RI
Design Exchange, Toronto
Joseph S. Stauffer Library, Queen's University, Kingston

1995   Gluskin Sheff + Associates, Toronto
Fields Institute for Research in Mathematical Sciences, Toronto
Ontario Ministry Building, Niagara Falls

1996   Walter Carsen Centre, Toronto
Grand Valley Institution for Women, Kitchener
Alliance Communications, Toronto
Hummingbird Centre, Phase 1, Toronto
Playdium, Mississauga

1997   Ettore Mazzoleni Concert Hall, Royal Conservatory of Music, Toronto
Ammirati Puris Lintas, New York, NY
Fort Lasalle Royal Military College, Kingston
Stratford Festival Theatre, Stratford
Alias/Wavefront, Toronto
Indigo Books Music & More, Toronto
Disney Television Animation Studios, Toronto

1998   McKee Public School, North York
Crabtree & Evelyn Flagship Store, Philadelphia, PA
Chinese Cultural Centre, Phase 1, Scarborough
Mitchell Field Community Centre, North York
Hilton Toronto Airport Hotel, Toronto

1999   Air Canada Club, Air Canada Centre, Toronto
Douglas Library, Queen's University, Kingston
500 Queen's Quay West, Toronto

2000   Japanese Canadian Cultural Centre, Don Mills
Hilton Hotel, Toronto
Cardinal Ambrozic Houses of Providence, Scarborough
Richmond City Hall, Richmond, BC
Munk Centre for International Studies, University of Toronto
Penthouse on the Waterfront, Toronto
TechSpace, Toronto
Goodman Theatre, Chicago, IL

2001   Ravine House, Toronto
Jackson-Triggs Niagara Estate Winery, Niagara-on-the-Lake
Granite Club, Toronto
Star Alliance Lounge, Zurich International Airport

2002   Roy Thomson Hall, Toronto

2003   McGill University and Genome Quebec Innovation Centre, Montreal
Central Park Lodge, Burlington and Richmond Hill
Trinity College, Hartford, CT
Hamilton Hall, McMaster University, Hamilton
St. Andrew's College, Aurora
Sprague Memorial Hall, Yale University, New Haven, CT
Maple Leaf Lounge, Toronto International Airport

2004   School of Management, University of Toronto
Centennial College Applied Research and Innovation Centre, Scarborough

2005   Canadian Embassy, Berlin
Le Quartier Concordia, Phase 1: Engineering and Computer Science and Visual Arts Integrated Complex, Concordia University, Montreal
Art Gallery of Hamilton, Hamilton
Woodbridge Office Renovation, Toronto
Canada's National Ballet School, Toronto
Mid-Century Bungalow Renovation, Toronto
Okanagan Campus Master Plan, University of British Columbia, Vancouver

2006   Gardiner Museum, Toronto
Young Centre for the Performing Arts, Soulpepper Theatre Company and George Brown College, Toronto

2007   Charles R. Walgreen Jr. Drama Centre and Arthur Miller Theatre, University of Michigan, Ann Arbor, MI
North Campus Auditorium, University of Michigan, Ann Arbor, MI
Marc Laurent, Hazelton Lanes, Toronto
180 Queen Street West/Federal Judicial Centre, Toronto

2008   SugarCube, Denver, CO
Japanese Canadian Cultural Centre, Phase 3, Don Mills
Centre for Addiction and Mental Health Phase 1A, Toronto
The Study at Yale Hotel, New Haven, CT
Torys LLP Offices, Toronto
Ryerson University Master Plan, Toronto
Nota Bene Restaurant, Toronto
Rockcliffe Redevelopment — Community Design Plan, Ottawa

2009   Le Quartier Concordia, Phase 1: John Molson School of Business, Concordia University, Montreal
Royal Conservatory TELUS Centre for Performance and Learning, Toronto
Manitoba Hydro Place, Winnipeg

2010   Canadian Museum of Nature, Ottawa
One Bedford Residential Development, Toronto
Maple Leaf Square (Bremner Boulevard), Toronto
TIFF Bell Lightbox and Festival Tower, Toronto

2011   Vaughan City Hall, Vaughan
Centre for International Governance Innovation (CIGI) Campus, Waterloo
18 York and Southcore Financial Centre, Toronto
Gluskin Sheff + Associates Offices, Toronto

2012   Art Gallery of Ontario, David Milne Centre, Toronto
Torys LLP Offices, Calgary and Toronto
Munk School for Global Affairs, University of Toronto
George Brown College, Waterfront Campus, Toronto
Joseph L. Rotman School of Management Expansion, University of Toronto, Toronto
Mike & Ophelia Lazaridis Quantum-Nano Centre, University of Waterloo, Waterloo
Toronto Community Housing, Block 32, Toronto

2013   Orchestra Hall Renewal, Minneapolis, MN
Elementary Teachers' Federation of Ontario, Toronto
Bridgepoint Health, Toronto
Library District Condominiums (Block 36), Toronto
Alumni Centre, University of British Columbia, Vancouver
Ponderosa Commons, University of British Columbia, Vancouver

2014   Fort York Bathurst Branch Library, Toronto
Bremner Tower, Southcore Financial Centre, Toronto

2015   Remai Art Gallery of Saskatchewan, Saskatoon
2015 Pan/Parapan American Games Athletes' Village/Canary District, Toronto
Centre for Addiction and Mental Health (All Phases), Toronto

2016   20 Washington Road, Princeton University, Princeton, NJ
Kellogg School of Management, Northwestern University, Evanston, IL

2017   The Globe and Mail Centre, Toronto

Selected Bibliography

BOOKS

Goodfellow, Margaret and Phil Goodfellow. 'Kuwabara Payne McKenna Blumberg Architects.' In *A Guidebook to Contemporary Architecture in Toronto*. Vancouver, Toronto: Douglas & McIntyre (D&M), 2010, pp. 30, 42, 108, 120, 124.

Duran, Sergi and Mariana R. Eguaras. Kuwabara Payne McKenna Blumberg Architects. In *1000 Ideas by 100 Architects*. Beverly, MA: Rockport Publishers, 2009, pp. 84-87.

Stanwick, Sean and Jennifer Flores. *Design City Toronto*. Chichester, West Sussex: John Wiley & Sons, 2007, pp. 42-47, 56-61, 62-69, 186-193, 212-219, 236-239.

Baird, George, Ian Chodikoff and Larry Wayne Richards. *Canadian Architect — RAIC Gold Medal 2006*, Bruce Kuwabara. Toronto: June 2006.

Rochon, Lisa. *Up North: Where Canada's Architecture Meets the Land*. Toronto: Key Porter Books, 2005, pp. 168, 195, 215-216, 221, 236, 240-241, 254-255, 263.

'Kuwabara Payne McKenna Blumberg Architects.' In *1000 Architects K-Z. Vol. 2*. Mulgrave, Victoria: The Images Publishing Group, 2004, p. 334.

Lambert, Phyllis, Detlef Mertins, Bruce Mau and Rodolphe el-Khoury. *The Architecture of Kuwabara Payne McKenna Blumberg*. Basel, Berlin, Boston: Birkhäuser — Publishers for Architecture, 2004.

Kuwabara Payne McKenna Blumberg, a monograph in the *Contemporary World Architects* series. New York: Rockport Publishers, 1998. [foreword by George Baird; introduction by Detlef Mertins]

PERIODICALS

Fisher, Thomas and Steven Fong. 'Emerging Talent: Kuwabara Payne McKenna Blumberg.' *Progressive Architecture* [New York: October 1992]: pp. 96-99.

Kingwell, Mark. 'Building Cities, Making Friends.' *Queen's Quarterly* 119, no. 3 [Kingston: Fall 2012]: pp. 358-377.

'Kuwabara Payne McKenna Blumberg: The First Three Projects.' *Contract Magazine* 10, no. 2 [Toronto: April/May 1991]: pp. 32-42.

ESSAYS AND PAPERS

Kuwabara, Bruce. 'Ourtopia: Ideal Cities and the Role of Design in Remaking Urban Space.' In *Ourtopias: Cities and the Role of Design*, edited by: Paola Poletto, Philip Beesley and Catherine Molnar. Toronto: Canadian Design Research Network, Design Exchange, Riverside Architectural Press, 2008, pp. 7-20.

Kuwabara, Bruce. 'Architecture and Urbanism.' *Building* [Toronto: April/May 2008]: pp. 20-21.

Kuwabara, Bruce. 'The Shape of Ambiguity.' *ROM* 40, no. 1 [Toronto: Summer 2007]: pp. 44-47. [on Michael-Lee Chin Crystal Pavilion]

Kuwabara, Bruce. 'Bruce Kuwabara on Canadian Design.' *VISUAL 1*, no. 2 [Toronto: December 2004]: pp. 16-19.

180 QUEEN STREET WEST, Toronto, Ontario

2007 OAA Annual Design Awards. *OAA Perspectives* 15, no. 2 [Toronto: Summer 2007]: p. 15.

American Institute of Architects. 'Federal Judicial Centre, 180 Queen St. West.' *Justice Facilities Review* [Washington: 2008]: pp. 36-37.

Barber, John. 'A Cold City Finally Finds its Heart.' *The Globe and Mail*, June 17, 2006.

Hume, Christopher. 'Bohemian Queen gets New Elegance.' *Toronto Star*, May 18, 2006.

Hume, Christopher. 'Getting Over our Fear of Heights.' *Toronto Star*, September 4, 2005.

'Canada Life to Build New 15-Storey Tower.' *Canadian Building* [Toronto: December/January 2004]: p. 7.

BRIDGEPOINT HEALTH, Toronto, Ontario

'Award of Excellence: Bridgepoint Health.' *Canadian Architect* 53, no. 12 [Toronto: December 2008]: pp. 30-33.

CANADA'S NATIONAL BALLET SCHOOL, Toronto, Ontario

Ashenburg, Katherine. 'Great Leap Forward.' *Toronto Life* 39, no. 12 [Toronto: December 2005]: pp. 45-50.

Boudova, Petra. 'Kultura Phhybu — Baletna Skola.' *ATRIUM*, no. 3 [Bratislava: May/June 2008]: pp. 110-116. [Slovak]

'Canada's National Ballet School.' In *The Phaidon Atlas of 21st Century World Architecture*. London: Phaidon Press, 2008, p. 618.

'Canada's National Ballet School.' *2008 National Urban Awards = Prix nationaux de design urbain 2008* [Ottawa: Royal Architectural Institute of Canada, 2008]: pp. 14-20.

Falzano, Rebecca. 'Ballet on Display.' *Lighting Design + Application* [New York: August 2007]: p. 44.

Slessor, Catherine. 'Dance Class.' *The Architectural Review* 222, no. 1325 [London: July 2007]: pp. 36-43 and cover.

Sobchak, Peter. 'The Whole Pointe.' *Canadian Interiors* 43, no. 1 [Toronto: January/February 2006]: pp. 56-61.

Stanwick, Sean and Jennifer Flores. 'Canada's National Ballet School.' In *Design City Toronto*. Chichester, West Sussex: John Wiley & Sons, 2007, pp. 186-193.

Wikke, Helle Bøcken, and Karin Skousbøll. 'Canada's National Ballet School, Toronto.' In *Arkitektur, Krop, Rum. 1. udg.* ed. [København: Kunstakademiets Arkitektskoles Forlag, 2010]: pp. 56-63.

CANADIAN MUSEUM OF NATURE, Ottawa, Ontario

Debanné, Janine. 'Glass Menagerie.' *Canadian Architect* 56, no. 9 [Toronto: September 2011]: pp. 32-37 and cover.

DiCosimo, Joanne. 'The Canadian Museum of Nature: A New Vision of National Service.' *Museum Design & Function 1*, no. 1 [Toronto: November/December 2004]: pp. 4-13.

O'Reilly, Dan. 'Victoria Memorial Museum Building.' *Award* 23, no. 4 [Vancouver: August 2009]: pp. 45-48.

Van Uffelen, Chris. 'Canadian Museum of Nature.' In *Contemporary Museums*. Berlin: Braun Publishing AG, 2011, pp. 30-33.

CENTENNIAL COLLEGE APPLIED RESEARCH AND INNOVATION CENTRE, Scarborough, Ontario

Carter, Brian. 'Practical Experiment.' *The Architectural Review* 216, no. 1292 [London: October 2004]: pp. 72-75.

'Centennial HP Science & Technology Centre.' *Interiors* no. 234 [Korea: March 2006]: pp. 200-204. [Korean]

'Centennial HP Science & Technology Centre.' In *Lobby Design*. Cologne: DAAB, 2006, pp. 230-235.

Stanwick, Sean and Jennifer Flores. 'Centennial HP Science and Technology Centre.' In *Design City Toronto*. Chichester, West Sussex: John Wiley & Sons, 2007, pp. 212-219.

Venafro, Roberto. 'Centro de Scienca e Technologia — Science & Technology Centre.' *iiC — l'industria italiana del Cemento* no. 832 [Rome: June 2007]: pp. 418-431. [Italian/English]

CENTRE for INTERNATIONAL GOVERNANCE INNOVATION (CIGI) CAMPUS, Waterloo, Ontario

'Balsillie School of International Affairs, CIGI.' *The Architects' Journal: RIBA Awards 2012* [London: June 2012]: p. 38.

'CIGI Campus, Waterloo, Ont. — Award "Best of Canada, Project of the Year".' *Canadian Interiors* 49, no. 7 [Toronto: Fall 2012]: p. 10.

Rapoport, Irwin. 'CIGI Campus.' *Award* [Vancouver: August 2011]: pp. 53-55.

Mercer, Greg. 'New Balsillie School will be "Functional, not Fancy".' *The Record* [Kitchener-Waterloo] January 8, 2009.

'KPMB Will Design Balsillie School.' *Market Watch/Wall Street Journal Digital Network*, November 20, 2008.

GARDINER MUSEUM, Toronto, Ontario

Bleiwas, Ellen. 'Emerging: Toronto's Contemporary Architectural Renaissance.' *Mimarlik Dekorasyon* [Istanbul: September 2007]: pp. 36-49. [Turkish/English]

Chapman, Tony. *Architecture 08: The Guide to the RIBA Awards*. London: Merrell Publishers, 2008, pp. 130-131.

'Gardiner Museum of Ceramic Art, Toronto.' *Architecture & Detail* [Dalian, China: June 2008]: pp. 414-420. [Chinese/English]

Goodfellow, Margaret and Phil Goodfellow. *A Guidebook to Contemporary Architecture in Toronto*. Vancouver, Toronto: Douglas & McIntyre (D&M), 2010, pp. 30-31.

Pagilari, Francesco. 'Gardiner Museum.' *The Plan: Architecture & Technologies In Detail*, no. 25 [Bologna: April 2008]: pp. 68-81. [Italian/English]

Sobchak, Peter. 'Good Things in Small Boxes.' *Building* 56, no. 5 [Toronto: October/November 2006]: pp. 58-63 and cover.

Stanwick, Sean and Jennifer Flores. 'Gardiner Museum of Ceramic Art.' In *Design City Toronto*. Chichester, West Sussex: John Wiley & Sons, 2007, pp. 56-61.

Tamborini, Susanne. 'Städtebaulicher Akzent/Town Planning Accent.' *md: International Magazine of Design/Möbel Interior Design* [Leinfelden-Echterdingen, Germany: October 2007]: pp. 80–85. [German/English]

Tanase, Oana. 'Toronto Muzeul Gardiner.' *Igloo habitat & arhitectură* VII, no. 83 [Bucharest: November 2008]: pp. 140–150.

Tasarim, Mimari. 'Gardiner Muzesi.' *Yapi* [Istanbul: December 2007]: pp. 78–83. [Turkish/English]

Van Uffelen, Chris. 'Gardiner Museum.' In *Contemporary Museums*. Berlin: Braun Publishing AG, 2011, pp. 36–37.

Yilmaz, Burcin. *Müzeler Projeler/Yapilar 5, Yapı-Endüstri Merkezi, Yem Yayin*. 190 [Istanbul: 2011]: pp. 50–55. [Turkish]

Zhang, Yunhua. 'Gardiner Museum of Ceramic Art.' In *Top Canadian Contemporary Architects*. Beijing: Phoenix Publishing Ltd., 2012, pp. 70–79. [Chinese]

GEORGE BROWN COLLEGE, WATERFRONT CAMPUS,
Toronto, Ontario

Dubowski, Stefan. 'Waterfront Health Sciences Campus — George Brown College.' *Award* 26, no. 5 [Toronto: October 2012]: p. 61.

LE QUARTIER CONCORDIA, CONCORDIA UNIVERSITY,
Montreal, Quebec

'Big Urban Projects — Kuwabara Payne McKenna Blumberg Architects/ Fichten Soiferman et Associés.' *MIPIM/ Architectural Review Future Project Directory — MIPIM Architectural Review Future Project Awards* [London: 2005]: p. 76.

Carroll, Michael. 'A Lesson in Contrasts: Montreal's New Academic Pavilions.' *Detail* [Munich: November/December 2006]: pp. 612–613.

Carroll, Michael. 'Urban Studies,' *Azure* 22, no. 166 [Toronto: March/April 2006]: pp. 78–83.

Dunton, Nancy and Helen Malkin. *A Guidebook to Contemporary Architecture in Montreal*. Vancouver/Toronto/Berkeley: Douglas & McIntyre (D&M), 2008, pp. 34–35.

Gruft, Andrew. *Substance Over Spectacle: Contemporary Canadian Architecture*. Vancouver: Arsenal Pulp Press; and Morris and Helen Belkin Art Gallery, 2005, pp. 58–63.

Molteni, Christina. 'Montréal: A Metropolis that has been Experiencing for Many Decades now the Charm and Contradictions Typical of Pluralism and of Multicultural Societies.' *ARCH* (International Magazine of Architecture and Design), no. 90 [Milan: May/June 2006]: pp. 60–63. [Italian/English]

Quartino, Daniela Santos (ed.). 'The Quartier Concordia.' *New Lobbies & Waiting Rooms*. New York: Collins Design, 2008, pp. 164–171.

Sobchak, Peter. 'Higher Learning.' *Building* 55, no. 5 [Toronto: October/November 2005]: pp. 52–55.

Theodore, David. 'Concordia's Campus Goes Vertical: KPMB's Iconic Solution for a Very Tight Site.' *Competitions* 14, no. 4 [Louisville, KY: Fall 2004]: pp. 4–11.

Zhang, Yunhua. 'John Molson School of Business.' In *Top Canadian Contemporary Architects*. Beijing: Phoenix Publishing Ltd., 2012, pp. 122–125. [Chinese]

MANITOBA HYDRO PLACE, Winnipeg, Manitoba

Armenciu, Daniel. 'Arhitectură Bioclimatica Manitoba Hydro Place Building.' *Igloo habitat & arhitectură*, 117 [Bucharest: September 2011] pp. 42–43.

Auer, Thomas, Joshua Vanwyk and Erik Olsen. 'Sustainability Beyond LEED: Integrating Performative Delight in the Built Environment.' *Perspecta: The Yale Architectural Journal* 45 [Cambridge, MA: MIT Press, 2012]: pp. 177–184.

'Award of Excellence — Manitoba Hydro Head Office.' *Canadian Architect* 51, no. 12 [Toronto: December 2006]: pp. 32–35.

Brunet, Robin. 'Manitoba Hydro Place.' *Award* 23, no. 6 [Toronto: December 2009]: pp. 73–75.

Dassler, Friedrich H. 'Extreme Conditions.' *XIA International* [Leinfelden-Echterdingen, Germany: January 2008]: pp. 32–37.

Dassler, Friedrich H. 'Manitoba Hydro — Corporate Head Office — Winnipeg, MB, Can: Extreme Randbedingungen.' *XIA Intelligente Architektur* [Leinfelden-Echterdingen, Germany: January/March 2007]: pp. 18–25. [German/English] [interview with Bruce Kuwabara and Thomas Auer]

Duran, S.C. and J.F. Herrero. 'Manitoba Hydro Place.' In *The Sourcebook of Contemporary Green Architecture*. New York: Collins Design and Loft Publications, 2010, pp. 169–175.

Fraser, J. Lynn. 'Manitoba Hydro Headquarters.' *SAB Mag: Sustainable Architecture & Building Magazine*, no. 9 [Gatineau, Quebec: January/February 2008]: pp. 37–38.

Gourluck, Russ. *Powering the Province — Sixty Years of Manitoba Hydro*. Winnipeg: Great Plains Publications, 2011, pp. 188–210.

Guly, Christopher. 'High-Performance Buildings Reaching New Heights.' *Architecture* [Royal Architectural Institute of Canada, Ottawa: Summer/Fall 2008]: pp. 12–15. [comments and quotes by Bruce Kuwabara]

'Harnessing Climate.' *High Performance Buildings®* 4, no. 4 [Atlanta: Fall 2012]: pp. 6–16.

Killory, Christine and René Davids. *Details, Technology, and Form*. New York: Princeton Architectural Press, 2012, pp. 106–115.

Kwok, Alison G. and Walter T. Grondzik (eds.). 'Manitoba Hydro Place.' In *The Green Studio Handbook: Environmental Strategies for Schematic Design*, second ed. Burlington, MA: Architectural Press, 2011, pp. 351–358.

Linn, Charles, FAIA. 'Cold Comfort.' *Green Source* 5, no. 2 [New York: March/April 2010]: pp. 52–57.

'Manitoba Hydro Downtown Office Project.' *Architecture and Detail* [Dalian, China: February 2008]: pp. 140–144. [Chinese/English]

'Manitoba Hydro Place: Integrated Design Process Exemplar.' In *PLEA 2009: Architecture, Energy and the Occupant's Perspective*. Quebec City: Les Presses de l'Université Laval (PUL), 2009, pp. 551–556. [Proceedings of the 26th International Conference on Passive and Low Energy Architecture; Bruce Kuwabara was a keynote speaker]

'Manitoba Hydro Place: Preis als das "beste Hochhausprojekt in Amerika".' *Forum. XIA Intelligente Architektur* [Leinfelden-Echterdingen, Germany: October/December 2009]: p. 4.

'Manitoba Hydro Place, SAB Awards Winning Project.' *SAB Mag: Sustainable Architecture & Building Magazine*, no. 24 [Gatineau, Quebec: July/August 2010]: pp. 31–37.

'Manitoba Hydro Place,' *XIA Intelligente Architektur* 10–12 [Leinfelden-Echterdingen, Germany: 2010]: pp. 26–33. [German]

Moe, Kiel. *Integrated Design in Contemporary Architecture*. New York: Princeton Architectural Press, 2008, pp. 18–22.

'Nominated Project 2010' In *Best High-Rises 2010/11: The International High-Rise Award 2010*. Berlin: Jovis Verlag, 2010, pp. 96–97.

Nyre, Ron. 'ULX Working for Green.' *Urban Land* 71, no. 9/10 [Washington: Urban Land Institute, September/October 2012]: p. 52.

Olsen, Erik. 'Client Blind Spots.' In *SOM Journal* 7. Stuttgart: Hatje Cantz Verlag, 2011, pp. 22–25.

Parker, Dave and Anthony Wood. 'Case Study 4: Manitoba Hydro Place.' In *The Tall Buildings Reference Book*. London: Routledge, 2013, pp. 382–389.

Sampson, Peter. 'Climate-controlled.' *Canadian Architect* 55, no. 1 [Toronto: January 2010]: pp. 16–22.

Slavic, Dijane. 'IBS Awards 2008: And the Winner is...' In *XIA International 8*, no. 2 [Leinfelden-Echterdingen, Germany: December 2008]: pp. 16–17.

Thierfelder, Anja and Matthias Schuler. 'In Situ: Site Specificity in Sustainable Architecture.' *Harvard Design Magazine* [Cambridge, MA: Spring/Summer 2009]: pp. 50–59.

Yudelson, Jerry and Ulf Meyer, 'Manitoba Hydro Place,' In *The World's Greenest Buildings*. New York: Routledge, 2013, pp. 52–55.

Wood, Anthony (ed.), *Best Tall Buildings 2009: CTBUH International Award Winning Projects*. New York: Routledge, 2009, pp. 20–27.

Wood, Anthony and Ruba Salib (principal authors). 'Case Study 2.12: Manitoba Hydro Place.' In *Natural Ventilation in High-Rise Office Buildings*. New York: Routledge, 2013, pp. 112–121.

Zhang, Yunhua. 'Manitoba Hydro Place.' In *Top Canadian Contemporary Architects*. Beijing: Phoenix Publishing Ltd., 2012, pp. 178–183. [Chinese]

MIKE & OPHELIA LAZARIDIS QUANTUM-NANO CENTRE, UNIVERSITY OF WATERLOO, Waterloo, Ontario

Sobchak, Peter. 'Going Big to Go Small. Really Small.' *Building* 60, no. 2 [Toronto: April/May 2010]: pp. 25-26.

NOTA BENE RESTAURANT, Toronto, Ontario

Smith, Leslie. 'Three Way.' *Canadian Interiors* 45, no. 5 [Toronto: July/August 2009]: pp. 20-23.

'Presenca Urbana.' *Lighting and Design Magazine* [New York: July 2009]: pp. 48-51.

2015 PAN/PARAPAN AMERICAN GAMES ATHLETES' VILLAGE/ CANARY DISTRICT, Toronto, Ontario

Canadian Architect 57 [Toronto: December 2012]: pp. 24-25.

REMAI ART GALLERY OF SASKATCHEWAN, Saskatoon, Saskatchewan

'Canadian Architect Awards of Excellence: Remai Art Gallery of Saskatchewan.' *Canadian Architect* 56, no. 12 [Toronto: December 2011]: pp. 13, 20-21 and cover.

JOSEPH L. ROTMAN SCHOOL OF MANAGEMENT EXPANSION, UNIVERSITY OF TORONTO, Toronto, Ontario

'Business Expansion.' *U of T Magazine* [Toronto: Spring 2009]: p. 14.

Magarrey, Paige. 'Manager's Special.' *Canadian Architect* 57, no. 11 [Toronto: November 2012]: pp. 18-25.

ROYAL CONSERVATORY TELUS CENTRE FOR PERFORMANCE AND LEARNING, Toronto, Ontario

'Award of Excellence — Royal Conservatory of Music TELUS Centre for Performance & Learning, 37th Annual Awards.' *Canadian Architect* 50, no. 12 [Toronto: December 2005]: pp. 38-39.

Bleiwas, Ellen. 'Emerging: Toronto's Contemporary Architectural Renaissance.' *Mimarlik Dekorasyon* [Istanbul: September 2007]: pp. 36-49. [Turkish/English]

Brown, Barry. 'Toronto's Architectural & Cultural Renaissance.' *Condo Monde* [Toronto: Winter 2007]: pp. 33-39.

Crabb Michael. 'Boxing Clever.' *Auditoria Magazine Annual* [Surrey, England: 2009]: pp. 34-40.

Gonchar, Joann. 'The Royal Conservatory, Toronto.' *Architectural Record* 199, no. 7 [New York: July 2011]: pp. 82-94.

Goodfellow, Margaret and Phil Goodfellow. 'TELUS Centre for Performance and Learning.' In *A Guidebook to Contemporary Architecture in Toronto*. Vancouver, Toronto: Douglas & McIntyre (D&M), 2010, pp. 42-43.

'Governor General's Medal Winner: TELUS Centre for Performance and Learning.' *Canadian Architect* 55, no. 5 [Toronto: May 2010]: pp. 20-21.

Kapusta, Beth. 'Chamber Music.' *Azure* 25, no. 195 [Toronto: October 2009]: pp. 66-72.

Lam, Elsa. 'Instrumental Composition.' *Canadian Architect* 55, no. 2 [Toronto: February 2010]: pp. 20-25.

Johnson, Bernadette (ed.). 'Koerner Hall, the Royal Conservatory.' In *Celebrating Excellence in Wood Structures, 2009-2010 North American Wood Design Award Winners*. Ottawa: Canadian Wood Council, 2010, pp. 170-175.

Newhouse, Victoria. *The Architecture and Acoustics of New Opera Houses and Concert Halls — Site and Sound*. New York: The Monacelli Press, 2012, pp. 148-151.

'Royal Conservatory of Music.' In *Architecture Canada 2010: The Governor General's Medals in Architecture/ Architecture Canada 2010: les médailles du Gouverneur général en architecture*. Ottawa: Royal Architectural Institute of Canada, 2010, pp. 56-63.

Scott, Sarah. 'All Ears.' *Azure* 21, no. 164 [Toronto: November/December 2005]: pp. 56-57.

Stanwick, Sean and Jennifer Flores. 'TELUS Centre for Performance and Learning.' In *Design City Toronto*. Chichester, West Sussex: John Wiley & Sons, 2007, pp. 236-239.

SUGARCUBE, Denver, Colorado

Fangs, Yang. 'SugarCube, Denver, U.S.A.' In *Innovative Residence*. Hong Kong: Hong Kong Architecture Science Press, 2012, pp. 364-370.

'Generation Green.' *RFP Magazine, Eco Build* 51 [Hong Kong: March 2009]: p. 32.

'Sweet: SugarCube, Kuwabara Payne McKenna Blumberg Architects.' *Hinge* 173 [Hong Kong: December 2009]: pp. 78-79.

Zhang, Yunhua. 'SugarCube.' In *Top Canadian Contemporary Architects*. Beijing: Phoenix Publishing Ltd., 2012, pp. 70-79.

TIFF BELL LIGHTBOX AND FESTIVAL TOWER, Toronto, Ontario

Baird, Daniel. 'City of Cinema.' *The Walrus*, August 9, 2010, pp. 74-77.

Jen, Leslie. 'See the Light.' *Canadian Architect* 56, no. 2 [Toronto: February 2011]: pp. 18-23 and cover.

Johnson, Brian D. 'Lightbox Fantastic: The Toronto Film Festival's New Home.' *Maclean's Magazine*, September 13, 2010, pp. 72-74.

Sobchak, Peter. 'Ready for its Close-up.' *Building* [Toronto: February/March 2011]: pp. 16-19.

Stanwick, Sean and Jennifer Flores. 'Toronto International Film Festival (TIFF), Festival Centre and Tower.' In *Design City Toronto*. Chichester, West Sussex: John Wiley & Sons, 2007, pp. 42-47.

Wood, Antony (ed). *Best Tall Buildings 2011: CTBUH International Award Winning Projects*. Chicago: Council for Tall Buildings and Urban Habitats (CTBUH) in conjunction with IIT & Routledge/Taylor and Francis Group, 2011.

TORYS LLP OFFICES, Toronto, Ontario

Jen, Leslie. 'Core Identity.' *Canadian Architect* 54, no. 6 [Toronto: June 2009]: pp. 19-23.

'Oficinas del bufete de abogados Torys.' *Oficinas* [Madrid: February 2010]: pp. 34-38. [Spanish]

Sokol, David. 'Oh Canada!' *Interior Design* 79, no. 10 [New York: August 2008]: pp. 198-205.

'Torys: un bufete customizado.' *Décollage* [Barcelona: June 2009]: pp. 12-14. [Spanish]

VAUGHAN CITY HALL, Vaughan, Ontario

'Governor General's Medal Winner: Vaughan City Hall.' *Canadian Architect* 57, no. 5 [Toronto: May 2012]: pp. 38-39.

'Vaughan City Hall,' *Canada 2012 Architecture — The Governor General's Medals in Architecture* [Toronto: January 2013]: pp. 48-55.

Pearson, Clifford A. 'Stimulus Plan.' *Architectural Record* 200, no. 10 [New York: October 2012]: pp. 132-135.

Phillips, Rhys. 'Refining City Halls.' *Building* 62, no. 1 [Toronto: May 2012]: pp. 38-39.

'Refined Wine in Old and New Bottles — Three New City Halls.' *Building Magazine*, 62, no. 1 [Toronto: February/March 2012]: pp. 18-24 and cover.

'Vaughan City Hall, Ont. — Award "Best of Canada".' *Canadian Interiors* 49, no. 7 [Toronto: Fall 2012]: p. 18.

'Vaughan Civic Centre.' *Canadian Architect* 49, no. 12 [Toronto: December 2004]: pp. 34-35.

YOUNG CENTRE FOR THE PERFORMING ARTS, Toronto, Ontario

Chodikoff, Ian. 'Young at Heart.' *Canadian Architect* 52, no. 9 [Toronto: September 2007]: pp. 41-44.

Goodfellow, Margaret and Phil Goodfellow. 'Young Centre for the Performing Arts.' In *A Guidebook to Contemporary Architecture in Toronto*. Vancouver, Toronto: Douglas & McIntyre (D&M), 2010, pp. 124-125.

Kieran, Christopher. 'Young Centre for The Performing Arts — Business Week/ Architectural Record Award-Winner.' *Architectural Record* 195, no. 11 [New York: November 2007]: pp. 92-95.

'Kuwabara Payne McKenna Blumberg Architects, Toronto, Canada.' *Hinge* no. 144 [Hong Kong: July 2007]: p. 99.

Stanwick, Sean and Jennifer Flores. 'Young Centre for the Performing Arts.' In *Design City Toronto*. Chichester, West Sussex: John Wiley & Sons, 2007, pp. 62-69.

Walters, Helen. '2007 Architecture Awards — Young Centre for the Performing Arts.' *Business Week* [New York: December 10, 2007]: p. 57.

George Baird is Emeritus Professor of Architecture, and the former dean of the John H. Daniels Faculty of Architecture, Landscape and Design at the University of Toronto. He is the founding principal of the Toronto-based architecture and urban design firm Baird Sampson Neuert Architects. Prior to becoming Dean at the University of Toronto in 2004, Baird was the G. Ware Travelstead Professor of the History of Architecture and Technology at the Graduate School of Design, Harvard University. He has published and lectured widely throughout most parts of the world.

He is co-editor (with Charles Jencks) of *Meaning in Architecture* (1969), and (with Mark Lewis) of *Queues Rendezvous, Riots* (1995). He is author of *Alvar Aalto* (1969) and *The Space of Appearance* (1995). His latest book *Public Space: Cultural/Political Theory: Street Photography* was published by SUN Publications in Amsterdam in 2011.

Baird's consulting firm, Baird Sampson Neuert, is the winner of numerous design awards, including Canadian Architect Magazine Awards over many years, and Governor General's Awards for Cloud Gardens Park in 1994, Erindale Hall on the campus of the University of Toronto at Mississauga in 2006 and the French River Visitor Centre in 2010.

Baird is a Fellow of the Royal Architectural Institute of Canada and a member of the Royal Canadian Academy of Arts. He has been the recipient of the Toronto Arts Foundation's Architecture and Design Award (1992), the da Vinci Medal of the Ontario Association of Architects (2000) and the Gold Medal of the Royal Architectural Institute of Canada (2010). Most recently, he has been selected as the 2012 winner of the Topaz Medallion of the American Institute of Architects and the Association of Collegiate Schools of Architecture.

Thomas Fisher is a Professor and Dean of the College of Design at the University of Minnesota. He was educated at Cornell University in architecture (1975) and at Case Western Reserve University (1980) in intellectual history.

His books include *In the Scheme of Things, Alternative Thinking on the Practice of Architecture* (Minnesota, 2000), *Salmela, Architect* (Minnesota, 2005), *Lake/Flato, Buildings and Landscapes* (Rockport, 2005), *Architectural Design and Ethics, Tools for Survival* (Elsevier, 2008), *Ethics for Architects* (Princeton Architectural Press, 2010), and *The Invisible Element of Place, The Architecture of David Salmela* (Minnesota, 2011), and *Designing to Avoid Disaster, The Nature of Fracture-Critical Design* (Routledge, 2012). He also co-edited with Wolfgang F.E. Preiser and Jack L. Nasar the book *Designing for Designers: Lessons Learned from Schools of Architecture* (Fairchild, 2007).

Prior to coming to the University of Minnesota, he served as the Editorial Director of *Progressive Architecture* and *Building Renovation* magazines, as the Historical Architect for the Connecticut State Historic Preservation Office, as a historian for the Historic American Engineering Record and as the Regional Preservation Officer for the Ohio Preservation Office.

He has served, as well, as the president of the Association of Collegiate Schools of Architecture, as a founding board member of the National Academy of Environmental Design and as a board member of several public and professional organizations, including the St. Paul Riverfront Development Corporation, the American Institute of Architects Minnesota, the Urban Land Institute, the Minneapolis Parks Foundation, the Weisman Art Museum, the Connecticut Architecture Foundation and *Faith & Form: The Interfaith Journal on Religion, Art, and Architecture*.

Mark Kingwell is a Professor of Philosophy at the University of Toronto and a contributing editor of *Harper's Magazine*. He is the author or co-author of many books on political, cultural and aesthetic theory, including the Canadian bestsellers *Better Living* (1998), *The World We Want* (2000), *Concrete Reveries* (2008) and *Glenn Gould* (2009). His articles on politics, architecture and art have appeared in, among others, *Harper's*, the *New York Times*, the *New York Post*, the *Wall Street Journal*, the *Guardian*, *Utne Reader, BookForum*, the *Toronto Star* and *Queen's Quarterly*; he is also a former columnist for *Adbusters*, the *National Post* and the *Globe and Mail*.

Mark Kingwell has lectured extensively in Canada, the United States, Europe, the Middle East and Australia on philosophical subjects and held visiting posts at Cambridge University, the University of California at Berkeley and at the City University of New York, where he was the Weissman Distinguished Visiting Professor of Humanities in 2002.

He is the recipient of the Spitz Prize in political theory, National Magazine Awards for both essays and columns, the Outstanding Teaching Award and President's Teaching Award at the University of Toronto, a research fellowship at the Jackman Humanities Institute, and in 2000 was awarded an honorary DFA from the Nova Scotia College of Art & Design for contributions to theory and criticism. His other recent books are a collection of essays on art and philosophy, *Opening Gambits* (2008); the edited anthology *Rites of Way: The Politics and Poetics of Public Space* (2009); with Joshua Glenn and cartoonist Seth, *The Idler's Glossary* (2008) and *The Wage Slave's Glossary* (2011); and a collection of political essays, *Unruly Voices* (2012). In order to secure financing for their continued indulgence, Mark Kingwell has also written about his various hobbies, including fly fishing, murder mysteries, baseball and cocktails.

Mirko Zardini, an architect, has been Director and Chief Curator of the Canadian Centre for Architecture (CCA), Montreal, since 2005. His research engages the transformation of contemporary architecture and its relationship with the city and the landscape. As director, Zardini has overseen the transformation of the CCA to address contemporary social, political and environmental issues.

Exhibitions by Zardini — or in collaboration with Giovanna Borasi — include Asfalto: Il carattere della cittá (2003), presented in Milan, and Out of the Box: Price, Rossi, Stirling + Matta-Clark (2003-2004), Sense of the City (2005-2006), 1973: Sorry, Out of Gas (2007-2008), Actions: What You Can Do with the City (2008-2009), Other Space Odysseys: Greg Lynn, Michael Maltzan, Alessandro Poli (2010), and Imperfect Health: The Medicalization of Architecture (2011) exhibited at the CCA.

He was editor of *Casabella* magazine from 1983 to 1988, *Lotus International* from 1988 to 1999, and served on the editorial board of *Domus* in 2004 and 2005. His writings have also appeared in journals like *Lotus International, Casabella, ANY, Archis, El Croquis, L'Architecture d'aujourd'hui, Domus, Log* and *Volume*.

Zardini has taught design and theory at architecture schools in Europe and the United States, including Graduate School of Design at Harvard University, Princeton University School of Architecture, Mendrisio Architecture Academy, Swiss Federal Institute of Technology (ETH) at Zurich, the Federal Polytechnic School of Lausanne (EPFL), University of Miami and Syracuse University.

Illustration Credits

Tom Arban Photography: p. 8, 11, 12, 20, 21, 24, 25 (top middle), 26 (top middle), 28 (middle), 29 (top middle), 31, 40–42, 50, 52 (bottom), 53 (bottom right),55, 56 (right), 57, 66 (bottom), 67, 70 (bottom), 71 (bottom), 72–79, 81, 84–88, 90 (top spread), 91 (bottom), 92–93, 98, 99, 110–113, 115, 117, 122, 128, 129, 133, 134 (bottom), 134–135 (top spread), 137, 138–143, 145, 147-151, 162, 167 (left), 177, 178 (top left, top right, bottom right), 179, 180, 184, 185, 186 (bottom left), 186–187 (top spread), 190, 191 (top spread), 191 (bottom), 192–193, 200, 201, 204–208, 228, 232–233, 235 (top), 238–239, 245, 246–247, 256 (bottom left), 259 (bottom right)

James Brittain: p. 156-157, 159–161, 163–166, 167 (right), 187 (bottom)

Bryan Christie Design: p. 218, 222, 224, 229

Collection Gemeentemuseum Den Haag, © 2013 Fondation Constant
c/o Pictoright/SODRAC 2013: p. 14

Marc Cramer: p. 181

Doublespace Photography: p. 95

Eduard Hueber, Arch Photo Inc.: p. 26 (bottom), 28 (bottom), 47–49, 51, 52 (top), 53, 58, 59, 65, 66 (top), 69, 70 (top), 90 (bottom), 135 (bottom), 136, 178 (bottom left), 182, 183, 186 (bottom right), 189, 190 (bottom), 226 (left)

Eric Fruhauf: p. 278

Shai Gill: p. 60–61, 63, 71 (top)

Pascal Grandmaison: p. 198

JS Models: p. 56, 119 (bottom), 171 (top)

Jesse Jackson: p. 243-245

Ramon Janer: p. 101 (bottom)

Sam Javanrouh: p. 241

Gerry Kopelow: p. 219, 226 (right), 229 (bottom)

Norm Li: p. 101 (top)

Luxigon: p. 249-253

Maris Mezulis: p. 15, 22, 23, 25 (bottom), 27, 28 (top), 29 (bottom), 34–37, 43–45, 82–83, 107–109, 114, 116, 119, 120–121, 123–127, 130–131, 152–155, 168–169, 194–197, 199, 202–203, 209, 215, 217, 221, 223, 224, 225, 227, 231, 234–235 (bottom spread), 236, 237, 255–261, 268, cover

Mehrdad Tavakkolian: p. 38

The Flat Side of Design: p. 103, 170, 172, 173, 210-211, 240, 242 (bottom)

Transsolar: p. 220

University of Toronto Archives, Robert Lansdale Photography Ltd.: p. 16

Nature Nocturne event at the Canadian Museum of Nature.

Acknowledgements

Historically, architecture in Canada has been discussed as a cultural response to nature and our northern geography, climate and sense of place. The reality of Canada today is that it is rapidly being transformed through immigration and growth into a highly urbanized culture and society, and its architecture is responding to both local diversity and global influences as we continue to form our cities.

Since we began our practice in 1987, we have engaged the project of architecture to embrace the pressing issues of building strong communities within our cities, urbanization, intensification and contemporary life, recognizing that we live and practice in one of the most vibrant models of social democracy. We have also pursued innovations in architecture that integrate sustainable technologies with place-making strategies that sponsor identity, diversity, social mixing and interaction.

For 25 years, we have focused on the making of public buildings — civic, cultural and academic — and urban buildings that reinforce and animate the public realm. This creative and intellectual investment has been rewarded by our own experience of our contribution to the city we live in. The form and content of our work is deeply integrated into the fabric of our lives.

While we are absolutely committed to the role of architecture at the urban level, we are simultaneously focused on the systems, details and materials that express bold ideas and forms. The importance that we place in making public buildings is rewarded by the pleasure that we gain from our cultural and academic buildings. For us, the city is a cultural artefact and architecture provides the agency of transformation.

Our deep appreciation is extended to our talented and committed colleagues — principals, associates, directors, architects, interns, students and staff at KPMB — who have collaborated with us consistently and tirelessly. We have an extraordinary team of people who make the ever-evolving practice of architecture exciting, productive and gratifying. Every day is a learning experience.

We have had exceptional clients who have entrusted us, challenged us and given us extraordinary opportunities. We are deeply grateful for their vision and support. The complexity of building requires many partners. We are fortunate to have worked with great consultants, contractors and fabricators.

Thank you to George Baird, Thomas Fisher, Mark Kingwell and Mirko Zardini who have contributed insightful reflections and opened up new lines of thinking about architecture and its practice.

We are grateful to Tom Arban, Eduard Hueber and Maris Mezulis who have captured the image and essence of our work in their photographs featured in this publication.

And our special thanks are extended to Amanda Sebris and Colin Geary who so ably directed the enterprise of creating this monograph; to Ria Stein of Birkhäuser who has been a remarkable and supportive editor; and to Anita Matusevics who has designed this beautiful book.

Finally, to our families our enduring gratitude for their constant support, understanding and patience.

Bruce Kuwabara

Thomas Payne

Marianne McKenna

Shirley Blumberg

Book design: Anita Matusevics, Wonder Incorporated, Toronto

Editor: Ria Stein, Berlin

Project director: Amanda Sebris, Toronto

Typesetting: Richard Hunt, Archetype, Toronto

Text editors: Joan Gardner, Kate Pocock, Amanda Sebris, Norbert Sebris,
Ria Stein, Dawn Stremler

Book production and design assistance: Colin Geary

Production support: Dawn Stremler, Anne Sewell, Alexander Robinson,
Alexandra Varvarikos, Patrick Cheung, Liwei Wang

Copy editor: Kate Pocock

Advisors on design, drawings, content: Joy Charbonneau,
Kevin Bridgman, Steven Casey, Jason Halter, Mitchell Hall,
Colin Geary, Maris Mezulis, Paulo Rocha, Glenn MacMullin,
Lucy Timbers, Robert Hill, Joseph Kan

Many individuals contributed to the realization of this book.
Special thanks to: Tom Arban, Kevin Bridgeman, Steven Casey, Joy Charbonneau,
Phyllis Crawford, Stuart Elgie, Robert Faber, Joan Gardner, Colin Geary, Jason Halter,
Robert Hill, Eduard Hueber, Mitchell Hall, Robert Hill, Richard Hunt, Krystal Koo,
Marc Letellier, Glenn MacMullin, Anita Matusevics, Maris Mezulis, Mary Mcintyre,
Michael Moxam, John Peterson, Adrian Pfeiffer, Kate Pocock, Guy Poulin, Johanna
Radix, Paulo Rocha, Amanda Sebris, Armand Sebris, Norbert Sebris, Lola Skytt,
Ria Stein, Dawn Stremler

A CIP catalogue record for this book is available from the Library of Congress,
Washington D.C., USA.

Bibliographic information published by the German National Library.
The German National Library lists this publication in the Deutsche
Nationalbibliografie; detailed bibliographic data are available on the Internet at
http://dnb.d-nb.de.

© 2013 Birkhäuser Verlag GmbH, Basel
P.O. Box, 4009 Basel, Switzerland
Part of De Gruyter

Printed on acid-free paper produced from chlorine-free pulp. TCF

Printed in Germany

ISBN: 978-3-0346-0828-2

9 8 7 6 5 4 3 2 1
www.birkhauser.com

Cover: Joseph L. Rotman School of Management Expansion,
University of Toronto, photograph by Maris Mezulis